Bicycling
MIDDLE
TENNESSEE

A Guide to Scenic Bicycle Rides in Nashville's Countryside

ANN RICHARDS & GLEN WANNER

4th Edition

PENNYWELL PRESS

4th Edition (2003), second printing (2007)

Cover photography by Ed Wanner
Cover design by Linda Nelson
Inside photography by Ann Richards, Glen Wanner
Maps by TN Dept. of Transportation and KY Dept. of Transportation. Adapted by Ann Richards, Glen Wanner. Topographical information courtesy of Tennessee Division of Geology.

Pennywell Press
P.O. Box 50624
Nashville, TN 37205

Publisher Cataloging Data

Richards, Ann
   Bicycling Middle Tennessee: A Guide to Scenic Bicycle Rides in Nashville's Countryside /by Ann Richards and Glen Wanner
   4th edition
   ISBN 0-9637798-5-0
   1. Bicycle Touring—Tennessee—Guidebooks. 2. Tennessee—Guidebooks. I. Richards, Ann II. Title.

Distributed by John F. Blair Publisher, Winston-Salem, NC
Printed by McNaughton & Gunn, Inc. Saline, MI

Disclaimer

Every effort has been made to make the information presented herein accurate and current; however, conditions, services, and street names may have changed since these routes were researched. The authors and publisher accept no responsibility for any inaccuracies contained within.

Bicycling activities involve risks and dangers; participants should be aware of their riding skills and abilities. The authors and publisher assume no responsibility for any personal injuries, death, and/or property damage caused or sustained by anyone engaged in the activities described in this book.

Printed on Recycled Paper

ACKNOWLEDGMENTS

To our families and friends who have given us wonderful advice and became willing "sounding boards" for our ideas and thoughts on this project which we have loved so much.
Our gratitude as well goes to those who, on occasion, shared the trails--cycling buddies and club members, and to all the dogs who chose *not* to chase us as we researched, rode, and rerode all of our routes!

We wish to express our appreciation to those who have shared their expertise--Durwood Edwards for all kinds of computer help; Linda Nelson for her artistic eye and flair for design; Morris Adkins for his sage advice on the business end; John and Bonnie Lukes in California for literary support; and Ed Wanner for his photographic talents.

Ann & Glen

P.S. Glen, I'm sorry about the time I sent through the wash your bicycle jersey with a whole day's worth of mileages in the pocket!

A.R.

TABLE OF CONTENTS

LOCATOR MAP

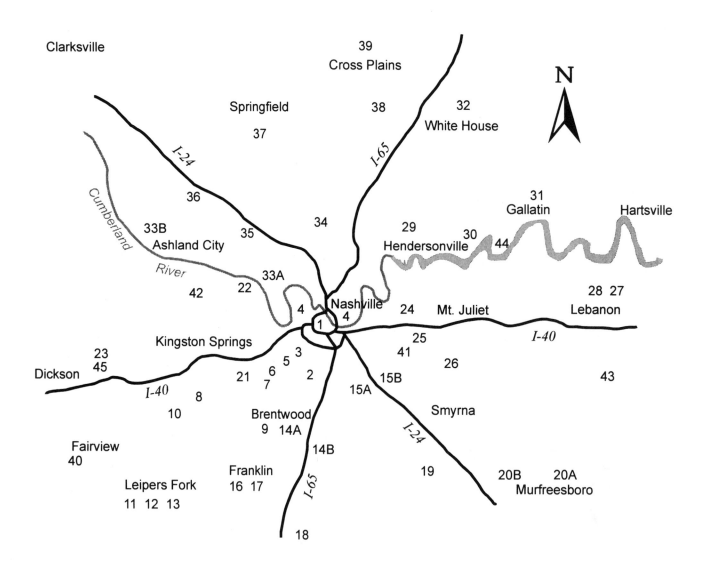

INTRODUCTION

The possibilities for great cycling are unlimited in Middle Tennessee. Nashville, the city in the country, is surrounded by a network of scenic rural roads, and only a few miles outside the city limits, cyclists will discover mixed hardwood forests, meandering rivers, tumbling creeks, old farmhouses, pastures, corn fields, and dilapidated barns. While touring these roads, you will often feel as if you have gone back in time to an era when life was simpler. The bustle of the city soon seems very distant.

We hope this book will enable both the novice and the experienced cyclist to discover wonderful places to ride. Since much of the fun of cycling evolves from exploring new territory, we encourage you to continue searching for new and even more challenging bike routes. Because this guide contains only some of the many route possibilities, we have included a list of available maps (see *Appendix*) to help you plan your own rides or variations of our rides.

It is impossible for any single guide to cover all aspects of bicycling. Fortunately, many bike books dealing with repair, equipment, training, technique and diet are available. For our purposes here, we will touch briefly on such basics only as they pertain to bicycling in Middle Tennessee.

GENERAL INFORMATION

TERRAIN

Middle Tennessee is hilly! If you haven't noticed this while driving your car, you will on a bicycle. The climbs are not long (rarely over one mile), but some of the grades are very steep. The Cumberland River flows through Nashville at 385 ft. above sea level, and some of the knobs (hills) are over 1,100 ft. in elevation. These two features provide the challenge of climbing several hundred feet at a time and the thrill of cycling the fast descents. For efficiency and safety, you will need appropriate gearing (at least a 10-speed) and good brakes for these rides. If you find climbing the hills too strenuous, the problem may be in the gearing, so see a bike shop about changing your freewheel and/or front chainrings. Of course, the more often you ride in hilly areas, the easier and more enjoyable it becomes.

TRAFFIC AND ROAD CONDITIONS

Tennessee law considers the bicycle a vehicle, and cyclists should ride appropriately. The principles of *Effective Cycling* by John Forester, a leading bicycle advocate, are based on the concept that "bicyclists fare best when they act, and are treated in return, as drivers of vehicles, with the same rights and responsibilities that motorists have." In other words, if you behave like a responsible and predictable cyclist, motorists are more likely to be courteous and share the road.

Most of our routes are on lightly traveled, paved roads which are often narrow with no shoulders. We've found that most drivers are courteous, allowing us plenty of room, and passing only when it's safe. In some areas, it's not uncommon to cycle 15 minutes or more without even seeing a vehicle. However, traffic can become hectic near urban areas especially during commuting hours, so use caution! Even in rural areas, the roads are often busy when school dismisses or on weekend afternoons. If you're willing to forgo "sleeping in," the best time to ride is in the early morning hours on weekends.

We've tried to select routes with smooth road surfaces, but at times it may be necessary for you to cycle on slightly bumpy pavement in order to ride in the more enjoyable scenic areas. Be aware that the pavement can become unsafe due to construction, flooding and weather conditions. On several occasions, we have encountered a gravel road surface where there had been a paved road only a few months earlier. Also, loose gravel accumulated on the pavement can be a hazard at intersections and curves.

CYCLING IN TENNESSEE'S CLIMATE

Tennessee's climate allows for enjoyable bicycling year-round, but you must plan properly. It's crucial always to carry plenty of water (especially on hot, humid days) and to drink frequently. Buy a large bicycle water bottle, a necessary item for the Tennessee heat. On rides over 15 miles with no reliable water supply, carry two water bottles. Drinking an electrolyte drink (Gatorade, etc.) will help keep your energy level up and may prevent muscle cramps. The country stores along the way sell such drinks (and they are cold!). Drinking too much of certain sport drinks sometimes causes nausea, so we suggest carrying both water *and* an electrolyte drink and drinking from each.

If you are perspiring profusely, feel exhausted, and look pale, you may have heat exhaustion and should immediately rest in the shade and drink plenty of fluids. To avoid overheating, it's a good idea to take a break in an air conditioned store if possible. (Ann often can be seen sticking her head in the freezer of some little grocery on a hot day!) Avoid the worst heat by riding early in the morning or late evening. Sunscreen is important for protecting skin from the relentless summer sun of the South. Besides endangering your skin, sunburn can drain energy by requiring more blood to nourish the skin cells. Bug repellent is essential when mountain biking in the summertime, and off-road cyclists should be aware of poison ivy as well.

Only freezing temperatures will keep us off our bikes in the wintertime; however, proper clothing is always essential, for even 60 degrees can seem cold when you add a 15-mph windchill factor. On the other hand, exercise generates body heat, so it will take some practice to find the right combination of clothing. Pay particular attention to your head, neck, hands, and feet, because these areas are especially vulnerable to the cold. Materials such as polypropylene, thermax, and wool will keep you much warmer and drier than cotton. We recommend wearing a windproof shell that you can easily unzip when you climb hills and zip up again for the chilly descents. It is wise also to carry along one more layer of clothing (a jacket, sweater, or rain parka) and a second pair of warm gloves.

Average Temperature (F) and Precipitation (inches)

	High	Low	Precip.		High	Low	Precip.		High	Low	Precip
Jan	46	28	4.5	May	79	57	4.6	Sept	83	61	3.7
Feb	51	30	4.0	June	87	65	3.7	Oct	72	48	2.6
Mar	60	38	5.6	July	90	69	3.8	Nov	59	38	3.5
Apr	71	48	4.5	Aug	89	68	3.4	Dec	50	31	4.6

EQUIPMENT

Please wear a proper bike helmet! Glen has saved his skull at least once by wearing his "brain bucket." Items such as padded Lycra bike shorts, gel saddles, bike gloves, etc. are not essential but will certainly make you a more comfortable and happy rider.

You will often be miles from nowhere, so carry necessary tools, spare tube(s), patch kit, and tire pump. Be sure you know how to fix a flat *before* you ride the backroads rather than when you're stuck in the pouring rain 30 miles from your starting point! Always carry money to buy energy food in case you "bonk" and also take along spare snacks (like an energy bar or trail mix) should there be no markets nearby. You should also carry identification and emergency contact phone numbers. Finally, we recommend wearing sunglasses even when it is overcast (clear glasses are available) in order to protect your eyes from harmful UV rays, dust, and the wide assortment of bugs found in Tennessee.

SERVICES

We have listed the locations of food services along our routes, but keep in mind that some of these places may go out of business or have unpredictable hours. Many small markets are closed on Sundays or do not open until noon.

CANINE CREATURES

If you ride in rural areas, you will encounter dogs who, for their daily entertainment, love to chase bicyclists. Most dogs will simply run behind or alongside you, then turn back when you leave their "territory." Only on rare occasions do dogs ever bite cyclists. The biggest danger occurs when animals (wild or domestic) run in front of you and cause a collision.

Cyclists have improvised a number of ways to escape canine hazards, but none of them are foolproof. First, try yelling abruptly something like "No!" "Stay!" or "Go home!" and dogs with any discipline will most likely stop when they hear a loud voice. Some cyclists try to outrun the dog(s). If you opt for this solution, good luck! We have seen dogs run faster than 20 mph, and if there is even a slight incline or headwind, forget it--even Greg Lemond isn't going to outride them. However, if you're spinning at a fast cadence, the dog will probably not be able to zero in on your ankle. Some people use their tire pumps to whack the dog as they ride by, but here you take a chance of having an accident while trying to ward off the dog. Other cyclists attempt to kick the animal if it gets too close, and although this can sometimes be effective, it can also be disastrous. To begin with, you cannot pedal very fast using only one leg. Secondly, holding your leg out from the bike gives the dog a great target.

We prefer using the water bottle method which involves squirting the dog in the face. This has proven to be effective on some pretty nasty-looking dogs. There is some danger in this method, too, since it leaves you with only one hand for steering and braking while, at the same time, out-maneuvering an unpredictable animal. Finally, there are red pepper, mace, and ammonia sprays that stop dogs almost instantly. It has, we have heard, occasionally stopped downwind cyclists as well!

As a last resort, dismount and walk slowly away, keeping your bike between you and the dog while assertively yelling at it and showing no fear. Should any accident or injury occur involving a dog on a public road, the owner is liable under state (and sometimes county) leash laws.

KNOW YOUR ABILITY

Never attempt a trip that is beyond your ability. Even if you are capable of a 25-mile ride, a 12-mile ride over tough hills and with relentless headwinds may be more than you anticipated. For this reason, we have included information on terrain and elevation in the trip description of each of our rides. Remember, too, that the weather plays an important factor in your ability to have an enjoyable ride.

PARKING

Many of our rides start at public parking areas such as parks and schools, but in some cases, you are on your own. It is usually okay to leave your car at a market or gas station (with their permission), and we think that buying food or gas from them would be a nice gesture of appreciation. We sometimes park at churches (except on Sundays, of course) provided there are no signs to prohibit it.

USING THIS GUIDE

We have outlined our routes on county maps to provide the most detail possible. Even so, staying on course in Middle Tennessee's countryside can be a challenge since street signs are sometimes non-existent or turned the wrong way. By using both the maps and the written directions, you will be able to follow these routes even in areas where the road signs are missing. We recommend highly that you watch for hints in our written directions, such as "stop sign at the T-intersection," "first right," or "at the top of a hill" to help you stay on course. ALWAYS READ THE NEXT DIRECTION AHEAD OF TIME SO YOU WON'T MISS A TURN AND THEN WONDER WHERE YOU ARE!!!

Most maps in this book are based on the Tennessee Department of Transportation county maps. All roads that intersect our bike routes are shown with the exception of a few residential streets in populated areas. Street names in towns or urban areas may not appear on the maps but will be indicated in the route directions. In some areas, the completion of I-840 may alter a few roads from what appears on the maps, but we expect our routes in the affected areas will still be suitable for cycling. Since the rides differ in length, the map scale will also vary. However, mileages for each ride are included on the direction sheets. If you use a cyclometer, your mileage may (and probably will) vary slightly.

For easy reference and a lighter load, you may wish to cut out any of our maps and directions that you will be using rather than carrying this entire guidebook on your bike. (Helpful tip: Carry your map(s) in a clear plastic bag, thus preventing damage from rain and/or perspiration.)

Any sections of our rides may be shortened into simple "out-and-backs" of any length desired. Some especially nice stretches (ideal for novices) are listed in the *Short Ride* section.

OPTIONS: Several rides have two or more options of varying lengths, all of which share some of the same route. For example, this could allow you to ride the first 15 miles and then decide whether you feel like taking the 25-mile option or the 35-mile option. Be sure to read the italicized print at the end of each option to find where your route continues in the printed directions.

ROAD SIGNS: Signs may disappear, re-appear, or change names, so never depend entirely upon them. Since some roads are known by more than one name, we have listed in parentheses the name(s) not appearing on the street signs.

ELEVATION/TERRAIN: For each ride we have listed the Elevation Difference (the difference between the highest and lowest elevation on the route) and the Accumulated Climb (the total gross gain in elevation during the entire trip). Our estimates are based on topographical maps. If you use an altimeter, your accumulated climb read-out will most likely be substantially less than ours since most altimeters do not register climbs of under 30-40 feet. A general description of the terrain is also provided.

COMBINING RIDES: Some rides share common stretches with our other rides, or they meet at an intersection. This allows you to extend your trip by combining all or portions of two or more rides.

CONNECTOR ROUTES: Written directions are given for spurs that connect one ride with another, allowing for more extensive trips. The roads used in these connectors are usually found on our maps.

ALTERNATE PARKING SITES: All of our rides start at the point of the route closest to Nashville. Suitable alternate parking locations are suggested for those coming from a different direction. In some cases, it is necessary to ride a short distance from the parking location to the described route; therefore, the total mileage may vary.

DISTANCE FROM NASHVILLE: This indicates the approximate mileage from downtown Nashville to the starting point of the ride. Keep in mind that driving time increases when mostly surface streets, rather than interstates, are used to get to the start of a ride.

HELP US IMPROVE THIS BOOK

A book like *Bicycling Middle Tennessee* is never finished, and although we have tried to make it as complete as possible, we believe that fellow cyclists may find new information that could be included in future research. Please send ideas and comments to:

Ann Richards, Glen Wanner
c/o Pennywell Press
Box 50624
Nashville, TN 37205

Thanks and happy biking!

BIKE COMMUTING

Why Drive a Car?

We doubt that many of you could say that you have plenty of time to do all the cycling you want. However, the solution to this time crunch is often easy—commute by bike, whether it's to work or school, or to run errands and visit friends.

Although our music profession does not usually allow us to bike commute, we do so whenever possible. It takes us 25 minutes to drive a car to work, plus another 5-10 minutes to park and walk to our job location. When we bike to work, it takes about 40 minutes to ride 9 miles, plus 5 minutes to clean up and change clothes. So you can see, it doesn't take that much extra time, and it's fun. Trips under 3 or 4 miles are often quicker on a bicycle. One of the greatest advantages of bike commuting is that it provides a decent workout during the time that would normally be wasted in a car. There are, however, many other advantages in bike commuting—saving money in auto expenses (gas and maintenance), contributing to clean air, and reducing traffic congestion. Most bike commuters claim that their morning commute is better than a second cup of coffee and that they invariably feel better at work.

There are several logistical problems in bike commuting, and you will have to determine if this clean mode of transportation is right for you. Most problems such as wardrobe, distance, bicycle parking/security, cleaning up after your morning ride, and weather can be easily solved with a little ingenuity. To learn more, visit www.walkbikenashville.org.

Choosing Your Route

Buy a detailed city map and drive a few different routes to work before you begin to bike commute. Consider things such as volume and speed of traffic, visibility, width of curb lane or paved shoulder, frequency of stop signs/traffic lights, hills, and distance when planning your route. Fortunately, Nashville and surrounding communities have begun adding on-street bike lanes and signed bike routes to make traveling by bike more enjoyable.

It is very important that you know how to ride in traffic and properly position yourself under varying conditions. Many cyclists make the mistake of riding too far to the right in a narrow lane or passing on the right side of stopped cars. Practices such as these can be dangerous. We highly recommend reading *Effective Cycling* by John Forester or take a cycling course (contact Walk/Bike Nashville—see *Appendices*) to learn how to ride safely in all traffic conditions.

CREATING YOUR OWN NEIGHBORHOOD WORKOUT

It's not always possible to escape to the rural roads for a satisfying ride; however, with a detailed city map, you probably can plan a peaceful and pleasant neighborhood cruise starting from your front door. Try to avoid streets with several stop signs or traffic lights that interrupt your workout. Many cyclists establish a short loop where they can do several laps without stopping. Others will put up with traffic for a short distance in order to reach a nice area for cycling. By pedaling around your neighborhood during the week, you will invariably do better on your longer trips out in the country.

Ride # 1   MUSIC CITY BIKEWAY/SHELBY BOTTOMS GREENWAY

Distance: Up to 21 miles
Terrain: A few small hills west of town, flat east of the Cumberland River.
Services: Markets and restaurants are abundant for first 5 miles.
Traffic: Moderate for 2 miles on Demonbreun St. Otherwise, on-street bike lanes or paved multi-use paths.
Alternate Parking Sites: 1) Forrest Green Trailhead—from Gallatin Rd. in East Nashville, take Eastland Ave east, left on Porter Rd., right on Rosebanks Ave, right on Welcome Ln., and left on Forrest Green Dr. **2)** Parking is available almost anywhere along the route although free parking is scarce downtown.
Distance from Nashville: 3 miles; ride may be started from downtown.

As Nashville completed its Sidewalk and Bikeway Plan in 2002, Walk/Bike Nashville began to promote the concept of a 25-mile route from Andrew Jackson's Hermitage in the east to the Belle Meade Plantation in the west. Based on current and proposed bike facilities, the Music City Bikeway would be a great way to promote tourism, recreation, commuting, and physical fitness. If you are heading to a Titans' game or other big downtown event, you will certainly feel smug as you pedal past traffic gridlock and motorists looking for a place to park.

While still a concept, much of this "urban assualt" is ready to ride. For sightseeing, this route can't be beat with attractions such as the Country Music Hall of Fame, 2nd Ave/Broadway Entertainment District, the Ryman Auditorium, First Center for the Visual Arts, the future Symphony Hall, and Belmont Mansion just to name a few. In the near future, a pedestrian bridge will link Shelby Bottoms with Opryland and the huge Opry Mills Shopping Complex. From there, you can pedal the Stones River Greenway for 10 miles to Percy Priest Dam.

We begin the Music City Bikeway on Belmont Blvd. where you can pedal past beautiful historic homes on a tree-lined street complete with bike lanes. Next you will find yourself cruising the bike lanes past the recording studios on 16th and 17th Avenues, an area known as Music Row. The only significant stretch without bike lanes will be on Demonbreun St. as you head downtown. Fortunately, traffic is never fast nor is it very heavy so long as you avoid commute hours. Once downtown, you may want to leave our route to enjoy one of the many exciting eateries or hop on the Downtown Greenway which runs one mile from Riverfront Park to the Bicentennial Mall and Farmer's Market just north of the Capitol.

Our route then crosses the Cumberland River on the Shelby Street Pedestrian Bridge where another stretch on bike lanes awaits as you head to Shelby Park. If this route has been too flat for your liking, explore the roads through this 360-acre park and you'll get a good hill workout.

Finally, you enter the Shelby Bottoms Greenway to enjoy flat peaceful bike riding in an auto-free setting. As you pedal the 4-mile trail as it meanders among forests and floodplains, it will hardly seem possible that you were in the heart of Nashville only minutes ago. If you are not in a hurry, take time to walk the mulch paths or stop at one of the river overlooks. Upon reaching the Forrest Green Trailhead, it is time to turn around and head home. Those desiring to only ride the greenway, may start at the trailhead near the train trestle in Shelby Park.

1 MUSIC CITY BIKEWAY/SHELBY BOTTOMS GREENWAY

HOW TO GET THERE: From downtown Nashville, take Broadway/21st Ave N toward Green Hills. Turn left on Blair Blvd. and right on Belmont Blvd. Park in the vicinity of Gale Ln. which is between Wild Oats Market and Christ the King School.

Mile

0.0   Begin by biking toward town (north) on Belmont Blvd. (becomes Portland Ave.)

1.2   **Right** on 18th Ave S. (4-way stop). Market/restaurant. Numerous eateries are found between here and the Shelby Street Bridge.

1.3   **Right** on Magnolia Blvd. (traffic light).

1.5   Cross Wedgewood Ave. and continue on 16th Ave S. (Music Square)

2.5   Enter roundabout. Take second **right** and continue toward town on Demonbreun St.

2.8   Cross over I-40.

3.6   **Left** on 4th Ave

3.7   **Right** on access to Shelby Street Pedestrian Bridge (Access is also possible on 3rd Ave.).

4.2   **Right** on 1st St. which becomes Davidson St.

5.7   Enter Shelby Park (stay right by river).

6.7   Bear **right** onto multi-use path near train trestle. Always stay right next to the river.

10.6 Go left to complete the small loop and retrace your route. The Forrest Green Trailhead is 20 yards to the right. Water. Upon returning to the Music Row Roundabout, take the second right and get into the middle lane to turn left on 17th Ave N. Also, after crossing Wedgewood Ave., quickly merge to the left to turn onto 18th Ave.

21.2 End of Ride!

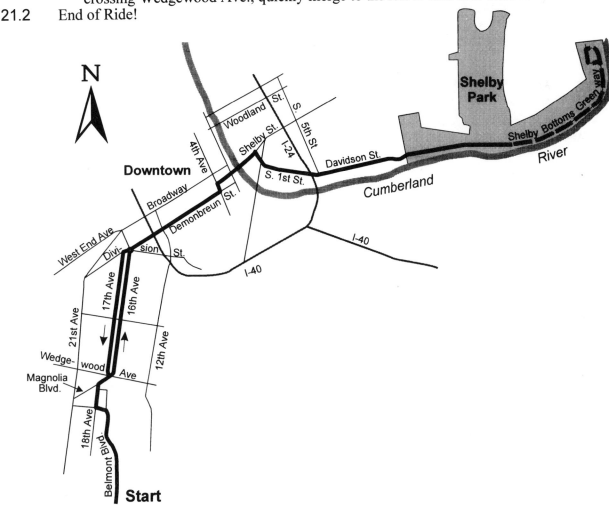

2 RADNOR LAKE EXCURSION

HOW TO GET THERE: Take West End Ave./Harding Rd. away from Nashville and turn left on Belle Meade Blvd. Continue on Belle Meade Blvd. until it ends at the Main Entrance of Percy Warner Park where the ride starts.

Mile

0.0	Bike away from the park on Belle Meade Blvd.
0.6	**Right** on Tyne Blvd.
2.2	Cross Hillsboro Pk./Hwy.431 (traffic light).
3.0	**Right** on Robert E. Lee Dr. (first right).
3.5	**Left** on Otter Creek Rd. (3-way stop).
4.3	Cross Granny White Pk. (stop sign). Market.
4.6	Visitors' Center/West Trailhead (water/restrooms).
5.8	East Trailhead (water/restrooms). Return the way you came.
11.6	End of Ride!

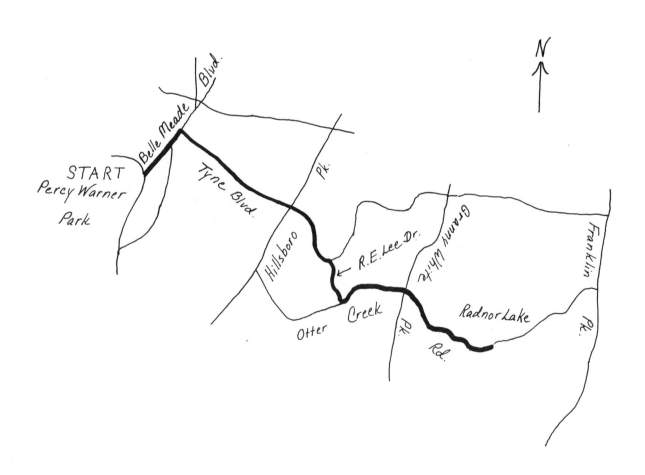

Ride # 2   RADNOR LAKE EXCURSION

Distance: 12 miles
Elevation Difference/Accumulated Climb: 240/350 ft.
Terrain: Moderately hilly.
Services: Market at miles 4.3 and 5.8.
Traffic: Moderate on Tyne Blvd. during commuting hours. Otherwise light on all roads.
Combining Rides: *# 3 Belle Meade Boulevard Cruise, # 5 Percy Warner Park Loop.*
Connector Routes: 5 mi. to *# 14 Brentwood/Old Smyrna Road Loop*--Continue east on
　　Otter Creek Rd. from the East Trailhead. Go right on Franklin Pk. and left on Church St.
Alternate Parking Sites: Radnor Lake - East or West Trailhead.
Distance from Nashville: 8 miles

　　This 12-mile ride cruises through the snazzy neighborhoods of Belle Meade and Forest Hills to a beautiful lake nestled among the steepest knobs in Davidson County. The trip starts at the Belle Meade Entrance of Percy Warner Park and after a short stretch on Belle Meade Blvd., turns onto Tyne Rd. An enjoyable flat stretch takes you through a lovely residential area and pockets of countryside. A few hills are encountered after you leave Tyne Blvd. and pick up Otter Creek Rd. which goes to Radnor Lake.

　　Radnor Lake State Natural Area is reminiscent of a typical New England pond, especially during autumn when the steep, forested hillsides surrounding the lake are aglow with brilliantly colored foliage. The dam, which created this lake, was constructed in 1914 by the L & N Railroad to insure a water supply for nearby Radnor Yard. The hills were stripped bare to supply wood for the railroad, but today the second growth forest is doing very well. Radnor Lake has several miles of hiking trails and is excellent for bird watching. On weekends and holidays, especially in the fall and spring, hundreds of people walk, jog, rollerblade, or bicycle on the road, so use caution when riding along the lake. This 1.2-mile section is usually closed to motor traffic on weekend afternoons in the spring and fall. Rangers *do* enforce the 20-mph speed limit for cyclists as well as cars.

When overtaking pedestrians or cyclists from behind, it is customary to pass on the left whenever possible and to call out, "On your left," before you pass.

Ride # 3   BELLE MEADE BOULEVARD CRUISE

Distance: 5 miles
Terrain: Flat
Traffic: Light to moderate. 2 lanes in each direction.
Combining Rides: *#2 Radnor Lake Excursion, #5 Percy Warner Park Loop.*
Distance from Nashville: 5 miles

The mostly level Belle Meade Boulevard is a pleasant 2.7-mile cruise which makes a very popular afterwork and weekend excursion for cyclists of all levels. The simple "out-and-back" ride takes you by opulent Belle Meade estates and the exclusive Belle Meade Country Club. Also, peaceful side streets which run through spacious residential areas offer additional cycling opportunities. An interesting side trip down Leake Ave. leads to the restored Belle Meade Plantation built in 1853 (tours available). The large carriage house and stables were home to the famous race horse Iroquois, the first American horse to win the English Derby.

The entire boulevard has two lanes in each direction, so traffic, which is usually light, can easily and safely pass cyclists. The Belle Meade Code requires bicyclists to ride in single file and the police do enforce all traffic laws pertaining to cyclists. The route has only one traffic light and one stop sign—not bad for a city bike ride.

HOW TO GET THERE: Take Harding Pk./Hwy. 70S West from Nashville. Turn left at the Belle Meade City Hall immediately before Belle Meade Blvd.
or
Go left on Belle Meade Blvd. and continue until it ends at Percy Warner Park.
Map/directions not included

Ride # 4   METROCENTER WORKOUT

Distance: 6 miles
Terrain: Flat.
Services: Restaurants in Fountain Square.
Traffic: Light.
Distance from Nashville: 2 miles

MetroCenter, an industrial park in-progress only 2 miles from downtown Nashville, is as flat as any place you'll find in Middle Tennessee. Originally a privately-owned and farmed floodplain area, it was a bird watcher's paradise and a haven for resident and migrating species.

However, today MetroCenter is home to office buildings, man-made lakes and lagoons and a public golf course. Traffic is usually light except during commuting hours. The divided streets are wide, and although there is usually a gentle prairie-like breeze, conditions are ideal for cyclists of all levels. From the starting point, cyclists may pedal Great Circle Rd., Mainstream Dr. and Freelands Station Rd. for a 5.6-mile roundtrip. Other loops are possible, plus there is a new 3.5-mile paved multi-use path along the Cumberland River levee.

HOW TO GET THERE: From I-65, take Metro Center Blvd. north to Metro Center. Turn right on Vantage Way and right on Great Circle Rd. (second intersection). Park at the end of Great Circle Rd. or in any of the parking lots if permitted.

Map/directions not included

Ride # 5   PERCY WARNER PARK LOOP

Distance: 2-11.2 miles
Elevation Difference/Accumulated Climb: 360/1100 ft.
Terrain: Constantly hilly. A thrilling and challenging roller coaster-type route.
Services: None.
Traffic: Light.
Combining Rides: *# 2 Radnor Lake Excursion, # 3 Belle Meade Boulevard Cruise.*
Connector Routes: 1) .7 mi. to *# 6 Edwin Warner Park Ride*--Bear right at the 4-way intersection at mile 4.8 and continue to Old Hickory Blvd., turn left on Old Hickory Blvd. and turn right at the first road into Edwin Warner Park. (Caution--the brief stretch of Old Hickory Blvd. is a narrow road with fast traffic.) **2)** 1+ mi. to *# 7 Old Natchez Trace/Del Rio Ride*--Bear right at the 4-way intersection at mile 4.8. Turn left on Old Hickory Blvd., then right on Vaughn Rd. or cut through Edwin Warner Park (see map). (Caution--Old Hickory Blvd. is a narrow road with fast traffic.) **3)** .8 mi. to *# 21 Bellevue/Kingston Springs Ride*--Bear right at the 4-way intersection at mile 4.8 and continue to Old Hickory Blvd. Turn right, then left onto Hwy. 100.
Alternate Parking Sites: 1) Hwy. 100 Entrance **2)** Chickering Road Entrance **3)** Old Hickory Blvd. Entrances.
Distance from Nashville: 7 miles

The *Percy Warner Park Loop* is a wonderful 11-mile ride among lush forests and meadows on a narrow winding one-way road with very little motorized traffic. In the past, few cyclists rode in the Warner Parks, and those of us who did had to worry about jarring our teeth out due to loose pavement and potholes. Fortunately, the entire road system in Percy Warner Park was resurfaced by the summer of 1991, and cyclists are now some of the most frequent users.

While cycling the Main Drive, we have occasionally encountered poor lost souls on foot, bike, or car, attempting to find their way out of the park. The Metro Park people plan eventually to have signs at every intersection, but until then, we suggest you follow our directions very carefully. Even if you get off the Main Drive, by following all the one-way signs you will eventually get back to the Belle Meade Entrance. We like to think of the road system as one big loop with five cutoffs or shortcuts which return to the Main Drive, thus creating shorter loops ranging from 2 to 10 miles. You can easily extend this trip by crossing Old Hickory Blvd. (Caution--blind hill with fast traffic) and continuing on the closed road system (no motor vehicles) in Edwin Warner Park. (See Connector Routes above and *Edwin Warner Park Ride*.)

The Warner Parks combine to form one of the largest city parks in the country, providing a 2,700-acre nature sanctuary for a large variety of trees, plants, and wildlife. Deer, chipmunks, squirrels, and raccoons are frequently-seen residents. A large number of birds, including red-tailed hawks and owls, live or migrate through the park. The park is mostly hillside forest with occasional grassy clearings and frequent picnic shelters (no water). In the autumn and spring, we especially enjoy observing the seasonal changes while we ride through these woods. From the Main Drive, a short .6-mile loop goes up to Lea's Summit (elevation 920 ft.) where there is a wonderful view of the Nashville Basin and the downtown skyline.

The route is very hilly with several steep climbs ranging from a 200-ft., .5-mile climb at mile 3 to the infamous "nine mile hill" which is a steep 220-ft., .6-mile climb. Be very careful when navigating the many sharp blind curves, watching out especially for two nasty hairpin turns near the end of the loop. Pedestrians (walkers, joggers, rollerbladers) frequently use these park roads, so for everyone's safety, never ride the wrong way on the one-way roads.

Ride # 6   EDWIN WARNER PARK

Distance: Up to 5 miles
Elevation Difference: 240 ft.
Terrain: Moderately hilly with a few steep climbs.
Services: None.
Traffic: None.
Combining Rides: *# 7 Old Natchez Trace/Del Rio Ride, # 21 Bellevue/Kingston Springs Ride.*
Connector Route: .6 mi. to *# 5 Percy Warner Park Loop*--Using the closed road just west of Vaughn Rd. that meets Old Hickory Blvd., cross into Percy Warner Park. (Dangerous crossing - use caution.)
Alternate Parking Sites: Picnic areas of Edwin Warner Park off Vaughn Rd.
Distance from Nashville: 9 miles

Edwin Warner Park, which borders Percy Warner Park on the south side of Old Hickory Blvd., has about 5 miles of roads closed to motor vehicle traffic. This road system has been recently resurfaced, allowing for pleasant, auto-free cycling through beautiful forest scenery that is equal to that of the popular Percy Warner Park. While gazing at the large variety of trees, be careful not to stray too close to the edge of the new asphalt; it often has a 1-2 inch drop which could easily cause an accident. (Not good planning, we think.)

Edwin Warner Park is not well-suited for fast riding because sticks and leaves often litter the roadway, creating cycling hazards if you are riding much over 12 mph. The park is excellent for leisurely cyclists and families who like to take their time to enjoy the solitude of the forest. A few picnic shelters are nestled among the hills, making it ideal for those wishing to bring a picnic into these pretty, secluded spots which are inaccessible to cars. Remember always to watch for pedestrians and warn them when you approach from behind. ("On your left," etc.)

5 PERCY WARNER PARK LOOP

HOW TO GET THERE: Take West End Ave./Harding Rd. away from Nashville and turn left on Belle Meade Blvd. Continue until it ends at the Main Entrance of Percy Warner Park where our ride begins.

Mile

0.0	Begin biking into the park on the one-way Main Drive.
0.7	Bear **right** at the first junction. (Cut-off # 1 goes left.)
1.8	Stay **left** at the next intersection. Don't take the road to Hwy. 100.
2.1	Deep Well Picnic Area and Trailhead.
3.3	Continue straight after the long climb. (Cut-off # 2 goes left.)
3.9	Stay **right** at the "Y" before the picnic shelter. (Cut-off # 3 goes left.)
4.2	Continue straight. (Cut-off # 4 goes left.)
4.8	Make a hard **left** (4-way intersection) immediately past the two picnic shelters. Several one-way roads with DO NOT ENTER signs will join the Main Drive.
6.5	Golf course and clubhouse on the right.
7.1	Continue straight at the 4-way intersection. (Cut-off # 5 goes left.) The road to the right leads to Chickering Rd.
8.5	Veer **right** at Beech Woods Picnic area. (Cut-off # 5 will enter from the left.)
9.1	Turn **right** where a one-way street (Cut-off # 2) enters from the left.
10.2	Road to Lea's Summit goes to the left, loops around, and comes back (.6-mi. roundtrip).
10.7	Turn **right** where a one-way street (Cut-off # 1) enters from the left.
11.2	End of ride--back into civilization!

6 EDWIN WARNER PARK

(See map to plan your own ride.)

HOW TO GET THERE: Take Harding Pk./Hwy. 70S West going away from Nashville. Bear left on Hwy. 100 West, continue past Old Hickory Blvd. (going east), and take the second left into Edwin Warner Park.

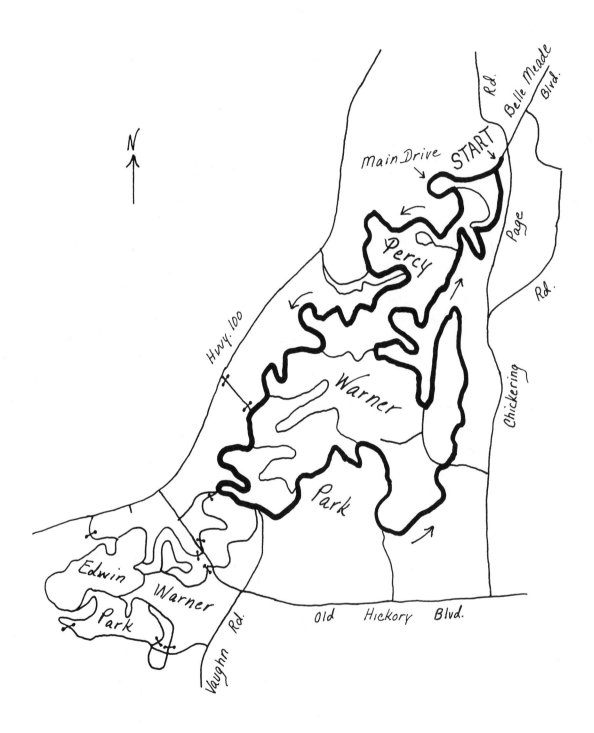

Ride #7   OLD NATCHEZ TRACE/DEL RIO RIDE

Distance: 26 miles
Elevation Difference/Accumulated Climb: 150/860 ft.
Terrain: Mostly flat to rolling. 1 very short but steep grade.
Services: Markets/restaurants in Franklin at mile 13.
Traffic: Light to moderate on Vaughn Rd. and Sneed Rd. Light on all other roads except near Franklin.
Combining Rides: *#6 Edwin Warner Park, #8 Harpeth Loop, #9 Brentwood/Beech Creek Loop, #16 Franklin/Nolensville Loop, #17 Williamson County Loop.*
Connector Routes: 1) .8 mi. to *#5 Percy Warner Park Loop*—Go left on Old Hickory Blvd. (watch for heavy traffic for .3 mi.) from Vaughn Rd. and take the first paved right into Percy Warner Park near the top of the hill. **2)** 1-3 mi. to *#21 Bellevue/Kingston Springs Ride*—Bike through Edwin Warner Park to Vaughn Rd. (see *Ride #6*).
Alternate Parking Sites: 1) Corner of Vaughn Rd. and Sneed Rd. **2)** Old Natchez Trace Rd. at the bottom of the hill 1.5 mi. south of Sneed Rd. **3)** Franklin Kroger (supermarket) on Hwy. 431/5th Ave and Del Rio Pk.
Distance from Nashville: 10 miles

This is probably the most popular ride in Nashville, and it's easy to see why. Along the route, several historic plantation homes stand majestically among the woods and fields through which the scenic Harpeth River meanders. Cyclists of all levels, from beginners to time trialists, enjoy this tour. The quiet and mostly flat roads are excellent for beginners, especially if they start at Sneed Rd. and Old Natchez Trace, thus eliminating one hill and some traffic. Another hill on the route can be avoided by starting near the intersection of Old Natchez Trace and Temple Rd. This ride is basically an out-and-back with a small loop through Franklin, so it can be shortened at any time by simply turning around. As many times as we have cycled this route, we never get tired of seeing this countryside and enjoying the fresh air.

The ride begins by going over a moderate hill (60 ft. climb) on Vaughn Rd. and then heading west across the Harpeth River. Old Natchez Trace is an amazingly wonderful stretch which frequently parallels the Harpeth River and passes several interesting landmarks. This route, used by white men since the late 1700s and by Indians long before that, was part of the Natchez Trace. You may notice that the roadway is sunken into the earth in certain areas as a result of two hundred years of foot, horse, and carriage travel. (Too bad mountain bikes weren't invented yet.) On the right at mile 4.9, there are stone pilings which are the remains of a bridge over Brown's Creek, built in 1801 by the U.S. Army and used until 1913. Andrew Jackson and his troops traveled this route on their way to New Orleans during the War of 1812. A short distance beyond are the Indian burial mounds which mark the Old Town site, a highly developed Indian society flourishing from 900-1400 A.D. Old Town (1856) located here and Montpier (1821) one mile to the south, are both beautiful historic homes along this road.

Del Rio Pk. takes you through open fields and by the Meeting of the Waters plantation (mile 7.4), built in 1800 near the confluence of the Harpeth and West Harpeth Rivers. This Georgian style mansion, one of the first in Williamson County, was almost destroyed in the Civil War but was spared when a Union officer who happened to have been a college mate of the owner Nicholas Perkins stopped his men from completely looting and setting fire to the property. After crossing the shaded West Harpeth River, Del Rio Pk. passes two other historic Perkins family homes and traverses the gradually rolling farmland as it heads toward Franklin.

Upon arriving at the Kroger supermarket in Franklin, many cyclists stop for a snack and retrace their route back. For a little variety, we usually go into Franklin and out Old Boyd Mill Rd. for a pleasant excursion that loops back to Del Rio Pk. Our directions take you into downtown Franklin, a cyclist's heaven complete with bakery, ice cream store, fruit stand, drug store soda fountain, and several good restaurants, all wrapped in a well-preserved small town atmosphere. The town, named after Ben Franklin, was founded in 1799 and is listed in the National Register of Historic Places. The Masonic Hall (1823) on Second Ave. was the first three-story building in the state (and possibly west of the Allegheny Mountains) and was also the location of an important meeting between Andrew Jackson and Chickasaw chiefs to discuss the sale of Indian territory. The Battle of Franklin was significant in the Civil War, with 8,000 Union and Confederate soldiers losing their lives in November of 1864.

If you are not interested in eating, we suggest you turn right on 11th St. from Hope St., cross Hwy. 96, and go right on Boyd Mill Pk. (first right). You will bypass several traffic lights and stop signs this way.

W. Main St. is a wide shady street which goes through the elegant and historic Hinchyville district of Franklin. Boyd Mill Pk. passes by Magnolia Hall (mile 13.7), an Italianate style mansion with a widow's walk on top, a rarity in this part of the South. A few miles later, you will have completed the small loop and be retracing your way home. Just remember to save some strength for that fun little drop you enjoyed on Old Natchez Trace Rd; it becomes a short, but very steep 70-ft. pull on the way back!

Head injury is *the* major cause of bicycle related fatalities. Studies show that over 90% of head-injured cyclists were not wearing helmets. The new helmets are light, well-ventilated, and inexpensive. Wearing a helmet is only a minor inconvenience compared to relearning the English language!

7 OLD NATCHEZ TRACE/DEL RIO RIDE

HOW TO GET THERE: Go south on Hwy. 100 and turn left on Old Hickory Blvd. Turn right at the bottom of the hill onto Vaughn Rd. Take the first left into the parking area for the model airplane flying field and athletic fields on the corner.

or

Go south on Hillsboro Pk./Hwy. 431 and turn right on Old Hickory Blvd. Go past the baseball fields on the left and turn left onto Vaughn Rd. Take the first left into the parking area for the model airplane flying field and athletic field.

Mile

0.0	Bike south on Vaughn Rd. (away from Old Hickory Blvd.)
2.0	**Right** on Sneed Rd. (stop sign at the T-intersection).
2.5	**Left** on Old Natchez Trace (first left).
6.6	**Right** on Old Hillsboro Rd./Hwy. 46. (stop sign at the T-intersection).
6.7	**Left** on Del Rio Pk. (first left).
8.6	**Right** (staying on Del Rio Pk.) at the 3-way stop.
10.2	**Left** (staying on Del Rio Pk.) at the next 3-way stop.
11.8	**Right** on Magnolia Ln. at the cemetery. Market/fast food restaurants.
12.1	**Left** on Hope St. (first left).
12.5	**Right** on Fifth Ave. North/Hwy. 431 (Hillsboro Pk.)
12.8	**Right** on W. Main St. at the 5-way intersection (third traffic light). Restaurants, etc. toward town square in the other direction on Main St.
13.2	**Right** on Eleventh Ave. N.
13.3	**Left** on Boyd Mill Pk.
15.3	Cross Hwy. 96 (stop sign) and continue onto Carlisle Ln.
16.0	Go straight onto Del Rio Pk. at the 3-way stop. You are now retracing your route back.
26.3	End of a great ride!

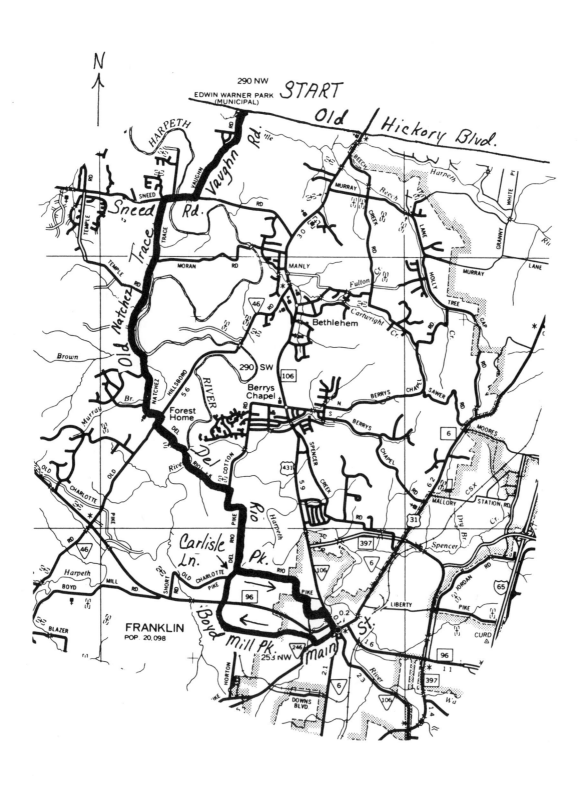

Ride #8   HARPETH LOOP

Distance: 16, 36, or 41 miles

Elevation Difference/Accumulated Climb: Option 1 - 450/500 ft., Option 2 - 450/1610 ft., Option 3 -410/1680 ft.

Terrain: Option 1 has two challenging climbs while Options 2 and 3 contain at least three substantial climbs. Terrain varies from flat to steep rolling hills.

Services: Option 1 has no services. Option 2 has a market/restaurant at mile 21.6. Option 3 has a market/restaurant in Leipers Fork at mile 22.

Traffic: Light on all roads except for moderate to heavy traffic on Hwy. 100 (no more than 1 mi.). Option 1 uses Hwy. 96 which is busy but has a wide paved shoulder.

Combining Rides: #7 *Old Natchez Trace/Del Rio Ride*, #9 *Brentwood/Beech Creek Loop*, #10 *Fernvale Loop*, #11 *Fly Loop*, #12 *Snow Creek Loop*, #13 *Burwood Loop*, #21 *Bellevue/Kingston Springs Ride*.

Connector Routes: 1) 4 mi. to #17 *Williamson County Loop* and #16 *Franklin/Nolensville Loop*—From Boyd Mill Rd. and Hwy. 96, go right (east) onto Hwy. 96 and take the first right onto Boyd Mill Pk. Turn right on 11th Ave and left on W. Main St.   **2)** 2 mi. to *Williamson County Loop*—From the corner of Southall Rd. and McMillan Rd., continue east (straight) on Southall Rd. to Carters Creek Pk.

Alternate Parking Sites: 1) Edwin Warner Park Model Airplane Field (4 mi. to loop)—Bike south on Vaughn Rd., right on Sneed Rd., left or straight at Old Natchez Trace   **2)** Corner of Vaughn Rd. and Sneed Rd. (3 mi. to loop)   **3)** Bellevue Park located on Harpeth Knoll Rd. near the intersection of Beech Bend Dr. and Old Harding Pk. (4 mi. to loop)—Bike to Old Harding Pk. and go left, then right on Poplar Creek Rd.   **4)** Franklin—(1.8 mi. to loop)—Bike west on Del Rio Pk.

Distance from Nashville: 15 miles

This loop tour combines portions of two excellent rides, the *Fernvale Loop* and the *Old Natchez Trace/Del Rio Ride*, into three scenic and challenging options, each encompassing the valleys of the South, West, and Big Harpeth Rivers. The recent completion of the northern terminus of the Natchez Trace Parkway has created several exciting loop tours in northwest Williamson County. To the frequently-cycled original route (Option 3), we have added two shorter options which will utilize the final segment of the Trace. A quick look at the map will reveal other loop variations which are bound to become favorites of local cyclists. Just remember that all these routes criss-cross Backbone Ridge which is guaranteed to increase your heart rate. The famous Loveless Cafe across the road from the Parkway Terminus is an extremely popular home-cooking eatery and is often packed for weekend brunches. Many hungry cyclists have frequented this charming cafe for a tasty post-ride meal!

You may want to stretch your muscles prior to embarking on this excursion because a steep 230-ft. climb commences immediately on Lewis Rd. The "payoff" of dropping down Griffith Rd. makes the effort worthwhile as you speed toward Poplar Creek, but use caution—it is easy to reach 40 mph here! The route now meanders 2 miles along Poplar Creek as it flows to the South Harpeth River. From here, the road is occasionally squeezed between the river and the vertical limestone bluffs with cedars clinging to their edges.

After successfully (we hope!) navigating four turns in 1.5 miles, Options 2 and 3 follow the *Fernvale Loop* (see *Ride #10* for more information) while Option 1 heads straight to the Trace on Hwy. 96. While Option 1 may be a relatively short ride, the 200 ft. "no-messin' around" climb up to the Parkway is guaranteed to give everyone a good workout.

The other options continue up the South Harpeth Valley for a pleasant 7-mile stretch. This is soon followed by a difficult 290-ft. climb guaranteed to break that nice rhythm you have lapsed into while taking in the sights of rural Tennessee. After winding around on top of Backbone Ridge, another well-deserved descent sends you into the charming, historic town of Leipers Fork (see *Ride #13* for more information).

Option 2 skirts Leipers Fork and enters the Parkway heading south while climbing a forested ridge before joining Option 1. Both of these options cross the magnificient Hwy. 96 Bridge whose mammoth yet graceful arches carry you 150 ft. above the valley. An overlook of this unique $14 million dollar bridge is located on the north side. A few miles later, an exhilarating drop off Backbone Ridge sends you to the end of the Trace.

Leaving Leipers Fork, Option 3 crosses both Leipers Creek and the West Harpeth River and traverses tranquil open countryside before turning onto McMillan Rd. where a short, but very steep hill awaits. The Boyd pioneer home (to your right after the turn onto Boyd Mill Rd.), situated on a knoll overlooking the West Harpeth River, was built in the early 1800s and remains in excellent condition. Boyd Mill Rd. is a beautiful country lane which makes its way over several roller coaster hills as it heads toward Franklin.

The route crosses Hwy. 96 near Franklin and proceeds onto Old Charlotte Pk., a narrow lane that passes two historic homes and several farms before coming to Del Rio Pk. For the next 7 miles, you are cycling the popular *Old Natchez Trace/Del Rio Ride* (see *Ride #7* for more details), which passes more magnificent antebellum Southern mansions and an Indian burial mound. The final climb of the day is on Temple Rd. and is actually the easiest major pull of this ride, but you may not think so after having pedaled 40 miles! Keep in mind that soon it's downhill to the famous Loveless Cafe. (The last half-mile on Hwy. 100 can be very busy at times, so use caution to finish this great ride on a pleasant note.)

#8 HARPETH LOOP

HOW TO GET THERE: Go west on Hwy. 100 toward Fairview. Continue .2 mi. past the Loveless Cafe at McCrory Ln. and park at the terminus of the Natchez Trace Parkway.

Mile

0.0	Bike south (away from Nashville) on Hwy. 100.
0.2	**Right** on Old Harding Rd. (first right).
0.4	**Right** on Lewis Rd. (first right).
1.0	**Left** on Griffith Rd. (first left).
2.5	**Left** on Poplar Creek Rd. (stop sign at T-intersection).
4.6	Poplar Creek Rd. angles to the left and becomes South Harpeth Rd.
6.8	**Right** on Hwy. 100 (stop sign).
7.1	**Left** on Old Harding Pk. (Old Charlotte Pk.). This is the first left *past* the South Harpeth River bridge, not the Old Harding Pk. before the bridge.
8.0	**Left** on Hwy. 96 (stop sign).

Go to Option 1, Option 2, or Option 3

OPTION 1
16 miles

10.9	**Right** on the Natchez Trace Parkway on-ramp.
11.5	**Right** on the Parkway going north toward Nashville.
16.4	Exit onto Hwy. 100. End of ride!

OPTION 2
36 miles

8.2	**Right** on Old Harding Rd. (first right).
13.1	At Fernvale, Old Harding Rd. becomes Old Hwy. 96. Continue going straight.
18.5	**Right** on Hargrove Rd. (first right after climbing Backbone Ridge).
18.9	**Left** on Wilkins Branch Rd. (Wilkie Branch Rd.)(first left).
21.6	**Right** on Old Hillsboro Rd./Hwy. 46 (stop sign at the T-intersection). Market/restaurant.
21.8	**Right** on Pinewood Rd./Hwy. 46 (first right).
22.4	**Left** on the Natchez Trace Parkway on-ramp.
22.7	**Left** on the Parkway heading north toward Nashville.
36.0	Exit onto Hwy. 100. End of ride!

OPTION 3
41 miles

8.2	**Right** on Old Harding Rd. (first right).
13.1	At Fernvale, Old Harding Rd. becomes Old Hwy. 96. Continue going straight.
21.7	**Left** on Old Hillsboro Rd./Hwy. 46. (stop sign at the T-intersection).
21.8	Market/restaurant in the town of Leipers Fork.
22.1	**Right** on Southall Rd. (Old Hwy 96).
24.0	**Left** on McMillan Rd. (first left).
24.7	**Left** on Boxley Valley Rd. (first left).
26.1	**Left** on Blazer Rd. (stop sign at the T-intersection).
26.4	**Right** on Boyd Mill Rd. (stop sign at the T-intersection).
29.2	**Right** on Hwy. 96 (stop sign).
29.3	**Left** on Short Rd. (Old Charlotte Pk.) (first left).
30.2	Straight at the stop sign.
31.0	Straight onto Del Rio Pk. (3-way stop).

33.7   **Left** (staying on Del Rio Pk.) at the next 3-way stop.
35.6   **Right** on Old Hillsboro Rd./Hwy. 46 (stop sign at the T-intersection).
35.7   **Left** on Old Natchez Trace. (first left).
37.1   **Left** on Temple Rd.
39.5   **Left** on Sneed Rd. (Union Bridge Rd.)(stop sign) which becomes Pasquo Rd.
40.7   **Left** on Hwy. 100 (stop sign at the T-intersection).
41.4   End of ride!

#8   HARPETH LOOP

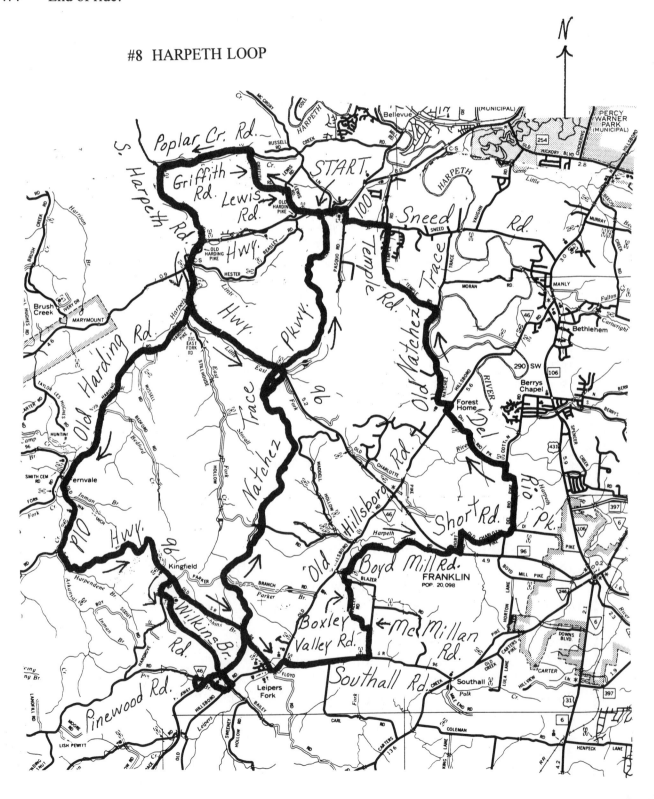

Ride # 9   BRENTWOOD/BEECH CREEK LOOP

Distance: 8 or 24 miles
Elevation Difference/Accumulated Climb: Option 1 - 210/660 ft., Option 2 - 400/1320 ft.
Terrain: Option 1 is moderately hilly with 1 fairly difficult climb and 2 easier ones. Option 2 is very hilly near Brentwood with 2 tough climbs going out and 2 moderate climbs on the return. Flat-to-rolling on western portion of loop with only 1 significant climb.
Services: None.
Traffic: Commuter traffic heavy on Granny White Pike, Murray Ln., and Holly Tree Gap Rd. Light to moderate at other times. Always heavy on the .7-mi. stretch of Hillsboro Pike (Option 2 only). Light on all other roads.
Combining Rides: # 7 *Old Natchez Trace/Del Rio Ride*, # 8 *Harpeth Loop*.
Connector Route: 4 mi. to # 14 *Brentwood/Old Smyrna Road Loop*--From Granny White Park, bike north on Granny White Pk., turn right on Maryland Way and continue to beginning of *Brentwood/Old Smyrna Road Loop*
Alternate Parking Sites: 1) Maryland Farms (1.5 mi. to loop)--Bike west to Granny White Pk., turn left and continue to loop. **2)** Old Natchez Trace and Sneed Rd. (1 mi. to loop)--Bike south on Old Natchez Trace.
Distance from Nashville: 12 miles

This trip provides a surprising variety of scenery for a short close-to-town excursion. One minute you're riding through a residential area, then suddenly you're passing by cows grazing in the pastures. The terrain varies from steep, forested hills (known as knobs) to flat, open fields along the scenic Harpeth River. There are several short, but very steep, hills to contend with on Option 2, including two consecutive grunt-and-groan pulls. If you are a real glutton for punishment, try pedaling this route in the other direction! Option 1 is a short 8-mile workout (with fewer less-excruciating hills) that cruises through sections of beautiful countryside between spacious neighborhoods.

Be advised that during commuting hours it gets trafficky near Brentwood. Once when we cycled this loop on a cold rainy Sunday morning in December, we enjoyed the misty countryside and had almost no traffic at all. These directions may look complex, but after completing this ride once or twice, you'll probably be able to ride it again without using the maps at all.

The tour begins by traveling through new suburban neighborhoods before entering the secluded valleys surrounded by steep knobs. Holly Tree Gap Rd. follows what was the primary passage to Franklin in pioneer days, and while camping near the gap, three Ft. Nashboro scouts were massacred by Indians in 1797.

Option 1 turns onto Manly Ln. and follows an upgrade through a residential area. Near the top, the new housing developments cease, and you breeze down to the rolling farmlands along Beech Creek.

Option 2 turns onto N. Berrys Chapel Rd. before reaching the gap and soon begins ascending the beautiful wooded knobs you have observed earlier from a distance. You may get a much different perspective of these knobs while huffing and puffing up this 220 ft. climb. (There is a nice view to the right at the top.) You did it! Good job! Now you get to blast down the hill and pedal up another 200 ft. climb. N. Berrys Chapel Rd. drops down to a much flatter terrain (certainly a welcomed relief to your quadriceps) and continues through residential areas. Shortly after crossing Hillsboro Pk., our route suddenly enters a rural area along the Harpeth River.

Del Rio Pk. and Old Natchez Trace meander through lovely pastoral areas with magnificent historic plantation homes. (See *Ride #7* for more information about this interesting area.) Old Natchez Trace follows the wooded banks of the Harpeth River before a short, but very steep, 70-ft. climb takes you to Moran Rd. Next, you will pass some of the most spacious and opulent farm estates in Middle Tennessee. The old stone fences, fine horses, and lush green pastures create a feeling of being in the English countryside. Harpeth Side, a shaded historic home built in the early 1800s, sits on the right after you cross the Harpeth River.

Our route turns onto Boxwood Dr. and runs through a neighborhood before coming out on Hillsboro Pk. After crossing this busy highway, Manly Ln. narrows as it passes through fields and forests as you ride into the hills. Options 1 and 2 join on Beech Creek Rd., traveling through an enchanting secluded area and over a substantial climb (80-ft.) through a gap in the wooded knobs. The Owl Hill Nature Center (operated by Cheekwood Botanical Gardens) is nestled up in the picturesque hills on the other side of the gap.

After descending to Murray Ln., the route takes you back into suburbia and gradually climbs over a low forested gap. You will then proceed through the snazzy neighborhood of Belle Rive before returning to Granny White Park.

When climbing, it is most efficient to stay seated and maintain your regular pedaling cadence. It is, however, okay to stand during short pulls or briefly on long climbs to stretch the muscles. Move back slightly in the seat, keep your hands on the top of the bars or brake hoods, and keep your upper body relaxed. Avoid rocking your torso (a mistake made by many riders), because this drains energy that your legs need.

#9 BRENTWOOD/BEECH CREEK LOOP

HOW TO GET THERE: Go south on Granny White Pk. After crossing Old Hickory Blvd., continue 1 mi. and park at Granny White Park on the left.

Mile
- 0.0   From the park, turn **left** (south) on Granny White Pk.
- 0.3   **Right** on Murray Ln. (traffic light).
- 1.8   **Left** on Holly Tree Gap Rd. (3-way stop).

Go to Option 1 or Option 2

OPTION 1
8 miles

- 2.1   **Right** on Manly Ln. (first right).
- 3.1   **Right** on Beech Creek Rd. (stop sign at the T-intersection).

Go to Both Options

OPTION 2
24 miles

- 2.9   **Right** on North Berrys Chapel Rd.
- 3.1   Turn **right** at the first street which is the new straightened North Berrys Chapel Rd. The old road simply loops around to this new road.
- 6.4   **Left** on Farmington Dr.(N. Berry's Chapel Rd.) (3-way stop).
- 6.5   **Right** on S. Berrys Chapel Rd. (first right).
- 7.2   Cross Hillsboro Rd./Hwy. 431 at the traffic light.
- 7.8   Road curves to the left and becomes Cotton Ln.
- 9.4   **Right** on Del Rio Pike (3-way stop) after leaving a residential area.
- 11.3   **Right** on Old Hillsboro Rd./Hwy. 46 (stop sign at the T-intersection).
- 11.4   **Left** on Old Natchez Trace Rd. (first left).
- 14.4   **Right** on Moran Rd. at the top of a steep climb.
- 16.5   **Right** on Boxwood Dr. (first right) after crossing river.
- 17.1   Cross Hillsboro Rd./Hwy. 431 and continue on Manly Ln. (traffic light).
- 19.0   Continue going straight on Beech Creek Rd. Manly Ln. goes to the right.

Go to Both Options

BOTH OPTIONS

- 4.6, 20.5   **Right** on Murray Ln. (stop sign).
- 5.5, 21.4   **Left** on West Johnson Chapel Rd. (easy to miss)
- 6.8, 22.7   Road becomes Belle Rive at 3-way stop. Continue straight.
- 7.5, 23.5   **Right** on Granny White Pk.
- 7.8, 23.8   End of ride!

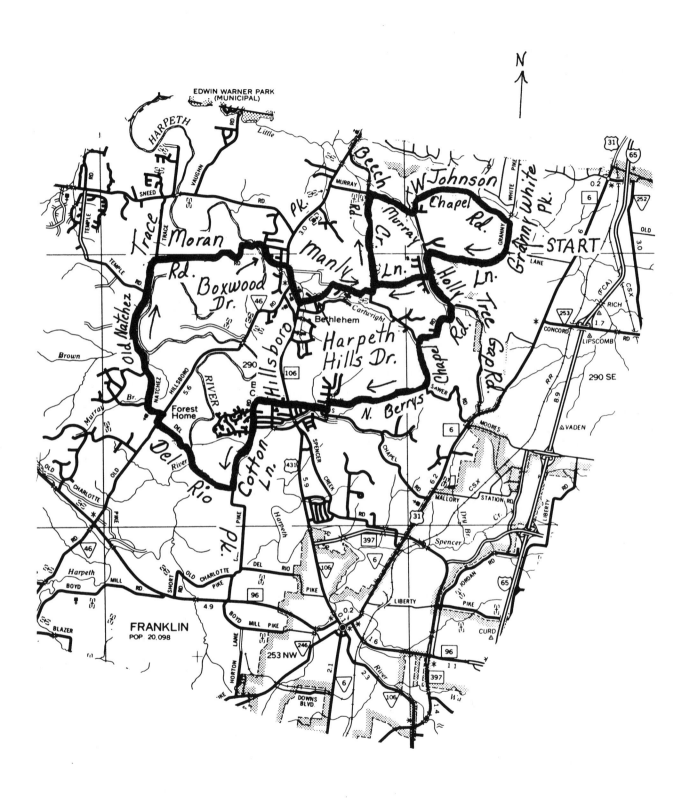

Ride # 10 FERNVALE LOOP

Distance: 26, 37, or 42 miles
Elevation Difference/Accumulated Climb: Option 1 - 400/1160 ft., Option 2 - 400/975 ft., Option 3 -390/1220 ft.
Terrain: Hilly with 1 or 2 challenging climbs. Several sections of easy, flat-to-rolling terrain.
Services: Option 1 has a market/restaurant at mile 13. Option 2 has a market at mile 18. Option 3 has markets/restaurants at miles 13 and 14 and another market at mile 22.
Traffic: Moderate on Old Hillsboro Rd. and New Hwy. 96. Light to moderate on Pinewood Rd. Light on all other roads.
Combining Rides: *#8 Harpeth Loop, #11 Fly Loop, #12 Snow Creek Loop, #18 Burwood Loop.*
Connector Route: 15 mi. to *#23 Montgomery Bell Loop*—From Hwy. 46 and Deer Ridge Rd., continue west on Hwy. 46. Cross Hwy. 100 and continue on Spencers Mill Rd. Left on Hwy. 96 to Hwy. 47.
Alternate Parking Sites: 1) South Harpeth Church of Christ (see "HOW TO GET THERE") **2)** Leipers Fork.
Distance from Nashville: 20 miles

This wonderful area around Leipers Fork and Fernvale has been a popular cycling destination long before the construction of the Natchez Trace Parkway. After a 2.5 mile warm up on the wide-shouldered Hwy. 96, you turn onto Old Harding Rd. which meanders through a beautiful broad valley with rock bluffs carved by the South Harpeth River. As you ride up the valley and are enjoying this relatively flat stretch, notice the great views of the cliffs on either side of the river.

The site of the Mayfield Spring Resort (mile 7.3) is on the left immediately before Fernvale and is marked with an interesting historical marker. A white lattice gazebo currently covers the sulphur spring which today is only a trickle. Around the turn of the century, several log cabins and an expansive 114-room white hotel with 32 columns was constructed on either side of Old Harding Rd. A connecting breezeway spanned the road, allowing horse and carriage traffic to pass underneath. The resort, complete with its fountains, gardens, and ice house, offered activities such as fishing, hunting, bowling, tennis, and live music in addition to the recreational and therapeutic sulphur spring. From as far away as the Gulf Coast, patrons were attracted to the cool waters of the plush Mayfield Spring Resort and came to escape the hot, humid, mosquito-infested summers. Visiting resort springs was a nationwide trend in this era, and several resorts such as this one were constructed in Tennessee. Unfortunately the Mayfield Spring Resort burned to the ground in 1910.

Don't blink or you'll miss Fernvale! Named for the lush green foliage growing in the area, the town today consists merely of a shut-down gas station and a few homes. Here Old Harding Rd. joins Old Hwy. 96 and continues up the narrowing valley. In approximately 2 miles the road turns to the left, and a 290-ft. climb awaits. (Some cyclists have given this hill a very affectionate name which we have chosen not to print!) Try admiring the densely wooded hillside rather than thinking about the climb up Backbone Ridge. Old Hwy. 96 levels out on top of the ridge for awhile and travels by a home that has, we think, one of the finest examples of yard-art in Middle Tennessee.

Option 1 turns right on Hargrove Rd. and quickly drops down into a secluded hollow known as Wilkie Branch before hooking up with the Natchez Trace. The Natchez Trace Parkway (see *Ride #12* for historical information) climbs once again up Backbone Ridge and meanders along the thickly forested hilltops, offering occasional peeks of the surrounding countryside.

Option 2 also cuts off on Hargrove Rd. and stays on the ridge, thus eliminating the climbs encountered on the other options. A well-deserved descent on Option 3 takes you into the peaceful community of Leipers Fork (see *Ride #13* for historical information) and then proceeds up a friendly grade on Pinewood Rd. (200 ft.) For the next 4 or 5 miles, Options 2 and 3 follow the Duck River Ridge, which separates the Harpeth and Duck Valleys.

Option 2 turns off on South Harpeth Rd. for a fun descent along the headwaters of the cascading South Harpeth River into Fernvale. Option 3 follows Caney Fork Rd. as it winds through a picturesque hollow that looks very similar to what one might see in the Appalachians. This stretch along a tumbling creek and shady woods is surprisingly cool and pleasant on hot summer days. The remains of the Caney Fork Iron Furnace can be seen on the left at mile 30.7. Iron was processed in the furnace to make cannonballs used in the Battle of New Orleans (1815) and the pillars of the Williamson County Courthouse (1857) in Franklin. Caney Fork Rd. transits the length of this hollow which gradually opens into a small valley with green pastures. Upon crossing the South Harpeth at Fernvale, Option 2 is joined, and both routes retrace the lovely stretch on which you started.

Update: We felt we had to mention that Big East Fork/Still House Hollow Rd. (at mile 3) is one of the most beautiful roads in the area. It was not paved when we first came out with this book which is why it is not utilized on this ride. Now that it is paved, it simply has to be used! This country lane traveling along a crystal clear creek and lovely farms would make a great beginner ride until the big hill which awaits 4 miles from our route on Old Harding Rd. From the top, it is usually possible to walk up steep embankment to the Natchez Trace Parkway. You may also continue down to Old Hillsboro Rd. (a total of 8 miles) where you can easily hop on the Harpeth Loop.

When riding in the rain, decrease your tire pressure (mountain/hybrid bikes need not do this) by 20 psi. This will give you better traction. The roads are most hazardous immediately after it begins to rain, due to the dust and oil mixing with the water. Be aware of slick hazards such as painted lines and steel surfaces (railroad tracks, manhole covers, etc.)

10 FERNVALE LOOP

HOW TO GET THERE: Take Hwy. 100 West (it actually goes south) and turn left on Hwy. 96 East. Park in the provided parking spaces along the on-ramp to the Natchez Trace Parkway. For Options 2 & 3, this ride may be reduced 5 miles by parking at the S. Harpeth Church of Christ (only if permitted and the church is not being used) on Old Harding Pk. which runs between Hwy. 100 and Hwy. 96.

Mile

0.0   From the Natchez Trace access ramp, turn **left** on Hwy. 96 going west.

2.6   **Left** on Old Harding Rd. (easy to miss).

7.5   Continue straight on Old Hwy. 96 (3-way stop) in the community of Fernvale.
Go to Option 1, Option 2, or Option 3

OPTION 1
26 miles

12.9   **Right** on Hargrove Rd. (first right after climbing Backbone Ridge).

13.3   **Left** on Wilkins Branch Rd. (Wilkie Branch Rd.)(first left).

16.0   **Right** on Old Hillsboro Rd./Hwy. 46 (stop sign at the T-intersection). Market.

16.2   **Right** on Pinewood Rd./Hwy. 46 (first right).

16.8   **Left** on the Natchez Trace Parkway on-ramp.

17.1   **Left** on the Parkway heading toward Nashville.

25.5   **Right** at the Hwy. 96 exit.

26.1   End of ride!

OPTION 2
37 miles

12.9   **Right** on Hargrove Rd. (first right after climbing Backbone Ridge).

15,8   **Right** on Pinewood Rd./Hwy. 46 (stop sign at the T-intersection).

21.3   Market.

22.5   **Right** on S. Harpeth Rd. (first right past the Pinewood School).

23.5   Bear **right** (staying on S. Harpeth Rd.) where Magnum Rd. enters from the left.

25.2   Bear **right** (staying on S. Harpeth Rd.) where Coldwater Rd. enters from the left.

27.7   **Left** on Old Hwy. 96 (stop sign at the T-intersection). Retrace your route to the starting point.

36.9   End of ride!

OPTION 3
42 miles

15.9   **Right** on Old Hillsboro Rd./Hwy. 46 (stop sign at the T-intersection) in the town of Leipers Fork. Market/restaurant .1 mi. off the route in the other direction (north) on Old Hillsboro Rd./Hwy. 46.

16.9   Market.

17.0   **Right** on Pinewood Rd./Hwy. 46. Look for the Natchez Trace Parkway sign.

24.9   Market.

27.3   **Right** on Deer Ridge Rd. (easy to miss) in a small residential area of brick homes.

28.8   **Right** on Caney Fork Rd. (second right). There are two confusing intersections on this road. Follow the creek all the way down to the South Harpeth River.

34.3   **Right** on Old Hwy. 96 and immediately cross the South Harpeth River at Fernvale.

34.4   **Left** on Old Harding Rd. (3-way stop). Retrace your route to the starting point.

41.9   End of ride!

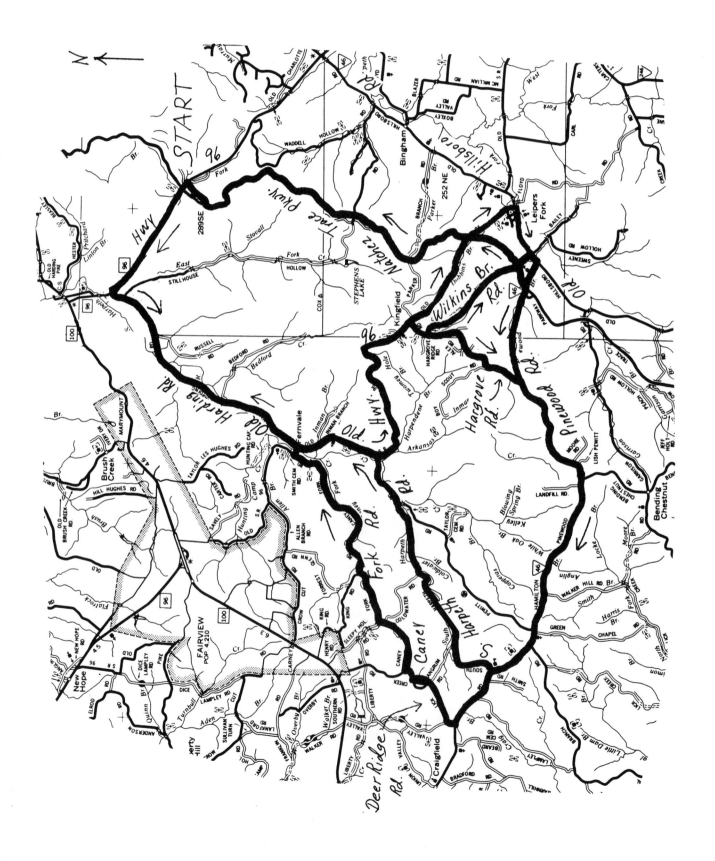

11 THE FLY LOOP

Distance: 29 miles
Elevation Difference/Accumulated Climb: 380/1050 ft.
Terrain: Moderately hilly to gently rolling.
Services: Water/restrooms at mile 2.3. Markets at miles 15.9, 19.1, and 25.3.
Traffic: Light on the Natchez Trace Pkwy. Light to moderate on Leipers Creek/Old Hillsboro Rd.
Combining Rides:# 8 Harpeth Loop, # 10 Fernvale Loop, # 12 Snow Creek Loop, # 13 Burwood Loop.
Alternate Parking Site: Garrison Branch Picnic Area 1.5 mi. south on the Natchez Trace Pkwy. from Hwy. 46.
Distance from Nashville: 22 miles

We call this tour the *Fly Loop* because it goes through a town named Fly, which consists of only a market, a garage, and a lumber mill. This loop is another great ride that begins from the town of Leipers Fork (see *Ride # 13* for historical information) and incorporates 13 miles of the wonderful Natchez Trace Parkway.

We begin by going south on the Trace where two substantial climbs await within the first 6 miles. The Trace reaches the top of the Duck River Ridge (also known as the Tennessee Valley Divide) at mile 5.9 where the Parkway thankfully flattens out for the next 8 miles. At a parking area on the left, there is a marker which explains that the Tennessee Valley Divide was the boundary between the United States to the north and the Chickasaw Nation to the south.

Peace and solitude are prevalent on the Natchez Trace, and there are times when you are as likely to encounter a deer silently grazing as you are another vehicle. On nice weekends, the traffic usually increases (as do the cyclists), but never enough to detract from the serenity of the area. Commercial traffic is not permitted. (More about the history of the Trace in *Ride # 12*.)

After exiting the Natchez Trace onto Hwy. 7, a thriller descent with no sharp curves takes you into Fly, Tennessee. "There's no place like Fly" as their sign reads. Leipers Creek Rd. follows the route of an old railroad grade through a particularly satisfying segment of Tennessee countryside along Leipers Creek. Notice the old train depot to the right at mile 17.7. Because this road follows what used to be a railroad grade, the ascent up the Duck River Ridge is more subtle than other roads in the area. After accomplishing this climb, you immediately drop down to the Leipers Fork Valley (not the same as Leipers Creek Valley) which soon becomes a very wide valley as it approaches the West Harpeth River. At mile 24, you roll through the community of Boston, dating back to the early 1800s. This town, which today consists of only a general store, was supposedly given its name by the first settlers because of the resemblance in landscape to Boston, Massachusetts. From here, the road hugs the west slope of the valley as it returns to Leipers Fork.

11 THE FLY LOOP

HOW TO GET THERE: Take Hillsboro Pk./Hwy. 431 South and go right on Old Hillsboro Rd./Hwy. 46 West. Cross Hwy. 96 and continue for 5.5 mi. into the town of Leipers Fork. Turn right on Pinewood Rd./Hwy. 46 at the sign for the Natchez Trace Pkwy. Park at Hillsboro School (.2 mi. on Pinewood Rd.) when school is not in session or at the Williamson County Rescue Squad building on the corner of Pinewood Rd. and Old Hillsboro Rd.

Mile

0.0	From the corner of Pinewood Rd. and Old Hillsboro Rd., bike west toward the Natchez Trace Parkway.
0.7	**Left** on the Natchez Trace Parkway on-ramp.
0.8	**Right** on the Trace going south.
2.3	Garrison Branch Picnic Area (water/restrooms).
4.6	Burns Branch Picnic Area (no facilities).
14.0	**Right** at the Hwy. 7 exit (first exit).
14.2	**Left** on Hwy. 7 (toward Columbia) at the bottom of the ramp.
15.9	Market in the town of Fly.
16.1	**Left** on Leipers Creek Rd. (second left past the market).
19.0	Market in the town of Bethel.
25.3	Market in the town of Boston.
28.8	End of Ride!

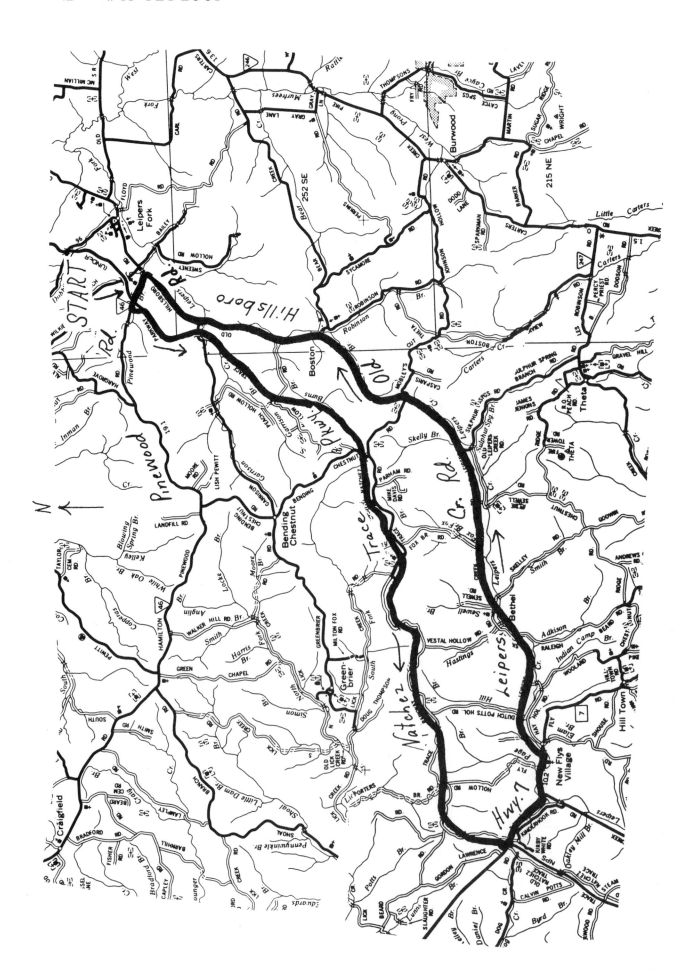

Ride # 12   SNOW CREEK LOOP

Distance: 40 or 48 miles
Elevation Difference/Accumulated Climb: Option 1 - 440/1780 ft., Option 2 - 490/2210 ft.
Terrain: Moderately hilly. Option 1 has 3 gradual grades and 2 steep climbs. Option 2 has 4 long gradual grades.
Services: Option 1 has markets at miles 3.5, 9.8, 16.3, and 24.4. Restaurant at mile 16.3. Water/restrooms at mile 37.5. Option 2 has markets at miles 3.5, 9.8, and 16.3. Restaurant at mile 16.3. Water/restrooms at miles 25.6 and 45.1.
Traffic: Light to moderate on Old Hillsboro Rd., Hwy. 50, and Hwy. 7. Light on all other roads.
Combining Rides: *# 8 Harpeth Loop, # 10 Fernvale Loop, # 11 Fly Loop, # 13 Burwood Loop.*
Connector Route: 5.9 mi. to *Burwood Loop*--We recommend beginning on the *Burwood Loop* and going south on Carters Creek Pk./Hwy. 246 when you get to the town of Burwood. Go right on Hwy. 247 which goes up to Theta on the *Snow Creek Loop.*
Alternate Parking Site: Garrison Branch Picnic area 1.5 mi. south of Hwy. 46 on the Natchez Trace Pkwy.
Distance from Nashville: 22 miles

This is truly a gem of a ride. It is easy to see why it's a favorite excursion of the Nashville Bicycle Club and other cyclists who have discovered how to combine Snow Creek Rd. and the Natchez Trace Parkway. Our route contains two options, both of which cross the Duck River Ridge and proceed down along Snow Creek. Option 2 goes all the way down to the Duck River at the Gordon House and Ferry site on the Trace while Option 1 leaves Snow Creek and cuts over into beautiful Water Valley. Both options return via the Parkway.

This trip starts in the town of Leipers Fork (see *Ride # 13* for historical information) and follows an old railroad bed up a gentle grade over the Duck River Ridge. After dropping down the other side, you take Sulphur Springs Branch Rd. up another gentle climb through an isolated hollow with several springs. At the turn of the century, this hollow was known for its sulphur spring resort which has long since disappeared like other similar resorts that were once popular in Tennessee.

After leaving the community of Theta, Snow Creek Rd./Hwy. 247 winds along the ridge for a couple of miles before dropping (and we mean a nearly vertical descent) down to the Snow Creek Valley. Cyclists can easily do 40-50 mph down this hill, but there is a *dangerous* sharp left at the bottom. You need to slow down well before you get to the turn.

The next 4 miles lead you down a flat tranquil valley with plenty of corn and cows. Upon arriving at Hwy. 7, you are in the community of Santa Fe (pronounced "Santa Fee" in Tennessee), boasting two markets and a country restaurant. When we indulged in veggies, cornbread, and pie, we discovered that the big hills before Water Valley had become noticeably tougher! This is the last chance for food on both options until the end of the ride; however, water is available later on Option 2, and there is a market .4 mile off the loop on Option 1.

Option 1 turns north on Hwy. 7 and passes through the Santa Fe community. After conquering two tough ascents (200 ft. and 130 ft.) on Water Valley Rd., you will cruise down to the community of Water Valley with its deserted store fronts. Next there is a nice, flat stretch (whoopee!) along Leipers Creek to Hwy. 7 near the town of Fly. From here, a long steady upgrade (170 ft.) awaits as you pedal up to the Natchez Trace Parkway.

From Santa Fe, Option 2 continues the length of Snow Creek for more of the same flat, peaceful, and scenic pedaling. Several lovely old white farmhouses overlook the pastures and corn fields in this broadening valley. From Hwy. 50, a moderate grade over a hill is followed by a long steady descent to the Natchez Trace Parkway.

Once you enter the Parkway, you may wish to detour to Gordon's Ferry Historic Site and Rest Area which is .4 mile to the south. The brick Gordon home, built in 1818, stands adjacent to the picnic shelters. An important ferry was established here in the early 1800s, making travel from Natchez to Nashville much easier. It was operated by John Gordon's wife Dorothea, under an agreement with Indian Chief George Colbert. If you have the time and strength, you may wish to ride 3 miles south on the Trace to a scenic overlook of the Duck River Valley and to the unique geological feature of Jackson Falls. There are also water and restroom facilities at Jackson Falls.

From Hwy. 50, our tour heads north on the Trace up a long gradual rise (300 ft.) to the Duck River Ridge. The Water Valley Overlook offers a panoramic view of the countryside which we have found to be particularly spectacular in the autumn. For the last 10 miles, Options 1 and 2 follow the Trace as it meanders along the rolling ridge and then drops and rises out of a couple of hollows before finally arriving at the Leipers Fork exit.

The Natchez Trace Parkway, run by the National Park Service, follows the route of the historic wilderness road that was officially established in 1800, although it was used as early as 1785 by white settlers. Boatmen floated their goods on the Cumberland, Tennessee, and Ohio Rivers to the Mississippi River and then down to Natchez or New Orleans. They sold their goods, dismantled their boats and sold the timber, and headed overland on the Natchez Trace to Nashville and points north. It was a perilous 500-mile journey through land controlled by the Choctaw and Chickasaw Nations. Wild animals, poisonous snakes, mosquitoes, swamps, flooded rivers, and worst of all, bandits were some of the hazards encountered along the Trace. Outlaws such as the Harpe brothers and Samuel Mason preyed upon the boatmen who carried money and other goods along this passage, and grisly murders were not uncommon. Should you be struggling up a hill in the heat of summer or attempting to fix a flat, just remember what these poor pioneers must have gone through compared to your current predicament. The arrival of the steamboat *New Orleans* in 1812 heralded a new age of travel, and the use of the Trace declined. Only recently have cyclists, hikers, equestrians, and motorists been able to enjoy this 450-mile national treasure. Cycling the Trace has other advantages besides its scenic and historic qualities--there are no commercial vehicles or loose dogs! (If you are interested in riding the entire Trace, see the *Appendix* for more information.)

#12 SNOW CREEK LOOP

HOW TO GET THERE: Take Hillsboro Pk./Hwy. 431 South and go right on Old Hillsboro Rd./Hwy. 46 west. Cross Hwy. 96 and continue 5.5 mi. into the town of Leipers Fork. Turn right on Pinewood Rd./Hwy. 46. at the sign for the Natchez Trace Pkwy. Park at Hillsboro School (.2 mi. on Pinewood Rd.) when school is not in session or at the Ranger Station by the Parkway.

Mile
0.0	Bike south (away from Leipers Fork) on Old Hillsboro Rd.
3.5	Market.
6.9	**Left** on Sulphur Springs Branch Rd. (first left after a substantial descent).
9.8	**Right** on Snow Creek Rd./Hwy. 247 (Dodson Rd.) (stop sign at the T-intersection). Market in the town of Theta.

Go to Option 1 or Option 2

OPTION 1
40 miles

16.3	**Right** on Santa Fe Pk. (Fly Rd., Old Hwy. 7) in the town of Santa Fe (stop sign at the 4-way intersection). Market/restaurant.
17.0	Go straight onto Water Valley Rd. where Fly Rd. curves to the right. Small park/gazebo.
17.9	Cross the new Hwy. 7 (stop sign).
20.9	**Right** on Leipers Creek Rd. in the community of Water Valley.
24.4	**Left** on Hwy. 7 (stop sign at the T-intersection).
25.6	**Right** on the on-ramp to the Natchez Trace immediately after going under the bridge.
25.8	**Left** on the Parkway (going north) at the end of the on-ramp.

Go to Both Options

OPTION 2
48 miles

16.3	Cross Santa Fe Pk. (Old Hwy. 7) at Santa Fe (stop sign). Market/restaurant.
16.7	**Left** on Hwy. 7 (stop sign at the T-intersection).
16.9	**Right** on Hwy. 247
22.6	**Right** on Hwy. 50 (stop sign at the T-intersection).
25.6	**Right** onto the Natchez Trace Parkway on-ramp. Take the Parkway north toward Nashville. Gordon Ferry historic site and picnic area (water/restrooms) are .4 mi. to the south on the Parkway.
33.4	Hwy. 7 exit. Continue on the Parkway.

Go to Both Options

BOTH OPTIONS

35.2, 42.8	Burns Picnic Area (no water).
37.5, 45.1	Garrison Creek Picnic Area (water/restrooms).
39.1, 46.7	**Left** at the Hwy. 46 exit.
39.2, 46.8	**Right** on Hwy.46/Pinewood Rd. at the bottom of the ramp.
39.9, 47.5	End of ride. Now you can say you've ridden a bicycle from Boston to Santa Fe in one day!

The map does not show the new Hwy. 7 in Santa Fe. The 4-mile segment of Leipers Cr. Rd. between Water Valley and Hwy. 247 may also be used to create additional loop rides.

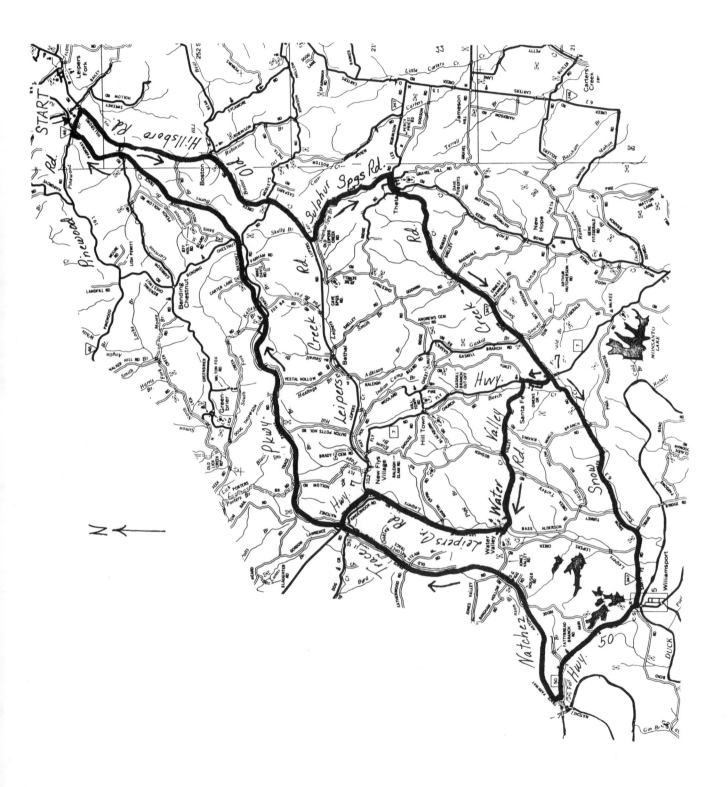

Ride # 13   BURWOOD LOOP

Distance: 20, 28, or 33 miles
Elevation Difference/Accumulated Climb: Option 1 - 260/640 ft., Option 2 - 260/1010 ft.,
   Option 3 - 380/1470 ft.
Terrain: Rolling and moderately hilly on All Options with 1 short but steep climb after
   Burwood. Option 3 has 1 additional very challenging climb.
Services: Option 1 has markets at miles 10 and 15.   Option 2 has markets at miles 14
   (1.5 mi. off the loop), 18, and 23. Option 3 has markets at miles 14 (1.5 miles off the
   loop), 18, and 28.
Traffic: Light to moderate on Old Hillsboro Rd., Southall Rd., and Carters Creek Pk. Light
   on all other roads.
Combining Rides: *# 8 Harpeth Loop, # 10 Fernvale Loop, # 11 Fly Loop, # 12 Snow Creek
   Loop, # 17 Williamson County Loop.*
Connector Routes: 1) .7 mi. to *Fernvale Loop*--From the town of Bending Chestnut on
   Option 2, take Bending Chestnut Rd. north to Pinewood Rd./Hwy. 46. An excellent
   choice is to go to Fernvale via Caney Fork Rd. or S. Harpeth Rd. and return to the town
   of Leipers Fork on Old Hwy. 96 or on the Natchez Trace Pkwy.   **2)** 5.9 mi. to *Snow
   Creek Loop*--Bike south on Carters Creek Pk./Hwy. 247 from Johnson Hollow Rd. in the
   town of Burwood to Hwy. 246, turn right and go up the hill to the town of Theta. Follow
   the rest of the *Snow Creek Loop* back to Leipers Fork.
Alternative Parking Site: Franklin (5 mi. to loop)--Bike west on W. Main St./Carters Creek
   Pk./Hwy. 246.
Distance from Nashville: 22 miles

The *Burwood Loop* follows wonderful meandering rural roads which pass through
quaint historic communities and by several antebellum homes. We begin this ride in the
town of Leipers Fork which is, in a sense, a bicycle hub offering miles and miles of excellent
cycling possibilities. Leipers Fork (originally known as Hillsboro) is also a town rich in
history. It was settled in the 1780s by the Leiper brothers, one of whom died in the Battle
of the Bluffs at Ft. Nashboro (1781). Many years later, another brother was accredited with
killing the notorious bandit Big Harpe who, along with his brother Little Harpe, terrorized
travelers on the Natchez Trace and elsewhere in the frontiers of Kentucky and Tennessee.
In 1800, Thomas Hart Benton, the famous senator from Missouri who was brought by his
widowed mother to Leipers Fork, also practiced law in Franklin and Nashville. He eventually left Tennessee with his brother Jesse who had shot and wounded Andrew Jackson in a
brawl.

After a short stretch on Old Hillsboro Rd., our route leaves town going west across
the creek which is also named Leipers Fork. Carl Rd. winds among forests and fields, crosses
Murfrees Creek, and then ascends a steep, wooded hillside before arriving at Carters Creek
Pk. Option 1 stays on Carters Creek Pk. into the community of Burwood while Options 2
and 3 follow a roundabout course on West Harpeth Rd. and Sedberry Rd. These peaceful
country lanes are picturesque with a mix of shaded woods and wide open pastures. After a
broken upgrade (150 ft.) to the top of the ridge on Sedberry Rd., you pass the Hilltop Manor
(1808) on the right.

Upon arriving at Thompson Station-Burwood Rd., you may choose to take either
Option 2 or Option 3 into Burwood. Both roads are scenic, but Evergreen Rd. has a few

minor climbs. Option 3 travels by the Eastview pioneer house (built by John Pope in 1806) at the corner of Evergreen Rd. and Chapel Rd. This building is reputed to be haunted by a ghost named "Crazy Mary" who is responsible for the mysterious lights which have appeared in the house throughout the years. She was seen also in the water at Cayce Springs near Burwood where a turn-of-the-century resort once stood. We recommend you avoid riding at night in this area!

All options come together in Burwood, a peaceful well-kept community founded by circuit preacher John Pope (a.k.a Parson Pope). This preacher, who was well-known at the time, donated land for large camp meetings that lasted for days on the site of the present Burwood Methodist Church.

After leaving Burwood, a short, steep uphill (60 ft.) out of Johnson Hollow is followed by a quick plunge into Robinson Hollow. Options 1 and 2 send you into the Boston community and back to Leipers Fork, with mostly downhill and flat stretches all the way. Hardy cyclists choosing Option 3 will test themselves on a very steep grade up Mobley Cut Rd. (200 ft.) which begins to level out near the top but keeps ascending for quite awhile after the initial "grunt-and-groan" pull. This route now winds along the rolling Duck River Ridge into the town of Bending Chestnut, named for a huge, bent chestnut tree which no longer exists (like all American Chestnuts). Young chestnut saplings, bent by Indians to mark the trails, grew into bent mature trees and created distinguishing landmarks. An exhilarating descent on Garrison Rd. brings you into a narrow hollow which gradually unfolds into a broad fertile valley. The final leg returns to Leipers Fork along the west side of the Leipers Fork Valley.

Joining a bike club is a great bargain for anyone who cycles. Besides meeting other riders, you also receive newsletters containing informative articles, ride calendars, and the latest on bike advocacy efforts. See the *Appendix* for local club listings.

13 BURWOOD LOOP

HOW TO GET THERE: Take Hillsboro Pk./Hwy. 431 South and go right on Old Hillsboro Rd./Hwy. 46 West. Cross Hwy. 96 and continue for 5.5 mi. into the town of Leipers Fork. Turn right on Pinewood Rd./Hwy. 46 at the sign to the Natchez Trace Pkwy. You can park at Hillsboro School (.2 mi. on Pinewood Rd.) when school is not in session or at the Williamson County Rescue Squad building on the corner of Pinewood Rd. and Old Hillsboro Rd.

Mile

0.0   From Pinewood Rd., turn **left** (north) on Old Hillsboro Rd. heading toward Nashville.

1.4   **Right** on Southall Rd. (Old Hwy 96).

2.4   **Right** on Carl Rd. (first right).

5.5   **Right** on Carters Creek Pk./Hwy. 246 (stop sign at the T-intersection).
Go to Option 1 or Options "2 and 3"

OPTION 1
20 miles

10.2   **Right** on Johnson Hollow Rd. which is .3 mi. before the market in the town of Burwood. Johnson Hollow Rd. becomes Robinson Rd.

15.0   **Right** on Old Hillsboro Rd. (Leipers Creek Rd.) (stop sign at the T-intersection). Market in the town of Boston.

19.8   End of ride!

OPTIONS "2 and 3"
28/33 miles

7.3   **Left** on West Harpeth Rd. (first left).

11.0   **Right** on Sedberry Rd. (3-way intersection). Do not cross the West Harpeth River.

14.2   **Right** on Thompson Station-Burwood Rd. (stop sign at the T-intersection). Market (1.5 mi. off the route) to the left on Thompson Station-Burwood Rd.
Go to Option 2 or Option 3

OPTION 2
28 miles

17.0   **Left** on Carters Creek Pk./Hwy. 246 (stop sign at the T-intersection).

18.1   **Right** on Johnson Hollow Rd. (first right). Market .3 mi. ahead on Carters Creek Pk. in the town of Burwood. Johnson Hollow Rd. becomes Robinson Rd.

22.9   **Right** on Old Hillsboro Rd. (Leipers Creek Rd.) (stop sign at the T-intersection). Market in the town of Boston.

27.7   End of ride!

OPTION 3
33 miles

14.3   **Left** on Evergreen Rd. (Martin Rd.)(first right).

16.6   Bear **right** (staying on Evergreen Rd.) as Lavender Rd. goes straight ahead.

17.6   **Right** on Pope's Chapel Rd. (stop sign at the T- intersection).

18.8   **Right** on Carters Creek Pk./Hwy. 246 in the town of Burwood (stop sign at the T-intersection). Market.

19.1   **Left** on Johnson Hollow Rd. (first left).

21.4   **Left** on Mobley Cut Rd. after descending into a hollow.

22.7   Cross Boston Theta Rd. (stop sign).

24.1   Cross Leipers Creek Rd. (stop sign) and continue on Natchez Trace Rd.

25.4   **Right** on Bending Chestnut Rd. which immediately goes under the Natchez Trace Pkwy.

27.7   **Right** on Garrison Branch Rd. (4-way stop) in the community of Bending Chestnut. Market.

31.5   **Left** on Old Hillsboro Rd. (stop sign at the T-intersection).

32.8   End of ride!

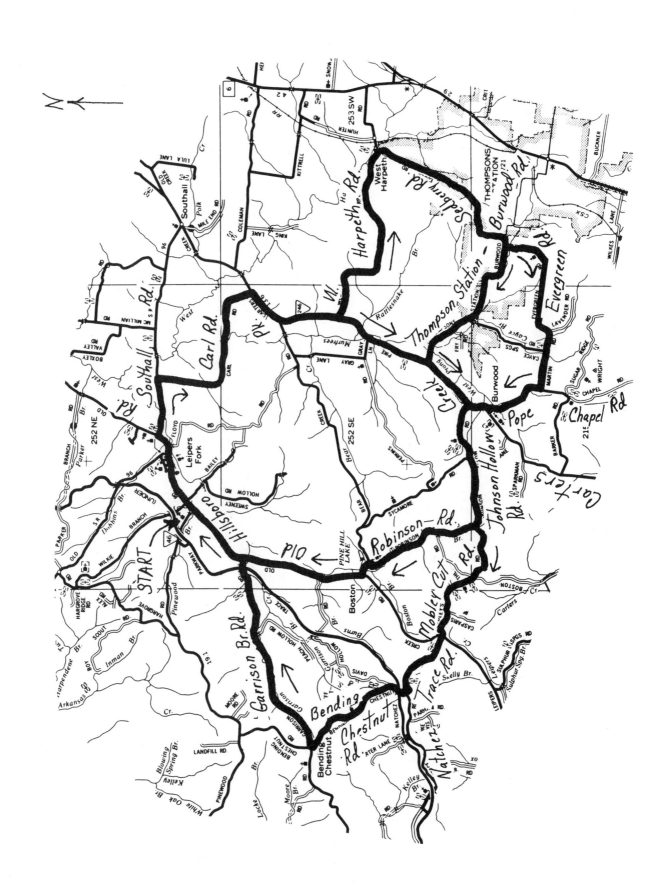

Ride #14A   BRENTWOOD/OLD SMYRNA ROAD LOOP

Distance: 19, 22, or 24 miles
Elevation Difference/Accumulated Climb: Option 1 - 200/1210 ft., Option 2 - 300/1690 ft., Option 3 - 340/1730 ft.
Terrain: Moderately hilly. No long climbs but a lot of ups and downs.
Services: None.
Traffic: Moderate (heavy during peak hours) on Wilson Pk., Crockett Rd., Concord Rd. and Edmondson Pk. Light on all other roads.
Combining Rides: *#15 Mill Creek Loop, #16 Franklin/Nolensville Loop.*
Connector Routes: 1) 2 mi. to *#9 Brentwood/Beech Creek Loop*—Bike west on Maryland Way to Granny White Pk., turn left (south) and go 1.2 mi. to beginning of loop. **2)** 1 mi. to *#17 Williamson County Loop*—From the intersection of Wilson Pk. and Split Log Rd. on Option 3, bike south on Wilson Pk.
Alternate Parking Sites: 1) Granny White Park (2.5 mi. to beginning of ride)—Bike north on Granny White Pk., turn right on Maryland Way, and continue to start of ride. **2)** Crockett Park/School on Crockett Rd. near Wilson Pk.
Distance from Nashville: 9 miles

This ride skirts the increasing suburban sprawl of Nashville and Brentwood, yet manages to traverse rural hills and pastures which have changed little in the last 100 years. Our route, which is only a short distance from Nashville and begins near I-65, makes a great after-work workout or quick bicycling getaway.

The premier section of the trip occurs after the first 2 miles. Suddenly, Old Smyrna Rd. becomes a cozy country lane lined by trees and old rock fences. Several antebellum plantation homes (dating 1800-1835) built by the Sneed family, stand in their quiet grandeur along this road. James Sneed came to Tennessee from North Carolina in 1798 along with the Perkins family whose historic homes lie along Del Rio Pk. and Old Natchez Trace. (See *Ride #7* for more information.) Holt Rd. goes through a spacious residential area before a short .2-mile busy stretch on Nolensville Pk. takes you to Bluff Rd. which briefly runs along a scenic section of Mill Creek. From here, the hills increase in size as you head south, but the nice views on Waller Rd. make the effort worthwhile.

Upon arriving at Sunset Rd. (no, it's nothing like Hollywood), you have the option of riding a straight stretch to Concord Rd. (Option 1), or tackling more hills and seeing lovely scenery on Split Log Rd. (Options 2 and 3). Split Log Rd. is great for cycling—smooth pavement, few cars, pastoral countryside, and challenging climbs.

Option 2 cuts back to Sunset Rd. on a pleasant downhill stretch on Ragsdale Rd.

Option 3 continues all the way down to Wilson Pk. where two opulent historic mansions stand majestically on wooded knolls on either side of Wilson Pk. The Ravenwood home, which is barely visible from the intersection of Wilson Pk. and Split Log Rd., was built in 1825 by James Wilson who owned several plantations in the deep South. He was reputed to be worth over two million dollars, an outrageous amount in those times. The Inglehame home (1858), built for Mr. Wilson's daughter, can be seen on the hill to the left as you approach Wilson Pk. on Split Log Rd.

Near Moore's Ln. at mile 15.5 on Option 3, you can see the Boiling Springs Academy (1833) which has been boarded up for quite some time. It stands next to an Indian mound which was excavated by archaeologists who sent several of the artifacts to the Smithsonian Museum for public display. Before Crockett Rd., you'll see the landmark historic plantation home known as Forge Seat. This mansion, built by Samuel Crockett in 1808, was visited by several famous people including Andrew Jackson and David Crockett. Rather than bike the sometimes busy Crockett Rd., you may turn into Crockett Park (by the schools) and go right on the greenway which, along with a few residential streets, allows you to connect with Green Hills Blvd.

The remainder of Option 3 goes through recently developed subdivisions before joining Options 1 and 2 on Edmondson Pk. From here all options take you back to lovely Old Smyrna Rd. and then into the hustle and bustle of Brentwood.

Updates: The northern segment of Wilson Pk., Concord Rd., and Crocket Rd. have become very busy unless you ride early on weekends. Consider parking at River Park on Concord Rd. just east of I-65. You can ride the greenway down to Wilson Pk. south of Crockett Rd. Cyclists may also avoid a portion of the moderately busy Concord Rd. and Edmondson Pk. by using Liberty Church Rd. to connect these two roads. This public road is gated near the church, but cyclists can easily get around the gate.

Ride #14B   BRENTWOOD GREENWAY

Distance: Up to 10 miles roundtrip
Terrain: Flat to slightly rolling.
Traffic: None
Combining Ride: *#14A Brentwood/Old Smyrna Road Loop.*
Distance from Nashville: 22 miles

The city of Brentwood boasts a network of paved greenways from the Lipscomb School near I-65 and Concord Rd. heading southeast to Crockett Park and onto Ravenwood High School. Twisting through forests and fields, this main path, known as the River Park Greenway or Red Trail, often parallels the Little Harpeth River. The cool cascading river, picnic tables, and two playgrounds make this an ideal family outing. At Crockett Park the path makes a one-mile loop with a mild 100 ft. climb. Also of interest at Crockett Park are two historic 1830s homes and several ballfields. Be alert and control your speed, because you are sharing the path with walkers, inline skaters, baby strollers, etc.

The Yellow Trail leaves the Red Trail and continues south, paralleling Wilson Pk. past the historic Boiling Springs Academy building and onto Ravenwood High where you can pick up the wide-shouldered Wilson Pk. and other great rural roads. There is additional road cycling on the bike lanes of Knox Valley Dr. (at River Park) and by taking a spur path from Crockett Park to the bike lanes of Arrowhead Dr. and Green Hills Blvd. The Blue Trail heads north of Concord Rd. for a 1-2 mile loop around the WSM tower. Erected in 1938, this tower which broadcasts the Grand Ol' Opry was once the tallest radio tower in the world.

HOW TO GET THERE: Take I-65 south, exit at Concord Rd./Hwy. 253 (exit 71), turn left (east) and then right on Knox Valley Dr. Park at River Park or the Brentwood Library.

or

From Concord Rd., turn right on Wilson Pk./Hwy. 252, and then left on Crockett Rd. Turn left at the school and continue to the ballfields at the bottom of the hill. The main bikeway goes to the left.

Map/directions not included.

14 BRENTWOOD/OLD SMYRNA ROAD LOOP

HOW TO GET THERE: Take Franklin Pk./Hwy. 31 South from Nashville to Brentwood. Go one light past Old Hickory Blvd. and turn right on Maryland Way. Park at any of the office parking lots after business hours. Be sure to obey all parking regulations.

Mile

0.0   Begin ride at the corner of Maryland Way and Franklin Pk. Cross Franklin Pk. and continue on Church St.

0.3   **Right** on Wilson Pk./Hwy. 252 which is the first right after going under I-65.

1.2   **Left** on Old Smyrna Rd. (easy to miss) immediately before the Brentwood Dolphin Swim and Tennis Club.

1.8   **Left** (staying on Old Smyrna Rd.) at the 3-way stop.

3.6   **Right** on Edmondson Pk. (stop sign at the T-intersection).

3.9   **Left** on Holt Rd. (first left).

6.0   **Right** on Nolensville Pk./Hwy. 31A (stop sign at the T-intersection).

6.2   **Right** on Bluff Rd. (first right).

7.4   **Left** on Concord Rd./Hwy. 253 (stop sign at the T-intersection).

7.6   **Right** on Waller Rd. (first right).

9.6   **Right** on Sunset Rd. (stop sign at the T-intersection).
Go to Option 1, Option 2, or Option 3

OPTION 1
19 miles

9.8   Continue straight on Sunset Rd.
Go to Options "1 and 2"

OPTION 2
22 miles

9.8   **Left** on Split Log Rd. (Owl Creek Rd.) (first left).

12.3   **Right** on Ragsdale Rd. after ascending a hill.

14.3   **Left** on Sunset Rd. (stop sign at the T-intersection).
Go to Options "1 and 2"

OPTIONS "1 and 2"

11.9, 15.2   **Left** on Concord Rd. (stop sign at T-intersection).

13.2, 16.5   **Right** on Edmondson Pk.

15.4, 18.7   **Left** on Old Smyrna Rd. and retrace your route back to the starting point.

19.0, 22.3   End of ride!

OPTION 3
24 miles

9.8   **Left** on Split Log Rd. (Owl Creek Rd.) (first left).

12.3   Stay **left** (on Split Log Rd.) at 3-way intersection near the top of a hill.

13.8   **Right** on Wilson Pk./Hwy. 252 (stop sign at the T-intersection).

15.8   **Right** on Crockett Rd.

17.2   **Left** on Green Hills Blvd.

18.1   **Right** on Concord Rd. (stop sign at the 4-way intersection).

18.4   **Left** on Edmondson Pk. (first left).

20.6   **Left** on Old Smyrna Rd. and retrace your route back to the starting point.

24.2   End of ride!

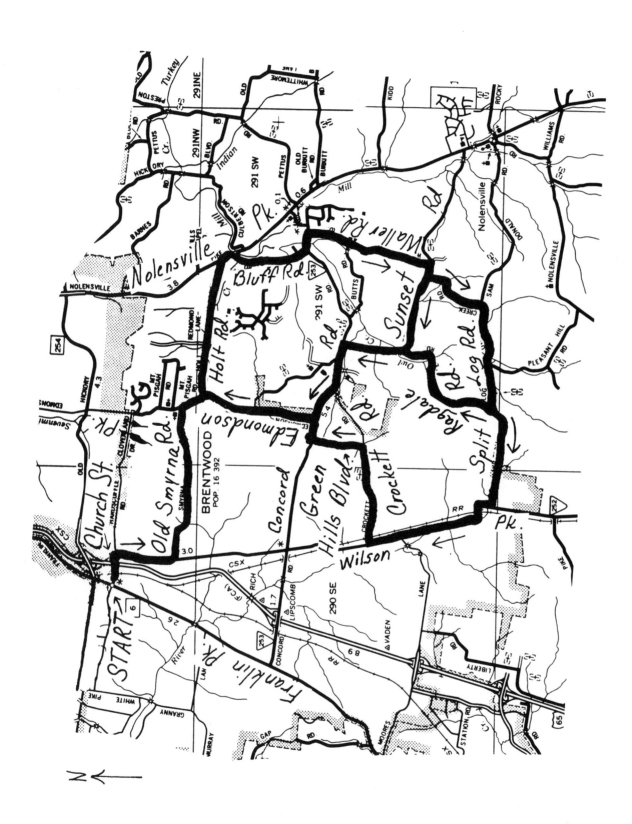

Ride # 15A   MILL CREEK LOOP

Distance: 12 or 29 miles
Elevation Difference/Accumulated Climb: Option 1 - 260/800 ft., Option 2 - 320/1,700 ft.
Terrain: Moderately hilly. No long climbs but frequent short ones.
Services: Market in Nolensville at mile 12.3 on Option 2.
Traffic: Light to moderate on all roads except for a very short stretch on busy Nolensville
  Pk. Traffic is heavier during commuting hours on Old Hickory Blvd. and Pettus Rd.
Combining Rides: #14 Brentwood/Old Smyrna Road Loop, #16 Franklin/Nolensville Loop.
Connector Routes: 1) .8 mi. to #19 Blackman Loop—From Nolensville, bike southwest
  on Clovercroft Rd. **2)** 3.2 mi. to #17 Williamson County Loop—From the intersection
  of Split Log Rd. and Sam Donald Rd., go right, then left on Wilson Pk.
Alternate Parking Sites: 1) Nolensville High School in Nolensville, 2) Cane Ridge Park on
  Battle Rd.
Distance from Nashville: 10 miles

It's hard to believe that only a few miles from the congested areas of Hickory Hollow Mall and the town of Antioch, cyclists can pedal through peaceful farm areas where horses, cows, and goats graze in the large pastures. This tour is an ideal quick getaway for people living southeast of Nashville. Even the areas close to busy Bell Rd. manage to retain a rural flavor despite the growing number of new homes. Both options of the *Mill Creek Loop* are somewhat of a maze to navigate at first, but they are well-worth the effort to avoid the busier roads.

You begin the ride by pedaling over a few rolling hills dotted with old barns and new homes. A fun drop on Culbertson Rd. sends you down to a lovely area along Mill Creek.

Option 1 soon crosses back over Nolensville Pk. and heads up a 200-ft. hill on Pettus Rd. This steep hill makes our 12-mile route a substantial workout. Another bonus is the panoramic view of the forested knobs of Brentwood and Franklin behind you on this climb. Your efforts will be rewarded by an opportunity to barrel straight downhill to Old Hickory Blvd.

Option 2 winds through more scenic countryside (and more hills, of course) toward Nolensville, a historic community dating back to the early 1800s. (See *Ride #16* for historical information.) Rocky Fork Rd. heads east from Nolensville along the broad open Mill Creek Valley where dairy farms have prospered for over one hundred years. The stretch on Rocky Springs Rd., Waldron Rd. and Lake Rd. is a real joy to cycle—plenty of relaxing scenery and almost no traffic. Cane Ridge Park makes a good water and restroom stop before the final 7 miles back to Nashville's bustling suburbia.

Ride # 15B   MILL CREEK GREENWAY

Distance: 1-2 miles
Terrain: Flat
Traffic: None
Distance from Nashville: 10 miles

Antioch residents can enjoy this delightful 1.5-mile greenway from Blue Hole Rd. to Antioch Pk. just south of Haywood Ln. Another 1-mile segment runs along the creek at Ezell Park. Both sections are ideal for families and novices. Future plans call for joining these trails to create an 8-mile multi-use path.

HOW TO GET THERE: Same as Mill Creek Loop except park at the community center on Blue Hold Rd. The Ezell Park segment can be reached by heading east on Harding Pl. from I-24.

15 MILL CREEK LOOP

HOW TO GET THERE: Go east on I-24 and exit at Bell Rd. (Exit 59). Turn right on Bell Rd./Hwy. 254, then right on Blue Hole Rd. immediately past the miniature golf course. Go .2 mi. and park by the athletic fields.

Mile

0.0   Bike south on Blue Hole Rd. toward Bell Rd.
0.2   Cross Bell Rd.
1.6   **Right** on Pettus Rd. (stop sign at the T-intersection).
2.1   **Left** on Old Hickory Blvd. (stop sign at the T-intersection).
2.9   Go **straight** onto Culbertson Rd. where Old Hickory Blvd. turns sharply to the left.
4.5   **Right** on Nolensville Pk./Hwy. 31A/Hwy. 41A (stop sign at the T-intersection).
4.7   **Left** on Bluff Rd. (first left).
5.9   **Left** on Concord Rd./Hwy. 253 (stop sign at the T-intersection).
Go to Option 1 or Option 2

OPTION 1
12 miles

6.1   **Left** staying on Concord Rd. (3-way stop).
6.4   **Right** on Nolensville Pk./Hwy. 31A/Hwy. 41A (stop sign at the T-intersection).
6.5   **Left** on Pettus Rd. (first left).
8.3   **Left** on Old Hickory Blvd. (stop sign at the T-intersection).
8.5   Continue **straight** onto Pettus Rd. as Old Hickory Blvd. angles to the left.
10.1   **Right** on Blue Hole Rd.
11.7   End of Ride!

OPTION 2
29 miles

6.0   **Right** on Waller Rd. (first right).
8.1   **Right** on Sunset Rd. (stop sign at the T-intersection).
8.2   **Left** on Split Log Rd. (Owl Creek Rd.)(first left).
9.3   **Left** on Sam Donald Rd. (first left).
12.0   **Right** at the White Methodist Church.
12.1   **Left** on Clovercroft Rd. (Clovercroft-Nolensville Rd.)..
12.3   Cross Nolensville Pk./Hwy. 31A/Hwy. 41A and continue straight on what is now Rocky Fork Rd. Market.
13.8   **Left** on Rock Springs Rd. (easy to miss) at the bottom of a small hill.
16.5   **Left** on Waldron Rd. immediately past the Rock Springs Church of Christ.
17.4   **Left** on Lake Rd. (Kidd Rd., McFarland Rd.) (first left at the top of a hill).
20.1   **Right** on Kidd Rd. (Battle Rd.) (stop sign at the T-intersection).
22.1   Cane Ridge Park. Restrooms/water.
22.3   **Left** on Burkitt Rd. (stop sign at the T-intersection).
23.9   **Right** on Whittemore Ln. (first right).
24.6   **Left** on Old Hickory Blvd. (stop sign at the T-intersection).
25.7   Go **straight** onto Pettus Rd. where Old Hickory Blvd. angles to the left. (Do not take the Pettus Rd. where Old Hickory Blvd. angles to the right.)
27.3   **Right** on Blue Hole Rd.
28.9   End of ride!

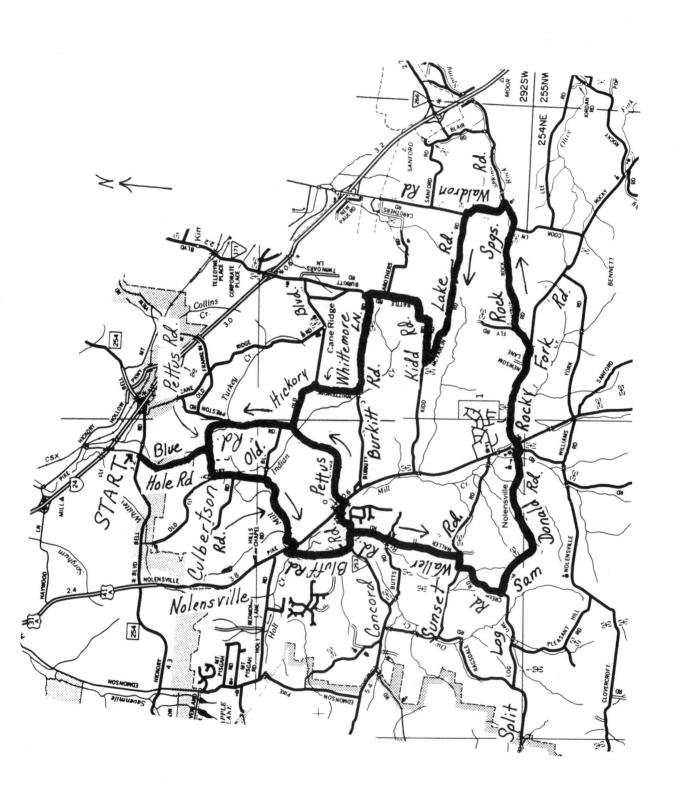

Ride # 16   FRANKLIN/NOLENSVILLE LOOP

Distance: 27, 33, or 38 miles
Elevation Difference/Accumulated Climb: Option 1 - 340/1860 ft., Option 2 - 340/2290 ft.,
Option 3 - 390/2750 ft.
Terrain: Moderate to very hilly with no long climbs but several steep ascents. Option 3 has
1 long ascent.
Services: Option 1 has a market/restaurant at mile 13.6. Option 2 has a market/restaurant
at mile 19.4. Option 3 has a market/restaurant at mile 25.2.
Traffic: Moderate on Liberty Pk. in the Franklin area and light to moderate on Wilson Pk.
Light on all other roads.
Combining Rides: *# 7 Old Natchez Trace/Del Rio Ride, # 14 Brentwood/Old Smyrna Road
Loop, # 15 Mill Creek Loop, # 17 Williamson County Loop, # 19 Stones River Battlefield
Loop.*
Alternate Parking Sites: 1) Nolensville--on the loop. **2)** Brentwood/Maryland Way (5 mi.
to loop)--Bike east on Church St. to Wilson Pk. and go south. **3)** There is also a gravel
area for possible parking .5 mi. north of Split Log Rd. on Wilson Pk.
Distance from Nashville: 18 miles

We begin this ride at the square in Franklin, a well-preserved historic town founded
in 1799. (See *Ride # 7* for more information). Cyclists enjoy riding to and from here because
it's easy to fit in a visit to the many unique shops and fine eateries. Our route goes east
from Franklin, avoiding the big ridges to the south and west, but instead encountering a
chain of knobby hills that will certainly challenge your quadriceps.

Liberty Pk. starts as a flat stretch through residential and business areas and fortunately
gives you a chance to warm up before attacking the hills. A very short distance after the
lane goes under I-65, rolling countryside replaces the sprawling suburbs of Franklin. The
first substantial climb is at mile 6 (240 ft.), and there is a wonderful view of the upper
Harpeth Valley to the south just before the top. Have fun on the quick descent to Wilson
Pk., but watch out for the bumpy wooden bridge at the bottom.

Clovercroft Rd. offers a challenging roller coaster-type ride with several climbs, each
followed immediately by a drop. The big hill on this section is called Pleasant Hill Knob
(.2 mile climb at mile 8.8) but on your way up you may choose to rename it! We often call
these "useless hills" because they seem to serve no purpose but to tire cyclists. In reality,
this scenic hilly area is a joy to ride provided you are in good shape and good spirits. Before
entering the town of Nolensville, Options 2 and 3 go right on Williams Rd., while Option
1 continues into Nolensville.

Option 2 follows quiet York Rd. on a less hilly loop that passes cedar groves and dairy
farms. On its way toward Nolensville, Option 3 tackles a more extended and challenging
route up Signal Knob, a long steady 280-ft. climb followed by a brief descent and another
200-ft. climb along the hilltop. Be sure to notice the view at 1,000 ft. (a very high elevation
for Middle Tennessee) immediately before turning left on Del Thomas Rd. On clear days,
you can see down to Smyrna and beyond. This route then heads over more of the gentle
yet unending hills on Rocky Fork Rd. Option 2 joins Option 3 on Rocky Fork Rd. and
proceeds through the wide Mill Creek valley. A series of interesting knobs to south include
Polk Knob and Signal Knob which Option 3 previously went up and over.

All of our options come back together in Nolensville (incorporated in 1838) which used to be a big dairy town with many grocery stores, etc. prior to World War II; however, the Great Depression and numerous devastating fires took their toll, for now there is only a market, gas station, cafe, and feed store. Some of the dairy farms have been made into residential subdivisions, but much farmland still remains intact. A few old frame farmhouses built over the original log cabins dating back to the early 1800s still stand along Rocky Fork Rd.

Going east from Nolensville, Sam Donald and Split Log Roads go back into more of the scenic roller coaster territory (including a steep .5 mile, 170-ft. pull) before rolling down to Wilson Pk. As you near Wilson Pk., the beautiful Inglehame Mansion, built in 1858, sits on a large knoll on the left. The opulent Ravenwood home (1825) is barely visible on a wooded hill .2 mile on the right after you turn onto Wilson Pk. James Wilson owned several plantations in the South besides this one and was reputed to be worth over two million dollars, an outrageous amount in those times.

Enjoy that short flat stretch on Wilson Pk. because you still have one final big climb (and a fun descent!) as you retrace your route on Liberty Pk.

Many cyclists do not ride with the proper saddle height. This is less efficient and may cause knee injuries. To find your proper seat height, multiply your inseam measurement by 1.09. This figure should be the distance (following the same angle as the seat tube) between the top of the seat and the axle of the pedal when it is all the way down.

#16 FRANKLIN/NOLENSVILLE LOOP

HOW TO GET THERE: This ride begins at the town square in Franklin. Hillsboro Pk./Hwy. 431, Franklin Pk./Hwy. 31, and I-65 all lead south to Franklin from Nashville. Parking is available on the residential streets near the square.

Mile

0.0	Bike north on Hwy. 31/E. Main St. (Franklin Pk.) toward Nashville.
0.4	**Right** on Liberty Pk. (traffic light).
0.8	Follow the short bike path under the RR and continue on Liberty Pk.
1.1	Market.
1.7	Cross Mack Hatcher Pkwy. (traffic light).
2.9	Go under I-65.
3.5	Bear **right** as an unnamed road goes straight ahead.
6.4	**Right** on Wilson Pk./Hwy. 252 (stop sign at the T-intersection).
7.0	**Left** on Clovercroft Rd. (first left).

Go to Option 1, 2, or 3

OPTION 1
27 miles

13.6	**Left** on Sam Donald Rd. which is immediately before busy Nolensville Pk. Market/restaurant less than a block north on Nolensville Pk.
13.65	**Left** immediately at the stop sign by the white Ebenezer Methodist Church.

Go to All Options

OPTION 2
33 miles

12.8	**Right** on Williams Rd. as Clovercroft Rd. bends to the left.
13.6	Cross Nolensville Pk. and continue onto York Rd. (stop sign).
16.2	**Left** on Rocky Fork Rd. (stop sign at the T-intersection).
19.4	Cross Nolensville Pk. (stop sign). Market in the town of Nolensville.
19.45	**Right** immediately on Sam Donald Rd. (first right).
19.5	**Left** immediately at the stop sign by the white Ebenezer Methodist Church.

Go to All Options

OPTION 3
38 miles

12.8	**Right** on Williams Rd. as Clovercroft Rd. bends to the left.
13.6	**Right** on Nolensville Pk. (stop sign).
13.7	**Left** on Sanford Rd. (first left).
16.7	**Left** on Del Thomas Rd. after passing a large modern wood house with a panoramic view.
19.9	**Left** on Rocky Fork Rd. (stop sign at the T-intersection).
25.2	Cross Nolensville Pk. (stop sign). Market in the town of Nolensville.
25.25	**Right** immediately on Sam Donald Rd. (first right).
25.3	**Left** immediately at the stop sign by the white Ebenezer Methodist Church.

Go to All Options

ALL OPTIONS

16.3, 22.1, 27.9	**Left** on Split Log Rd. (Owl Creek Rd.) (stop sign).
18.0, 23.8, 29.6	Bear **left** (staying on Split Log Rd.) at the 3-way intersection at the hill top.

19.5, 25.3, 31.1	**Left** on Wilson Pk. (stop sign at the T-intersection).
20.4, 26.2, 32.0	**Right** on Liberty Pk. (first right). Retrace your route back to Franklin.
26.8, 32.6, 38.4	End of Ride!

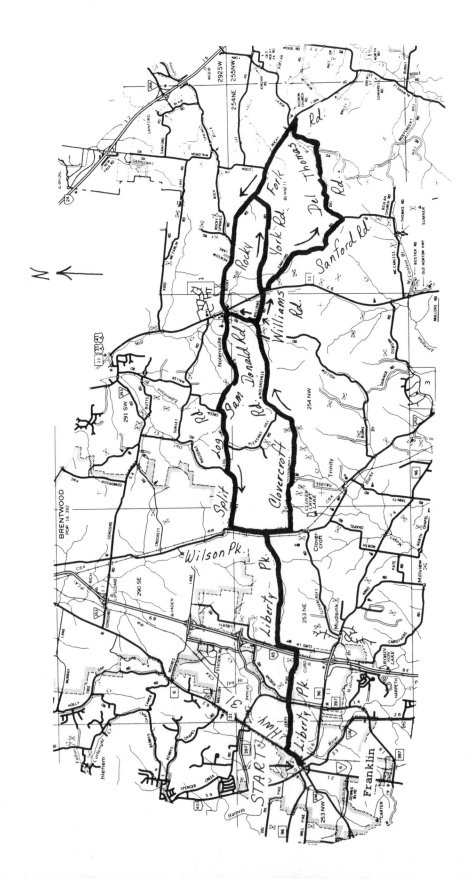

Ride # 17   WILLIAMSON COUNTY LOOP

Distance: 42 miles
Elevation Difference/Accumulated Climb: 330/1820 ft.
Terrain: Rolling to moderately hilly with 3 climbs over 150 ft.
Services: Markets at mile 4.0, 16.1, 16.6, 21.1, 25.7, 34.2, and 40.6.
Traffic: Moderate for the first 2-3 mi. on Carters Creek Pk. and for the final 3 mi. of the route. Light to moderate on Wilson Pk. Light on all other roads.
Combining Rides: # 7 Old Natchez Trace/Del Rio Ride, # 13 Burwood Loop, # 18 Peytonsville Loop, # 16 Franklin/Nolensville Loop.
Connector Routes: 1) .9 mi. to # 14 Brentwood/Old Smyrna Road Loop--From the corner of Liberty Pk. and Wilson Pk. at mile 35.1, continue north on Wilson Pk. **2)** 2 mi. to # 8 Harpeth Loop--From the town of Southall at mile 3.9, bike west on Southall Rd. **3)** 5.2 mi. to # 10 Fernvale Loop, # 12 Snow Creek Loop, # 11 Fly Loop, and # 13 Burwood Loop--From the town of Southall at mile 3.9, bike west on Southall Rd. and turn left on Old Hillsboro Rd./Hwy. 46.
Distance from Nashville: 18 miles

This delightful 40-mile tour encompasses a large area of Williamson County and combines portions of the *Burwood Loop, the Peytonsville Loop,* and *the Franklin/Nolensville Loop* into what could be considered a "greatest hits" loop. For the hard-core cyclists seeking long distances of 50 to 100+ miles, several combining rides and connector routes hook up to places such as Leipers Fork, the Warner Parks, Brentwood, Smyrna, and Murfreesboro, creating a nearly infinite number of route possibilities.

Our trip begins from the square in historic Franklin. This well-preserved town boasts numerous restaurants, ice cream store, bakery, fruit stand, and drug store with soda fountain--any of which would be a wonderful reward after completing this ride. (For cyclists who like to eat, Franklin is hard to beat.) Historical tour maps are often available at the Visitors' Information Booth on E. Main St. (See *Ride #7* for a brief history of Franklin.)

After the initial 2-3 miles, rolling pastures nestled among forested hills greet the rider leaving the town limits. The mild hills you encounter on Carters Creek Pk. are just enough to create some enjoyable downhills.

This ride joins the *Burwood Loop* shortly before turning onto West Harpeth Rd., a quaint country lane that is a joy to bicycle as it winds through open farmlands and shaded woods. A fairly gentle 180-ft. climb on Sedberry Rd. leads you through an area that has almost completely recovered from an old strip mine operation. Next the route heads up and over the first big hill of the day. The Hilltop Manor (1808) can be seen through the trees on the right as you reach the crest.

Soon you roll into Thompson Station (mile 16) with a country store and a few churches that are reminders of what a busy place it once was. Located along the railroad, this old community had a large broom factory, a bank (which is still standing by the market), several stores, and a blacksmith shop. It was also the sight of a important Civil War skirmish prior to the Battle of Franklin. From here, our route heads east along flat-to-gently rolling terrain and connects with the *Peytonsville Loop* near the town of Harpeth. If you wish to extend your trip and see some additional beautiful countryside, turn right on Bethesda Rd. from Hwy. 431 and follow Options 2, 3, or 4 of the *Peytonsville Loop* in the opposite direction of Peytonsville. The *Williamson County Loop* follows Harpeth-Peytonsville Rd. up a very gentle grade along the Duck River Ridge and dips into the small basin around Peytonsville.

Our trip turns north on Peytonsville-Trinity Rd., traverses more pastoral rolling terrain, crosses the upper portion of the Harpeth River, and eventually reaches Wilson Pk.

Soon you connect with the *Franklin/Nolensville Loop* and start muscling up a steep hill (150 ft.) at mile 36. Before you begin the long descent into the Franklin city limits, take a rest and check out the view of the Harpeth Valley and the vast territory which you just cycled.

17 WILLIAMSON COUNTY LOOP

HOW TO GET THERE: This ride begins at the town square in Franklin. Hillsboro Pk./Hwy. 431, Franklin Pk./Hwy.31, and I-65 all lead south to Franklin from Nashville. Parking is available on the residential streets near the square.

Mile

0.0	Begin ride by biking west on Main St./Hwy. 31 south.
0.2	Continue straight (don't veer to the left) onto W. Main St. at the busy intersection at 5th St. W. Main St. becomes Carters Creek Pk./Hwy. 246.
4.0	Market in the town of Southall.
7.8	**Left** on West Harpeth Rd. (easy to miss).
11.5	**Right** on Sedberry Rd. (first right).
14.7	**Left** on Thompson Station-Burwood Rd. (stop sign at the T- intersection).
16.1	Market in the town of Thompson Station.
16.3	**Left** at the stop sign and continue on Thompson Station Rd.
16.6	Cross Hwy. 31. Market.
19.1	Cross over I-65.
20.3	**Left** on Hwy. 431. (stop sign at the T-intersection).
21.1	**Right** on Harpeth-Peytonsville Rd. immediately after crossing the W. Harpeth River (really a small creek). Market in the town of Harpeth.
25.3	**Left** on Peytonsville-Trinity Rd. (second four-way intersection) at the bottom of valley. Look for the white Peytonsville Baptist Church on the left.
25.7	Market in Peytonsville.
30.7	Cross Hwy. 96 (second stop sign).
32.4	**Left** on Wilson Pk./Hwy. 252 (stop sign at the T-intersection).
34.2	Market in the town of Clovercroft.
35.3	**Left** on Liberty Pk. (first left after going under the RR tracks past the market).
38.8	Go under I-65.
40.0	Cross Mack Hatcher Pkwy. at the traffic light.
40.6	Market.
41.3	**Left** on Hwy. 31/E. Main St. (Franklin Pk.) at the traffic light.
41.7	End of ride!

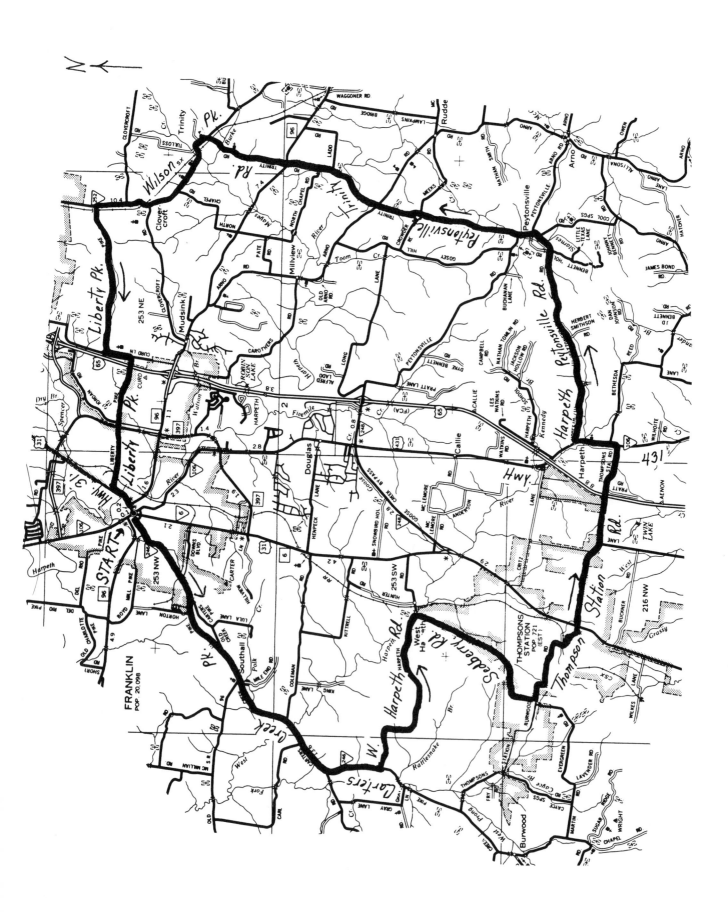

Ride #18 PEYTONSVILLE LOOP

Distance: 17, 28, 31, or 38 miles
Elevation Difference/Accumulated Climb: Option 1 - 250/1350 ft., Option 2 - 250/1870 ft.,
     Option 3 - 460/2360 ft., Option 4 - 280/2620 ft.
Terrain: Moderately hilly with a very hilly portion on Options 3 and 4.
Services: Option 1 has a market at mile 11.9. Option 2 has markets at miles 14.1, 18.9, and
     23.3. Option 3 has markets at miles 17.2, 22.0, and 26.4. Option 4 has markets at miles
     20.6, 24.1 28.9, and 33.3.
Traffic: Light to moderate on Arno Rd., Hwy. 431, and Peytonsville Rd. Light on all other
     roads.
Combining Ride: *#17 Williamson County Loop.*
Distance from Nashville: 22 miles

This ride goes through a delightful portion of southeastern Williamson County that few cyclists know. A network of quiet roads meander among pastures and the precipitous wooded hills of the Duck River Ridge. Our tour begins on Long Ln. which makes its way over several rolling hills. (With its 130-ft. climb, the initial mile will certainly wake up your muscles!) Next you follow Crowder Rd. to the old feed store in the community of Rudderville. Arno Rd. is an easy and pleasant ride with a few easy climbs before the big ones begin. Option 1 cuts off before really big hills, but the other options send you up the Duck River Ridge which, in this region, is a series of connected steep hills rather than the miniature plateau it becomes at Leipers Fork.

Option 1 leaves the McCrory Creek Valley, goes over a small hill (130-ft. climb) and leads down into Peytonsville, a sleepy little town nestled in the hills of the Duck River Ridge. After the Civil War, fugitives hid in these hills and hollows around Peytonsville, and it gained the nickname "Little Texas" because of the great number of similar fugitives who fled to the state of Texas. The old store in Peytonsville has been in business since 1901 and is still a meeting place for delightful local retired citizens.

Option 2 follows Bethesda-Arno Rd. up a surprisingly gentle climb to a gap (110 ft. climb) and down to Bethesda. Although this option is only 3 miles shorter than Option 3, it is a much easier ride due to the gentle grade into Bethesda. The beautifully built Blue Grass Home constructed around 1805 still stands on a knoll on the right and overlooks the green pastures of a small valley.

Options 3 and 4 continue on Arno Rd. over a long 210-ft. climb, followed by a fun descent into a scenic area known as "The Cove" which lies between a steep, forested hill to the east and the Duck River Ridge to the west. Option 3 turns off Arno Rd. and ascends Pull Tight Hill which was given this name because the wagon drivers had to "pull tight" on the brakes when coming down. After a very challenging climb (260 ft.) up the ridge, the cyclist is rewarded with nice views to the southwest and a narrow winding drop into the community of Cross Keys. The modest Hartley home, still standing, was built in 1785 of 3-foot thick, yellow limestone slabs and located on a hill to protect its inhabitants from hostile Indians and wild animals.

Option 4 continues further down The Cove before heading over Giles Hill on a not-quite-so tough 170-ft. climb over the Duck River Ridge. After descending, the route follows Flat Creek for several easy miles through wonderful farmland.

Options 2, 3, and 4 come together in Bethesda, a quiet community of new and old homes located at the headwaters of Rutherford Creek. The old white Presbyterian Church (1879) at the corner still has two separate front doors, for in the past, men and women were required to enter and sit on opposite sides of the church. Along this route, you may notice several other churches with separate doors as a result of this custom. Many log cabins dating back to the early 1800s still stand in the area although most are covered with weatherboarding today. As you leave town on Bethesda Rd, look for the well-preserved Irvin home (1850) sitting on a hilltop. A few old slave cabins still exist behind the home, drawing attention to the stark contrast of lifestyles between slaves and their masters. Several other antebellum homes, both large and small, can be seen in the hills and valleys around Bethesda.

Our route continues over rolling countryside with a few steep pulls to the town of Harpeth located at the source of the West Harpeth River. Harpeth has the distinction of having two historic churches and a notorious outlaw named John Murrell who specialized in slave stealing. After leaving Harpeth, a gradual climb through more beautiful country takes you to Peytonsville where Option 1 joins.

One more climb (170 ft.) awaits as you head up Talley Hill. Again, take note of the nice views of the Harpeth Valley to the north before you begin the final downhill of the day.

Walk/Bike Nashville is dedicated to creating communities where people of all ages can safely bicycle anywhere they choose. This 501c3 non-profit organization has accomplished much since it was founded in 1998. The city of Nashville has completed a bikeway plan and allocated $600,000 in 2003 to begin work on the first phase. Walk/Bike Nashville holds various promotional events and works with city and state officials. For more information, visit www.walkbikenashville.org. See Appendices for more information.

18 PEYTONSVILLE LOOP

HOW TO GET THERE: Take I-65 South to Peytonsville Rd./Hwy. 248 (Exit 61). Turn left at the top of the ramp and park on the east side of the interstate.

Mile

0.0	Begin ride by going **left** on Long Ln. (first left east of I-65) from Peytonsville Rd.
3.9	**Right** on Gosey Hill Rd. (stop sign at the T-intersection).
4.2	**Left** on Crowder Rd. (first left).
5.0	Continue straight onto Meeks Rd. (4-way intersection).
6.8	**Right** on Arno Rd. (4-way intersection).

Go to Option 1, Option 2, Option 3, or Option 4

OPTION 1
17 miles

9.6	**Right** on Peytonsville-Arno Rd. (4-way intersection).
11.6	**Right** on Peytonsville-Trinity Rd. (first right).
11.9	**Left** on Peytonsville Rd. Market in Peytonsville.
16.7	End of ride!

OPTION 2
28 miles

10.3	**Right** on Bethesda-Arno Rd. (next right past Peytonsville-Arno Rd.)
14.1	**Right** on Bethesda Rd. (stop sign at the 4-way intersection). Market in Bethesda.

Go to Options "2, 3, and 4"

OPTION 3
31 miles

13.2	**Right** on Pull Tight Hill Rd. after a long descent. (easy to miss).
15.4	Bear **right** on Cross Keys Rd. (3-way stop).
16.9	Bear **right** as Comstock Rd. enters from the left.
17.2	Continue straight onto Bethesda Rd. (4-way intersection). Market in Bethesda.

Go to Options "2, 3, and 4"

OPTION 4
38 miles

14.4	**Right** on Giles Hill Rd. (easy to miss).
16.7	Bear **left** (staying on Giles Hill Rd.) at the 3-way stop.
17.6	**Right** on Flat Creek Rd. (stop sign at the T-intersection).
20.6	**Right** on Comstock Rd. at the market.
23.8	**Left** on Cross Keys Rd. (stop sign at the T-intersection).
24.1	Continue straight onto Bethesda Rd. (4-way intersection). Market in Bethesda.

Go to Options "2, 3, and 4"

OPTIONS "2, 3, and 4"

18.1, 21.2, 28.1	**Right** on Hwy. 431/Lewisburg Pk. (stop sign at the T-intersection).
18.9, 22.0, 28.9	**Right** on Harpeth-Peytonsville Rd. (first right). Market in Harpeth.
23.0, 26.1, 33.0	**Left** on Peytonsville-Trinity Rd. (second 4-way intersection). Look for the Peytonsville Baptist Church.
23.3, 26.4, 33.3	**Left** on Peytonsville Rd. Market in Peytonsville.
28.0, 31.1, 38.0	End of ride!

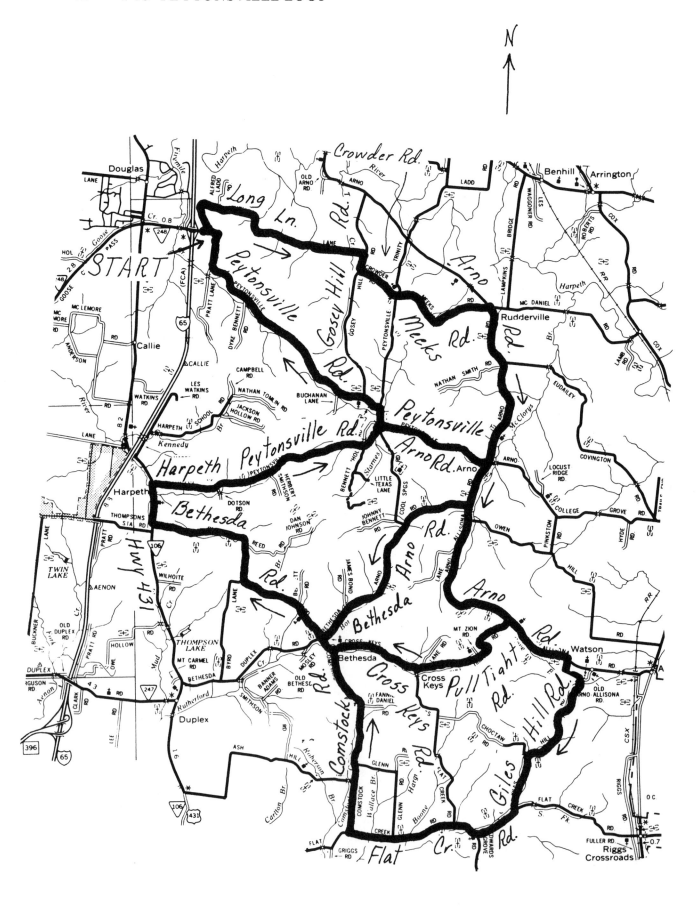

Ride #19   BLACKMAN LOOP

Distance: 15, 37, or 45 miles
Elevation Difference/Accumulated Climb: Option 1 - 270/500 ft., Option 2 - 300/1900 ft.,
   Option 3 - 450/2550 ft.
Terrain: Option 1 is flat to rolling. At least three significant hills are encountered on Options
   2 and 3, but there are long stretches of flat to rolling terrain.
Food Services: Option 1 has no services. Option 2 has markets at mile 19.9 and 30.5.
   Option 3 has markets at mile 19.9 and 37.8.
Traffic: Heavy traffic for .4 miles on Hwy. 96. Nolensville Pk. on Option 2 has moderate
   traffic and a small paved shoulder. Light on all other roads.
Combining Rides: *#16 Franklin/Nolensville Loop, #17 Williamson County Loop.*
Connector Route: .8 mi. to *#15 Mill Creek Loop*—Continue into Nolensville on Clovercroft
   Rd.
Alternate Parking Sites: 1) The markets at Hwy. 96 and Wilson Pk. (ask permission). **2)**
   The community of Trinity on Wilson Pk. 1 mi. north of Burke Hollow Rd. Park at the one
   of the churches, the market, or the closed elementary school.
Distance from Nashville: 25 miles

Our first edition of *Bicycling Middle Tennessee* featured a scenic and historic bike tour from Smyrna to the Stones River Battlefield. Today, more and more housing tracts occupy what were green pastures and cotton fields only a few years ago. Rutherford County is currently the fastest growing county in Middle Tennessee. While this may be good news for the local economy, the real estate boom is less than ideal for cyclists pedaling these narrow roads with fast and frequent commuter traffic. Hopefully our local planners and politicians will learn from other regions of the country that it is beneficial to establish bike lanes, sidewalks, and greenways *before* development begins.

The *Blackman Loop*, which replaces the original *Stones River Battlefield Loop*, rolls among the rural areas southwestern Rutherford county and eastern Williamson County on lightly traveled backroads that have not yet been largely impacted with new development. Our new tour begins in the rapidly changing community of Blackman which will be even further impacted when I-840 cuts a swath through this once rural community. Despite the changes, Blackman maintains it country charm. Fields of cotton, a crop that has grown well in this soil for many years, still line these rural roads. The local market/cafe makes an excellent stop after finishing your ride. Their grilled cheese sandwiches warmed our group up after a chilly November ride.

In December of 1862, the flat pastures and fields were bustling with activity as thousands of Union and Confederate troops positioned themselves for what was to be an important battle and one of the most bloody struggles of the Civil War. The Stones River National Battlefield, 3 miles to the east, has a visitor center and a 1.3-mile auto loop through the battlefield where over 23,000 soldiers lost their lives. A paved bike path is being constructed that will follow the Stones River from here to Fort Rosecrans at Old Fort Park in Murfreesboro. The best route from Blackman is via Manson Pk., which has fast and often frequent traffic, then left on Ashbury Ln. after crossing I-24, right on Ashbury Rd., and right on Nashville Hwy.

Beginning on Beasley Rd., you will be pedaling through remnants of the Old South when cotton was king. A few pioneer homes that survived the devastation of the Civil War can be seen along this road. Raiford Blackman, a large landowner whose mansion was burned to the ground by Union troops, spent his last years living in a simple slave cabin with dirt floors. Just south of the Beasley Church, the Solomon Beasley home, built in 1804, continues to overlook the flat fertile fields that have yet to be gobbled up by urban sprawl.

After a short hectic stretch on Hwy. 96, Kingwood Rd. leads through a residential area before connecting with Windrow Rd. which heads west into increasing pastoral territory. After 7 miles of enjoyably flat cycling, a steep 200 ft. climb interrupts the nice pace you have established. Option 1 turns north on Newman Rd. before cresting the hill and returns to Blackman on quiet country roads.

After a fun descent, Option 2 and 3 turn right on Patterson Rd. and begin to explore wonderful cycling territory with rolling hills and large open fields along Nelson Creek. Cox Rd. heads north over a minor hill and takes us to a welcomed market in the community of Arrington.

After a short segment on Wilson Pk., Option 2 turns onto Osborne Rd. where a minor 100 ft. climb precedes a drop down to Nolensville Pk. Our tour follows this moderately busy highway with a small paved shoulder as it climbs yet another hill. One of our favorite stretches is encountered on the twisting and rolling Spanntown Rd. The occasional views of the flat lands 200 ft. below these rugged knobs are well worth the effort it takes to struggle up the short, steep hills.

Option 3 continues on Wilson Pk. to Burke Hollow, a favorite training location for local racers. Even if you are not a "hammerhead", you will enjoy the scenery of this quaint valley, *and* definitely increase your heart rate after climbing 300 ft. from Wilson Pk. A long descent takes you into the Nolensville area where there is another 280 ft. climb up Signal Knob on Sanford Rd. Be sure to notice the view at 1,000 ft. (a very high elevation for Middle Tennessee) near the intersection with Del Thomas Rd. After another downhill, a moderate climb on Bell Church Rd. reveals another excellent view which we found stunning during the peak colors of autumn.

Option 2 and 3 come together in the community of Almaville. From here, Shores Ln. meanders through a region of poor rocky soil, cedar forests, and several modest homes before returning to the more fertile lands of the Blackman area.

Drafting, or riding close behind in the slipstream of one or more cyclists, can save 15-30% of your energy. A common drafting technique known as a paceline occurs when the front cyclists leads for a period of time (less than 30 seconds for racers), then moves to the left (sometimes the right), and slightly eases up on his/her speed, allowing the paceline to pass. He/she then pulls in behind the last cyclist, and the next person in line leads the paceline. Drafting is a frequent cause of cycling accidents, so be alert and always look ahead—not just at the rear wheel of the cyclist in front of you.

19 BLACKMAN LOOP

HOW TO GET THERE: Take I-24 East and exit on Almaville Pk./Hwy. 102 (Exit 70). Go right for .8 mi. and turn left on One Mile Ln. Turn left at the next stop sign (still One Mile Ln.). Go right on Baker Rd. at the T-intersection and right on Blackman Rd. at the next T-intersection. Our ride begins at the market at the intersection with Blackman Rd. Ask permission before parking here. There is also a church and community center less than a mile east on Manson Pk.

Mile

0.0   From the market, bike south on Blackman Rd. which becomes Beasley Rd.
2.5   **Right** on Hwy. 96 (stop sign).
2.9   **Left** on Kingwood Rd.. (second left, easy to miss).
5.6   **Right** on Windrow Rd. (stop sign at the T-intersection).
Go to Option 1 or Options "2 and 3"

OPTION 1
15 miles

7.6   **Right** on Newman Rd. before cresting a steep hill.
9.4   **Right** on Coleman Hill Rd.
10.3   **Right** on Hwy. 96 (stop sign at the T-intersection).
10.5   **Left** on Puckett Rd. (first left).
11.4   **Right** on Shores Ln. (stop sign at the T-intersection).
13.6   **Left** on Beasley Rd. (stop sign at the T-intersection).
15.0   End of ride!

OPTIONS "2 and 3"

8.3   **Right** on Patterson Rd. at the white Community Church.
12.1   **Left** on Patterson Rd. (stop sign at the T-intersection).
15.7   **Right** on Nolensville Pk. (stop sign at the T-intersection).
15.8   **Left** on Patton Rd. (first left).
17.8   **Right** on Cox Rd. (stop sign at the T-intersection).
19.8   **Left** on Hwy. 96 (stop sign at the T-intersection).
19.9   **Right** on Wilson Pk./Hwy. 252. Market.
Go to Option 2 or Option 3

OPTION 2
37 miles

20.6   **Right** on Osburn Rd. (easy to miss).
24.1   **Right** on Nolensville Pk./Hwy. 31A (stop sign at the T-intersection).
25.6   **Left** on Spanntown Rd. shortly after cresting a hill.
28.1   **Left**, staying on Spanntown Rd. at the stop sign.
30.5   **Right** on Almaville Pk./Hwy. 102 (stop sign at the T-intersection). Market one-half mile north (the other direction) on Almaville Pk.
31.1   **Left** on the new Shores Rd. after crossing I-840.
35.7   **Left** on Beasley Rd. (stop sign at the T-intersection).
37.1   End of ride!

OPTION 3
45 miles

22.4   **Right** on Burke Hollow Rd.
28.0   **Right** on Clovercroft Rd. (stop sign at the T-intersection).
28.3   **Right** on Williams Rd. (first right).

29.1	**Right** on Nolensville Pk./Hwy. 31A. (stop sign).
29.2	**Left** on Sanford Rd. (first left).
32.3	Continue straight onto McCanless Rd. (Del Thomas Rd. goes left.)
33.6	**Left** on Bell Church Rd. (Independent Hill Rd.) after going downhill.
37.1	**Right** on Almaville Pk./Hwy. 102 (stop sign at the T-intersection).
37.8	Market.
38.9	**Left** on the new Shores Rd. after crossing I-840.
43.5	**Left** on Beasley Rd. (stop sign at the T-intersection).
44.9	End of ride!

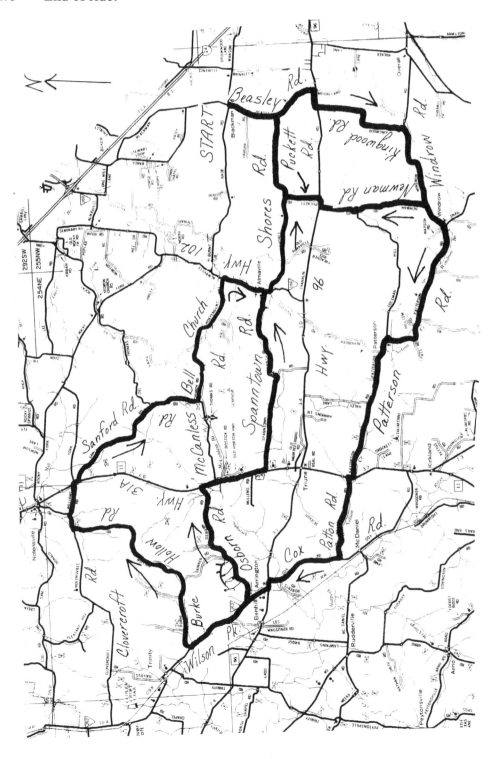

#19 BLACKMAN LOOP

I-840 (under construction) not shown on map

Ride #20   MILTON LOOP

Distance: 27 or 45 miles
Elevation Difference/Accumulated Climb: Option 1 - 170/790 ft., Option 2 - 380/1670 ft.
Terrain: Flat to rolling.
Services: Option 1 has markets at miles 13.5 and 18.5. Option 2 has markets at miles 31.5 and 37.2. Restaurant at mile 16.4.
Traffic: Moderate on Halls Hill Rd. within 2 miles of Murfreesboro. Light to moderate on Hwy. 266. Light on all other roads.
Combining Rides: *#26 Long Hunter State Park Loop, #27 Watertown Loop*
Distance from Nashville: 32 miles

This rolling countryside tour of Rutherford County begins in the town of Murfreesboro, the geographical center of the state. However, if you are driving from Nashville, you can start from the town of Walter Hill on Hwy. 266, thus eliminating 4 miles of driving and numerous traffic lights. This route also combines nicely with the *Watertown Loop* and the *Long Hunter State Park/Lacassas Loop* allowing for miles of great road cycling.

Our directions begin from the Middle Tennessee State University campus where this loop heads east on Halls Hill Rd. through modest residential areas which are gradually replaced by farmland. A series of gentle rolling hills is traversed as you head into the wide, shallow valley of the East Fork of the Stones River. It is always a pleasure to be in this peaceful region of dairy farms and occasional Beefalo herds while pedaling toward an impressive group of distant forested knobs comprising the foothills of the Cumberland Plateau.

After rolling through the community of Halls Hill, today consisting of only a few homes and a decaying abandoned store, Option 1 heads north and meanders along farm pastures nestled in the rocky cedar-covered hills. Option 2 continues on Halls Hill Rd. and passes quaint white farm houses and more recently constructed homes. Fortunately, Halls Hill Rd. swings to the north just before reaching the big hills, but you don't quite escape pumping up a few Tennessee rollers.

Milton, located at Halls Hill Rd. and Hwy. 96, would be just another farm community if it weren't for an unusual bit of culture that exists here. Manuel's Cajun Store and Restaurant draws more and more visitors who like the taste of Louisiana backwoods on Tennessee backroads. If Manuel's is open (and it isn't always on weekdays), you can take a break at this colorful joint, order some gumbo or crawfish etoufee, and meet Manuel, the popular Cajun cook and fiddle player from Louisiana.

Option 2 continues north over a small gap in a series of steep, wooded hills and drops down to the community of Greenvale (no services). Heading west from Greenvale, this trip follows Florida Creek out of the hilly country and proceeds south on Cainsville Pk. over a few more rolling hills.

Option 2 follows Hoover Rd. and Barlow Ln. where the complexion of the land changes. These narrow country lanes travel through an area of flat farmland at the base of Rucker and Casons Knobs before arriving into the town of Lascassas. The old general store here sells an interesting mixture of hardware, feed, and groceries.

Both options head west, then south, passing through expansive pastureland and occasional housing developments before crossing the East Fork of the Stones River. Just before crossing the river, our route travels by the gracious antebellum Rucker home built in 1832. After crossing Hwy. 96, Compton Rd. leaves the expanding suburbs of Murfreesboro and runs through a lightly developed rural area before arriving at Halls Hill Rd. The next 5 miles back to Murfreesboro follow the same segment on which you started.

Ride # 20B   STONES RIVER AND LYTLE CREEK GREENWAY

Distance: Up to 12 miles
Terrain: Flat
Traffic: None, except for street crossings and light traffic on the Battlefiled Loop.
Distance from Nashville: 30 miles

Middle Tennessee's first greenway stretches from historic Cannonsburgh Village on S. Front St. near downtown Murfreesboro to where Thompson Ln. crosses the Stones River. Most of this shaded greenway follows the Stones River and Lytle Creek. Several trailheads provide access to local streets. In addition to its scenic beauty, this 4.5-mile greenway boasts numerous historic sites mostly related to the infamous battle that occured here during the Civil War. From the General Bragg trailhead, a one-mile spur trail connects to the Stones River National Battlefield. Here you will find a visitor center and a 1.3-mile interpretive auto tour through flat cedar thickets where over 23,000 soldiers lost their lives in December of 1862.

HOW TO GET THERE: Take I-24 East from Nashville to Hwy. 96 (Exit 78B) and continue on Hwy. 96/Old Fort Pkwy. toward Murfreesboro. Turn left into Old Fort Park and proceed to the Fortress Rosecrans Trailhead.

maps/directions not included

Tired of drinking warm water on summer bike rides? Try putting your bottle in a wet white cotton sock, then keep the sock wet with water from a second bottle or another source. Your water (or sports drink) will stay noticeably cooler all day.

20 MILTON LOOP

HOW TO GET THERE: Take I-24 East from Nashville to Hwy. 96 East (Exit 78B) and continue on Hwy. 96 into Murfreesboro. Cross NW Broad St. and continue on Memorial Blvd/Hwy. 96. Turn right on E. Clark Blvd./Hwy. 96 which becomes Tennessee Blvd. Turn left on Greenland Dr. and park in MTSU parking lots on the right. Be sure you are not in a restricted parking area.

Mile

0.0   Begin by biking east on Greenwood Blvd. away from Tennessee Blvd. Mileage numbers begin at C St. and Greenland Dr.

0.6   Cross N. Rutherford Blvd. (traffic light) and continue on Halls Hill Rd.

1.1   Market.

Go to Option 1 or Option 2

OPTION 1
27 miles

7.6   **Left** on Trimble Rd. (easy to miss) in the town of Halls Hill.

8.2   **Left** on Browns Mill Rd. (first left).

9.7   Bear **right** (staying on Browns Mill Rd. at the 3-way intersection where Rob Taylor Rd. goes to the left.

13.6   Cross Hwy. 96 (stop sign). Market.

13.8   **Left** on Hwy. 266 in the town of Lascassas (first left). Market.

Go to Both Options

OPTION 2
45 miles

16.4   **Right** on Milton St. (Old Hwy. 96) (stop sign at the T-intersection) in the town of Milton. Restaurant.

16.5   **Right** on Hwy. 96 (stop sign at the T-intersection).

16.55   **Left** *immediately* on N. Milton Rd. (North Rd.).

22.5   **Left** on Greenvale Rd. in the town of Greenvale (stop sign at the T-intersection).

25.1   **Left** on Hwy. 266 South/Cainsville Pk. (stop sign at the T-intersection).

28.4   **Right** on Hoover Rd. (easy to miss) (first right after the Rutherford County line).

29.8   **Left** on Barlow Ln. (stop sign at the T-intersection).

31.5   **Right** on Hwy. 266/Barlow Ln. (stop sign) in the town of Lascassas. Market.

31.6   Stay **right** at the "Y" immediately past the market.

Go to Both Options

BOTH OPTIONS

15.8, 33.6   **Left** on Betty Ford Rd. (easy to miss) which is before you get to the large TVA powerlines.

17.2, 35.0   **Left** (staying on Betty Ford Rd.) after crossing the Stones River.

18.1, 35.9   **Left** on Hwy. 268/Compton Rd. (stop sign at the T-intersection).

18.4, 36.2   Cross Hwy. 96 (stop sign) and continue on Compton Rd. (Sharpsville Rd.). Market.

22.2, 40.0   **Right** on Halls Hill Rd. (stop sign at the T-intersection). You are now retracing your route to the starting point.

27.0, 44.8   End of ride!

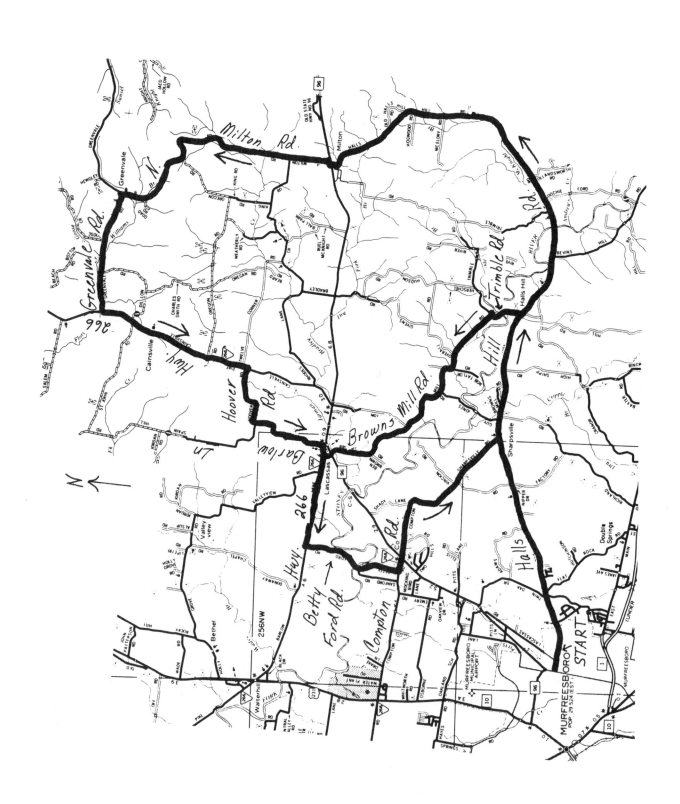

Ride # 21 BELLEVUE/KINGSTON SPRINGS RIDE

Distance: 44 miles
Elevation Difference/Accumulated Climb: 390/3000 ft.
Terrain: Very hilly. 9 challenging climbs on the roundtrip. Flat to rolling stretches interspersed between the big climbs.
Services: Market/restaurant at mile 14.4 (29.6 on return trip). Restaurant at mile 18.7 (25.3 on return trip).
Traffic: Moderate to heavy on short stretches on Hwy. 100, Old Harding Rd., and Hwy. 70 (total of 1.3 mi. each way). Light to moderate near Bellevue and I-40. Light on all other roads.
Combining Rides: # 6 *Edwin Warner Park*, # 8 *Harpeth Loop*, # 22 *Narrows of the Harpeth Loop.*
Connector Routes: **1)** .8 mi. to # 5 *Percy Warner Park Loop*--From Edwin Warner Park parking area, turn right on Hwy. 100, right on Old Hickory Blvd., first left into the park, then right on the Main Drive. **2)** 1.5-2.5 mi. to # 7 *Old Natchez Trace/Del Rio Ride*--Proceed on the closed roads through Edwin Warner Park to Vaughn Rd. (See *Ride # 6.*)
Alternate Parking Site: Bellevue Park located on Harpeth Knoll Dr. near Old Harding Pk. and Beech Bend Dr.
Distance from Nashville: 10 miles

The *Bellevue/Kingston Springs Ride* is an excellent hill workout as well as a scenic tour of Davidson and Cheatham Counties. Many cyclists whine over the inevitable hills encountered in Middle Tennessee, but the best way to increase the muscle and aerobic condition is to go for the big climbs. This trip provides five challenging pulls occurring at approximately 4-mile intervals, after which you get to turn around and struggle up them going the other way for a total of 3,000 ft. accumulated elevation gain--more than any of our other trips. Combine this trip with the *Warner Park Loop* (total of 57 miles), and you are worthy of the "King of the Mountain Jersey." For the insane cyclist, add the *Narrows of the Harpeth Loop* to both of these trips, and you have a good training ride for the mountain stages of the Tour de France.

The first 6 miles of this tour cruise among the quiet residential streets of the ever-expanding Bellevue community. The cyclist is greeted with the first workout grade (270 ft.) on Poplar Creek Rd. which continues for .7 mile up a wooded section of Backbone Ridge. At the top, the road immediately descends into a shady hollow and follows Poplar Creek through a small picturesque valley to the South Harpeth River.

From here, our route goes right and crosses into Cheatham County on a sparsely traveled road which was a bit bumpy when we last rode it. Be sure to notice the tall limestone cliffs to the right after you cross the river. Two .5-mile climbs (180 ft. and 240 ft.) await on South Harpeth Rd.

A speedy descent with a few sharp turns (be careful!) brings you to I-40 and past a multitude of truck stops. After the momentary shock of our interstate culture passes, you are rolling through the countryside once again. W. Kingston Springs Rd. leads you to Main St. in Kingston Springs (mile 16, no services). Several residential developments have recently sprung up in the area, causing this community gradually to become a distant suburb of Nashville. The original sleepy town along the old Main St. has changed little since the day the train no longer stopped at the depot. At one time, Kingston Springs was among the many popular sulphur spring resorts in Middle Tennessee and was a favorite destination for excursion by train from Nashville.

Leaving Kingston Springs, this tour parallels the RR tracks and soon crosses the Harpeth River before a steep grade on aptly named Pinnacle Rd. After the 160-ft. climb up Pinnacle Hill, the road winds on top of a narrow ridge that hosts newer homes and forests before descending to Hwy. 70.

Cedar Hill Rd. travels through a charming rural valley occasionally framed by magnificent rugged bluffs carved by the Harpeth River. After crossing Mound Creek, you'll be able to catch glimpses (especially when the trees are bare) of Indian mounds on the bend across the river. The *Bellevue/Kingston Spring Ride* finally heads out to conquer the final hill which is known as the Narrows of the Harpeth--actually a tall bluff in the middle of a river bend. (See *Ride # 22* for more information.)

This unique historical and geological area is a fascinating place for a walk before cycling the return trip. At this point, you can simply turn around (which obviously can be done at anytime--such as before climbing any of the previous hills), or do one of the following: bike down to bridge across the river on Cedar Hill Rd. and add another really tough climb to your day, or go left at the top of the hill. The latter option (stay left at all intersections) goes through the park and down to the river before a minor climb brings you back to Cedar Hill Rd. Enjoy your new perspective of all these hills on the return trip!!!

21 BELLEVUE/KINGSTON SPRINGS RIDE

HOW TO GET THERE: Take Hwy. 100 West (really south) from Nashville to Edwin Warner Park. Park at the second parking area past the traffic light at Old Hickory Blvd. This come before the second traffic light (which is also Old Hickory Blvd).

Mile

0.0	**Left** on Hwy. 100 from the parking area.
0.4	**Right** on Harpeth Bend Rd. (first right after Old Hickory Blvd).
1.5	**Right** on Harpeth Knoll Dr.
1.9	**Right** on Beech Bend Dr. (stop sign at the T-intersection).
2.0	**Left** on Old Harding Pk. (stop sign at the 4-way intersection).
2.3	**Right** on Morton Mill Rd. (first right).
2.9	**Left** on Bay Cove Trail.
3.5	**Left** on Rolling River Pkwy. (stop sign at the T-intersection).
4.4	**Right** on Poplar Creek Rd. (stop sign).
5.4	Cross McCrory Ln. (stop sign) and continue on Poplar Creek Rd.
8.7	**Right** on S. Harpeth Rd. as the road bends to the left.
13.8	**Right** on Luyben Hills Rd. (stop sign at the T-intersection).
14.4	Cross I-40. Markets/restaurants.
14.7	**Left** on W. Kingston Springs Rd. (stop sign at the T-intersection).
16.0	Bear **right** onto Main St at the Church of Christ in Kingston Springs.
16.2	Continue on Park St. (Pinnacle Rd.) which crosses the RR track.
18.7	**Left** on Hwy. 70/Charlotte Pk. (stop sign at the T-intersection).
19.3	**Right** on Cedar Hill Rd. immediately before crossing the Harpeth River.
22.0	Narrows of the Harpeth State Park. You can go left near the top of the hill and go through the park. Stay left at every intersection to come out on Cedar Hill Rd. Return the way you came.
44.0	End of Ride!

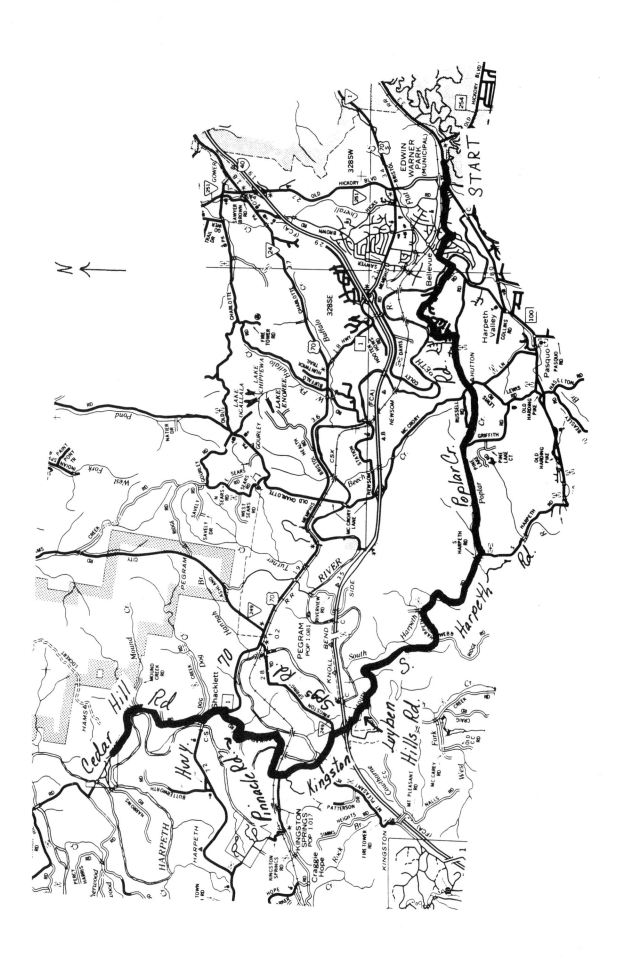

Ride #22   NARROWS OF THE HARPETH LOOP

Distance: 35 or 40 miles
Elevation Difference/Accumulated Climb: Option 1 - 440/1,900ft., Option 2 - 440/2,375 ft.
Terrain: Moderate to very hilly. 3 short steep climbs and 2 long gradual climbs plus many more ups and downs.
Services: Option 1 has markets at mile 11, 13.7, and 30.1. Option 2 has markets at mile 11, 13.7, 26.2, 30.7, 35.1. Restaurants at miles 13.7 and 17.7.
Traffic: Moderate to heavy on 2 stretches of Hwy. 70 (total of .8 mi.). Moderate on Hwy. 49 and River Rd. Light on all other roads.
Combining Ride: *#21 Bellevue/Kingston Springs Ride.*
Connector Routes: 1) 5.5 mi. to *#23 Montgomery Bell State Park Loop*—Bike south on Hwy. 250 from its intersection with Greenbrier Rd. (Cedar Hill Rd.) at mile 26.2. **2)** 2.1 mi. to *#35 Lower Sycamore Creek Loop*—Continue into Ashland City on Hwy. 49. Turn left on Hwy. 12 and continue for 1.1 mi. to Option 3 of the *Lower Sycamore Creek Loop.*
Alternate Parking Sites: 1) Narrows of the Harpeth State Park. **2)** Truck stops at Hwy. 249 and I-40 (Exit 188).
Distance from Nashville: 20 miles

From river to river and over the ridge that separates them, this challenging ride cruises through the delightful rural areas of southern Cheatham County. The route meanders among broad, grassy valleys and winds along densely forested ridges with plenty of hills in between to keep you entertained.

Leaving River Rd., a very gentle grade on Sams Creek Rd. heads up an open grassy valley encompassed by wooded hillsides. As is often the case, the incline suddenly increases and a steep 200-ft. pull takes you to what appears to be the top. Guess again? How many dips are there? We can never remember. We just enjoy gazing across the beautiful forests of the Cheatham Wildlife Management Area and try not to think about the repeated upgrades. A straight, speedy descent rewards you for your effort as you fly down to Hwy. 70 on the outskirts of Pegram. If you wish to avoid a difficult hill and shorten this trip by 5 miles, simply stay on Hwy. 70 to Cedar Hill Rd. Although this highway with a barely-usable shoulder often has frequent high speed traffic, we have found it tolerable to ride.

Our tour continues to follow Hwy. 249 through a mix of urban and country in the new areas of Kingston Springs, a growing bedroom community of Nashville. You may wish to take advantage of the interstate quick-stop markets, because the next food opportunity is 13 miles and several steep hills away. Downtown Kingston Springs has sadly lost its many thriving enterprises of the railroad days to the interstate 2 miles away. In bygone days, hundreds of people rode the train from Nashville to visit the cool sulphur springs for which the town was named.

After going down the block-long Main St., the route continues on a narrow country lane along the RR tracks and crosses the Harpeth River before a very challenging ascent (170 ft.) of aptly named Pinnacle Hill is encountered. The road winds on top of a narrow ridge hosting newer homes and forests before descending to Hwy. 70. In the community of Shacklett, there are two canoe rental businesses, so you may want to consider paddling the scenic Harpeth River for some post-ride relaxation. Cycling Cedar Hill Rd. as an out-and-back and then floating down the Harpeth makes an excellent fun-filled day for active families.

The premier part of the tour follows Cedar Hill Rd. through a charming pastoral valley occasionally framed by magnificent rugged bluffs carved by the Harpeth River. Past the small stream known as Mound Creek, you can sometimes catch glimpses (especially when the trees are bare) of the Indian mounds on the bend across the river. After a delightful stretch along the Harpeth River, a very steep ascent goes up to Narrows of the Harpeth, a narrow and often vertical bluff separating a horseshoe bend of the river. You immediately barrel down to a new bridge that has replaced (alas) an old metal truss bridge we used to enjoy. It is easy to pick up speed on this descent, but slow down and be careful of the bump as you enter the bridge (something you should expect at every bridge).

The Narrows of the Harpeth is a unique scenic, geologic, and historical area. If you have the time and walkable bike shoes, a short walk on the trail beginning to the left before the bridge can be taken through this inviting area. At the trail junction, the trail to the right leads to a 100-yard tunnel through the bluff where part of the diverted river gushes over a waterfall. This hole through the cliff was designed by Montgomery Bell and dug through the arduous work of his many slaves. (See *Ride #23* for more information on Montgomery Bell.) The tunnel, completed around 1815 after a year of drilling, was a major engineering feat of the time considering the tools of the day. Water was diverted through the tunnel to power the Pattison Iron Works, one of the largest iron furnaces in the region. The other trail goes up a series of wooden steps to the top of the bluffs where there are some of the best views in Middle Tennessee, including both sides of the river bend.

The next 5 miles journey over small forested hills and open pastures in an area situated among the bends of the Harpeth River. Often it seems that time has forgotten places like this, and the fields and farmhouses in this sparsely settled area must look almost the way they did 50 years ago. Option 1 takes off on a steep climb through the Cheatham Wildlife Management Area and drops you back down to River Rd.

From the community of Harpeth Valley, Option 2 heads north on Hwy. 250, crosses the Harpeth for the last time, and begins a long broken climb (280 ft.) up the ridge. Upon reaching Germantown with its market and a fire tower, you are once again on the ridge between the rivers. It is usually permissible to climb the tower, and there is a great panoramic view of this beautiful, forested Tennessee landscape. The route continues along the ridge into the woods of the Cheatham Wildlife Management Area before beginning a long steady descent to the Cumberland River on Hwy. 49.

While coasting (or madly pedaling) downhill, be sure to observe the sheer limestone cliffs within the green hills across the valley. Just past the junction of Hwy. 249, a short detour on Old River Rd. provides a view of 200-ft. Sidney's Bluff which is directly above this road. Hwy. 249 heads up and around the back of this bluff on a steep 220-ft. pull followed by a short exhilarating descent into the undulating flood plains of the Cumberland Valley. Only at a few places can you see the river from the road, but there are several views of the bluffs on the east side of the river. (On this final segment, it's an amusing sight when you can see only the top of a river barge moving along and appearing to be gliding through the pastures!)

#22 NARROWS OF THE HARPETH LOOP

HOW TO GET THERE: Take I-40 West and exit at Charlotte Pk./Hwy. 70 (Exit 201), go right (west) on Charlotte Pk. for .4 mi. and turn right onto River Rd. Go 1.5 mi. and turn right at the stop sign, and continue on what is still River Rd. Go approximately 12 mi. and park at Brush Hill Recreation Area on the right. Look for its brown sign in addition to a market on the left.

Mile

0.0	Begin ride by turning **left** on River Rd./Hwy. 249 going toward Nashville.
0.9	**Right** on Hwy. 249/Sams Creek Rd. (Ashland City Rd.)
10.9	**Right** on Hwy. 70 (stop at the T-intersection). Market.
11.2	**Left** on Hwy. 249 (first left). You may also continue on Hwy. 70 for 2.2 mi. to Cedar Hill Rd., thus shortening the entire trip by 5 miles. Hwy. 70 has moderate to heavy traffic and a 2-3 ft. paved shoulder.
13.7	Continue straight onto Kingston Springs Rd. (3-way stop). Markets/restaurants to the left.
15.0	Bear **right** onto Main St. at the Church of Christ in Kingston Springs.
15.2	Continue on Park St. (Pinnacle Rd.) which crosses the RR tracks.
17.7	**Left** on Hwy. 70/Charlotte Pk. (stop sign at the T-intersection).
18.2	**Right** on Cedar Hill Rd. Look for the sign to the Narrows of the Harpeth.
20.8	Narrows of the Harpeth State Park (no water or restrooms).
21.2	Cross bridge over the Harpeth River.
21.6	Cedar Hill Rd. turns sharply to the right as Leatherwood Rd. comes in from the left. Continue on Cedar Hill Rd.
22.8	Cross Harpeth River.

Go to Option 1 or Option 2

Option 1
35 miles

24.6	**Right** on Griffintown Rd.
30.0	Straight at the first 4-way intersection.
30.1	**Right** on Willy Pardue Rd. Market.
35.1	Cross River Rd. End of Ride!

Option 2
40 miles

25.1	Cross river again.
26.2	**Right** on Hwy. 250/Greenbrier Rd. (stop sign at the T-intersection). Market.
30.7	Market.
34.6	**Right** on Hwy. 49 (stop sign).
35.1	Market.
37.1	**Right** on Hwy. 249 (River Road).
40.0	End of Ride! Remember—if it weren't for the hills, this ride would not be nearly as scenic!

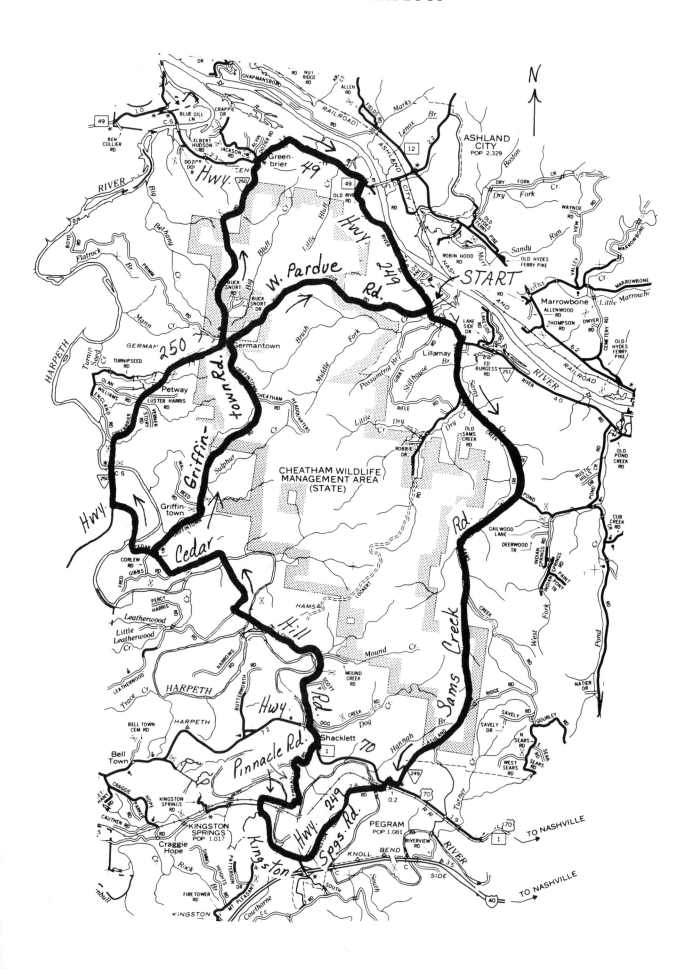

Ride # 23   MONTGOMERY BELL STATE PARK LOOP

Distance: 25 or 66 miles
Elevation Difference/Accumulated Climb: Option 1 - 340/1380 ft., Option 2 - 410/2690 ft.
Terrain: Moderately hilly with several long gentle grades.
Services: Option 1 has markets at miles 2.0, 5.3, and 23.2. Option 2 has markets at miles 2.0, 5.3, 14,6, 16.7, 23.6, 24.2, 30.2, 36.5, 38.8, 54.6, 55.3, 57.9, and 63.5.
Traffic: Moderate on Hwy. 70 (.5 mi.) and in the town of Dickson. Light to moderate on Hwy. 47 between Hwy. 70 and Charlotte. Light on all other roads.
Connector Routes: 1) 15 mi. to # *10 Fernvale Loop*--From the intersection of Hwy. 47 and Hwy. 96 on Option 2, turn right (west) on Hwy. 96, then turn right on Spencer Mill Rd. which becomes Pinewood Rd. after crossing Hwy. 100. **2)** 5.5 mi. to # *22 Narrows of the Harpeth Loop*--Go right on Hwy. 252 at mile 7.6.
Alternate Parking Sites: Dickson.
Distance from Nashville: 32 miles

As officers of the Nashville Bicycle Club, we have worked with the Leukemia Society of America in organizing the CURE 2000 Bicycle Classic which takes place at Montgomery Bell State Park on the second weekend in June. We love the route (mapped out by Nashville Bicycle Club member and local resident Jerry Clark) so much that we feel compelled to include it in this book even though it is out of our "surrounding counties" area. If there is such a thing as the "heartland" of Tennessee, it might be Dickson county. Much of the 66-mile loop traverses miles and miles of scenic rural countryside in lightly populated areas.

The ride begins at beautiful Montgomery Bell State Park and makes a great outing for families or individuals who want to do more than just bicycle. The park has hiking, fishing, picnicking, camping, nature study programs, and golf. There is also a refreshing swimming lake for a post-ride cool-down in the summer.

The park is named for Montgomery Bell (1769-1855), a Scotch-Irishman from Pennsylvania, who built an iron empire in Middle Tennessee and operated several iron works in Dickson County including the Cumberland Furnace. Bell also designed the tunnel at the Narrows of the Harpeth in Cheatham County. (See *Ride # 22* for more information.) Bell was said to be a man who had few friends, often would not pay his debts unless sued, and was a ruthless slave driver. His slaves labored throughout the region, digging iron ore from the limestone rock, crushing it by hand with sledge hammers, feeding it into the charcoal-fired smelters, and finally hauling it off by mules and oxen to the Cumberland River.

Our tour begins with a brief upgrade and continues for 2 miles through the forest within the state park. After 8 miles of mostly flat cycling, you will roll down a long, gentle hill and cross Jones Creek. From here the terrain becomes noticeably more hilly. Option 1 heads south into a scenic area on lightly traveled backroads, crosses Hwy. 70, and continues to Burns, Tennessee (where Ann went to Girl Scout camp) before returning to the park.

Option 2 continues on Hwy. 47 before turning onto Old Hwy. 47 for a short, pretty descent into the town of Charlotte (established 1805), the county seat of Dickson County. Because of its location away from the railroad, and more recently I-40, this little town has not grown much since its early days. You may wish to detour one block to the right and take a spin back in time around the charming town square with the old brick courthouse (1835) and a truly original country store known as Bernadine's Grocery.

From Charlotte, this tour follows Hwy. 49 northeast toward the town of Vanleer, situated high on the ridge above Yellow Creek. Before reaching Vanleer, a seemingly endless 200-ft. climb (but really only 2 miles long) heads from Bartons Creek to the ridge. Fortunately, the grades on this ride seem to be much friendlier than those in other sections of Middle Tennessee. The sleepy town of Vanleer has a couple of old markets to help you rejuvenate after accomplishing that last hill. Some of Ann's roots can be traced back to this region, and we can't help but wonder what her forefathers and mothers would have thought of their lycra/coolmax-clad descendant going up and down these hills on her 21-speed Terry bicycle.

Hwy. 46/Yellow Creek Rd. is a delight to ride as it winds through a gentle, green valley. Old farmhouses, woods, corn, and other crops are situated along beautiful Yellow Creek. Glen attempted to rescue and remove a large turtle off this road and was nearly bitten--by an angry snapping turtle! (It was quickly agreed that the turtle could stay on the road as long as it liked.)

The route passes by the entrances of Jewel Cave and Ruskin Cave (tours available for both). This area of Yellow Creek was once the home of the Ruskin Cooperative Association, a socialist colony which flourished from 1894 to 1899. Its members farmed the fertile soil in addition to selling books, clothing, questionable medicinal remedies, and other goods all over the nation. Julius Wayland, the colony's founder, published a national newspaper propagating the socialist writings of John Ruskin. The Ruskin Colony must have failed in its goal of communal living, because inner dissension led to its disintegration. In more recent years, Ruskin Cave has become known for its country music concerts.

Gilliam Hollow Rd. proceeds up another gradual ascent (210 ft.) before crossing Hwy. 70 in Tennessee City (no services). From here the route goes up and down the rolling hills in slightly more populated areas. After crossing the upper reaches of the Piney River, you make the final major climb (190 ft.) of the day and go into the bustling town of Dickson. Dickson was established as a train stop around 1865 and eventually grew as several rail lines intersected there. From the corner of Hwy. 48 and E. Walnut St., you may wish to detour to the old Main St. with its typical small town store fronts. Several restaurants (from fast food to country cookin') make a good lunch stop before the final 10 miles back to Montgomery Bell State Park.

Anytime your rims are wet, your braking ability will be greatly reduced. You can, however, dry your rims by lightly squeezing the brakes before you need to apply them. In general, always allow extra stopping distance when riding in wet conditions.

23 MONTGOMERY BELL STATE PARK LOOP

HOW TO GET THERE: Take I-40 West from Nashville to Bellevue/Hwy. 70S (Exit 196) and turn right (west) at the bottom of the ramp onto Hwy. 70S. Continue 1.8 mi. and turn left on Hwy. 70 toward Dickson. Continue approximately 19 mi. through the town of White Bluff and turn left into Montgomery Bell State Park. Park at the ball fields near the campground or any other suitable parking area.

Mile
0.0	Begin ride by going **right** (away from Hwy. 70) on the main road through the park (not the road to the Inn or swim area).
2.0	**Left** on Hwy. 47. Market.
4.8	**Right** on Hwy. 70 (stop sign at the T-intersection).
5.3	**Left** on Hwy. 47. Market. There are 3 more markets within the next 2 miles.
7.6	Continue straight on Hwy. 47 as Hwy 252. goes right.

Go to Option 1 or Option 2

OPTION 1
25 miles

12.1	**Left** on Liberty Rd. (4-way intersection) after climbing a hill (easy to miss).
12.5	**Right** on Shelton Rd. (first right).
13.2	**Left** on Rock Church Rd. (4-way intersection).
17.9	Cross Hwy. 70 (stop sign) and continue on Buddy Rd. Restaurant.
20.2	**Left** on Hwy. 47 (stop sign at the T-intersection) after crossing the RR tracks.
23.2	**Left** into Montgomery Bell State Park. Market.
25.2	End of ride!

OPTION 2
66 miles

13.6	**Right** on Old Hwy. 47 (easy to miss) as new Hwy. 47 bends to the left. (Note: There may be 2 other Old Hwy. 47's marked prior to this one.)
14.6	**Left** on Hwy. 49 (stop sign at the T-intersection) in the town of Charlotte. Market in the town square.
14.9	**Right** on Hwy. 48/Hwy. 49 (3-way stop).
15.2	**Left** on Hwy. 49 at the traffic light.
16.7	Market.
17.0	Stay **left** on Hwy. 49 as Old Hwy. 48 goes straight.
21.6	Continue straight on Hwy. 49 at the junction of Hwy. 235.
23.6	Markets in the town of Vanleer.
24.2	Bear **left** (staying on Hwy. 49) at the junction of Hwy. 235. Market.
30.2	**Left** on Hwy. 46/Yellow Creek Rd. Market.
36.5	Market/cafe at Jewel Cave.
38.8	Market.
40.0	**Right** on Gilliam Hollow Rd. (easy to miss).
42.7	Cross Hwy. 70 (stop sign).
42.9	**Left** on Pruett Rd. (first left).
43.4	**Left** (staying on Pruett Rd.) (T-intersection).
44.2	**Right** on CCC Rd. (stop sign).
48.0	CCC Rd. becomes Lock Hollow Rd. at a bend to the left.
50.6	**Right** on W. Piney Rd. (stop sign at the T-intersection).
53.4	**Left** on Hwy. 48/Center Rd. (stop sign at the T-intersection).

54.6   Market.

55.2   Straight at the 4-way stop.

55.3   **Right** on Hwy. 46/E. Walnut St. (traffic light) by the brick Church of Christ. Markets/restaurants straight ahead and to the left in the town of Dickson.

56.0   Straight onto Hwy. 47 (traffic light).

57.9   Market.

59.5   Cross Hwy. 96 (stop sign).

60.2   **Left** (staying on Hwy. 47) at the traffic light.

63.5   **Left** into Montgomery Bell State Park. Market.

65.5   End of ride!

#23   MONTGOMERY BELL STATE PARK LOOP

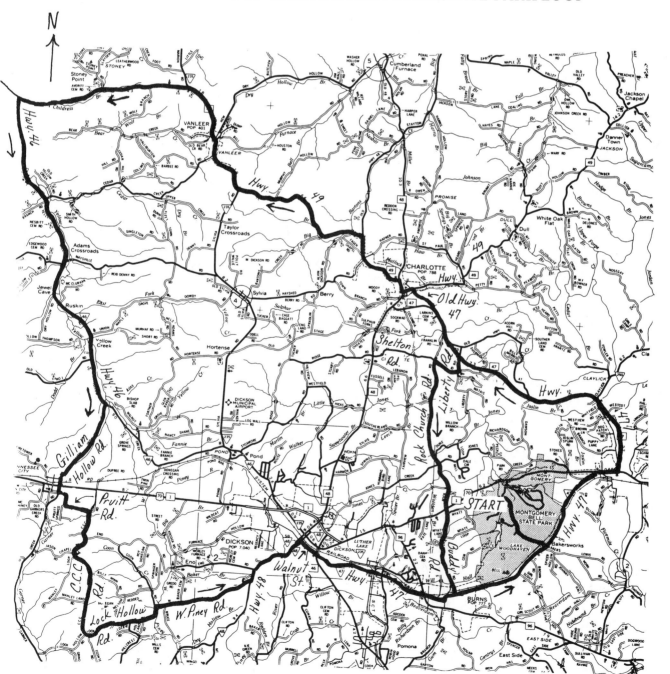

Ride # 24 OLD RAILROAD ROAD LOOP

Distance: 27 or 41 miles
Elevation Difference/Accumulated Climb: Option 1 - 370/1450 ft., Option 2 - 450/1770 ft.
Terrain: Flat to rolling. 1 moderate hill on Option 1 and 1 tough hill on Option 2.
Services: Option 1 has markets at miles 5.3 and 18.7. Restaurant at mile 8.0. Option 2 has
   markets at miles 5.3, 11.8, 17.7, 26.3, and 32.3. Restaurants at miles 8.0 and 11.8.
Traffic: Moderate on Chandler Rd. and Old Lebanon Dirt Rd. near Hermitage. Light to
   moderate on Old Railroad Rd./Leeville Pk. and Central Pk. Light on all other roads.
Combining Ride: *# 25 Percy Priest Lake Loop.*
Connector Routes: 1) 1.5 mi. to *# 26 Long Hunter State Park/Lascassas Loop*--Bike south
   on Gladeville Rd. from the market at mile 26.3 on Option 2. **2)** 1.3 mi. to start of *# 27
   Watertown Loop* and *# 28 Lebanon/Hartsville Ride*--Continue east on Leeville Pk. at mile
   17.7 on Option 2.
Alternate Parking Site: Mt. Juliet Library north of Division St. (Old RR Rd.) on Hwy. 171.
Distance from Nashville: 12 miles

In the mid-1980s, the Mt. Juliet Eagle Scout Troop 474 established a historical bike route on what is known as Old Railroad Bed Road. A pamphlet with the bike route and historical information can be obtained from the Mt. Juliet Library. Our tour follows this 18-mile route (8 miles on Option 1) and makes a convenient cycling escape for those living in the Hermitage area. Both options follow quiet rural roads connecting south to Central Pk. which returns to the starting point.

Old Railroad Rd. is one of the few places in Middle Tennessee (but hopefully not for long) where bicycle route signs are posted. Unfortunately the road has no shoulders or other accommodations for bicycle riding. At the very least, the signs might inform the few inconsiderate motorists that cyclists do indeed have a legal right to use the roads. The traffic has undoubtedly increased in the growing areas of Hermitage, Mt. Juliet, and Lebanon since this official route was established, yet we have still enjoyed some very peaceful segments which are flat and easy to ride. Certain areas will have moderately high volumes of traffic during commuting hours and afternoons when schools dismiss.

Old Railroad Road (at times marked as Chandler Rd., Division St., or Leeville Pk.) follows the course of the railroad operated by the N C and St. Louis Railroad between 1875 and 1935. During these sixty years of operation, many small towns sprung up along the line, allowing local farmers conveniently to sell their goods and purchase imported items. The train was also the main method of transportation for citizens traveling between Nashville and Lebanon and to points beyond.

Often, knowledgeable cyclists' eyes light up when they discover their route follows an old railroad bed because this usually means there are no steep grades; however, don't get too excited, because our trip does climb a few good hills on the return portion of the loop. After the route leaves the residential areas of Hermitage, grassy fields gradually replace suburban sprawl, and you roll into the old section of Mt. Juliet with its handful of well-kept wooden frame houses. The original Mt. Juliet was located on the hill south of here on Old Lebanon Dirt Pk., but the entire community found it profitable to move down to the railroad line after it opened. Unfortunately the train station is no longer there, but the Freeman

House (now a private residence) located on the right just before Hwy. 171, operated as a hotel during these active railroad days.

Outside Mt. Juliet, where the land becomes a little more rolling, Option 1 leaves Old Railroad Rd. and heads south on Rutland Rd. and Posey Hill Rd. into more hilly terrain. The premier part of this route follows Posey Hill Rd. as it winds its way through sleepy farmland. A .5-mile pull (200 ft.) up Posey Hill is rewarded by a wonderful view of the Stones River watershed to the south and (if you stop and look back) the Cumberland watershed to the north.

Option 2 continues the journey on the old rail bed and gradually ascends to Tuckers Gap, site of another railroad stop, before arriving in Lebanon. Our route bypasses most of busy Lebanon, but you may wish to go straight into town if you are interested in the many antique malls on the town square or the numerous fast food and coffee shop establishments along Hwy. 231/S. Cumberland St.

A very scenic stretch on Franklin Rd. meanders through open pastures before a broken ascent (250 ft.) with nice glimpses of the lowlands reaches the top of Big Hill. (We think you will agree with the name!) After a brief, flat reprieve on the summit, you immediately barrel down toward Central Pk.

Option 2 soon joins Option 1 on Central Pk., traverses an interesting area of lumpy hills, and hits one fast drop. More and more homes, both new and old, line the route, but plenty of pastures help maintain the characteristic rural quality.

We have chosen to follow a pleasant detour south of I-40, thus eliminating a portion of Central Pk. which gets busy near Hermitage. This detour travels Hager Rd., passes a new residential area, heads up a small hill, and is topped off by a refreshing broken descent into a   semi-forested region. The remainder of trip travels through residential areas to end the tour.

Do not panic if an angry motorist honks. An accident is more likely to occur if you suddenly try to move out of their way. Keep your course and remember, that if they honk, at least they know you're there and it is their responsibility to safely pass you. If they are unable to pass and their presence is making you uneasy, give the hand signal for slowing down and cautiously pull off the road when safe.

#24 OLD RAILROAD ROAD LOOP

HOW TO GET THERE: Take I-40 East and exit at The Hermitage/Hwy. 45 North (Exit 221A) which takes you north into the Hermitage area. Turn right onto Andrew Jackson Pkwy.—not Andrew Jackson *Way* which is the light just before Andrew Jackson Pkwy. Turn right onto Old Lebanon Dirt Rd. and immediately left on Chandler Rd. Park at the Dodson Chapel Elementary School or at the RR parking area.

Mile

0.0   Begin ride by cycling away from Old Lebanon Dirt Rd. on Chandler Rd. (which changes names to Division St., Old Railroad Rd., and Leeville Pk. in the 18-mile stretch to Lebanon).

5.3   Cross Hwy. 171/Mt Juliet Rd. at the traffic light in the town of Mt. Juliet. Market.
Go to Option 1 or Option 2

OPTION 1
27 miles

8.0   **Right** on Rutland Rd. (easy to miss).
9.7   **Right** on Posey Hill Rd. (Beckwith/Rutland Rd.) (stop sign at the T-intersection).
9.8   Cross over I-40.
10.7   **Left** (staying on Posey Hill Rd.) at the 4-way intersection.
13.7   **Right** on Central Pk. (stop sign at the T-intersection).
Go to Both Options

OPTION 2
41 miles

11.8   **Right** on Hwy. 109 (stop sign). Market/restaurant.
11.9   **Left** on Leeville Pk.
17.7   **Right** on Castle Heights Ave. (4-way stop) after passing the small airport. Market.
18.5   **Right** on Franklin Rd. (stop sign at the T-intersection). Markets/restaurants (.2 mi. off the loop) to the left (east) on Franklin Rd. Restaurants 1 mile east on Hwy. 231.
19.4   Cross over I-40.
21.2   Go under I-840.
26.0   **Right** on Central Pk. (stop sign at the T-intersection).
26.3   Market.
Go to Both Options

BOTH OPTIONS

18.7, 32.3   Cross Hwy. 171 (stop sign). Market.
19.9, 33.5   **Left** on Hager Rd. which is immediately before Central Pk. crosses I-40.
22.4, 36.0   **Right** on Earhart Rd. (stop sign at the T-intersection).
23.2, 36.8   Go under I-40.
23.5, 37.1   **Left** on Central Pk. (stop sign at the T-intersection).
24.2, 37.8   **Right** on New Hope Rd. past the Central Pk. Church of Christ.
25.5, 39.1   **Left** on Old Lebanon Dirt Rd. (stop sign at the T-intersection).
27.0, 40.6   **Right** on Chandler Rd. (traffic light).
27.4, 41.0   End of Ride!

NOTE: State Route 840 is not shown on this map.

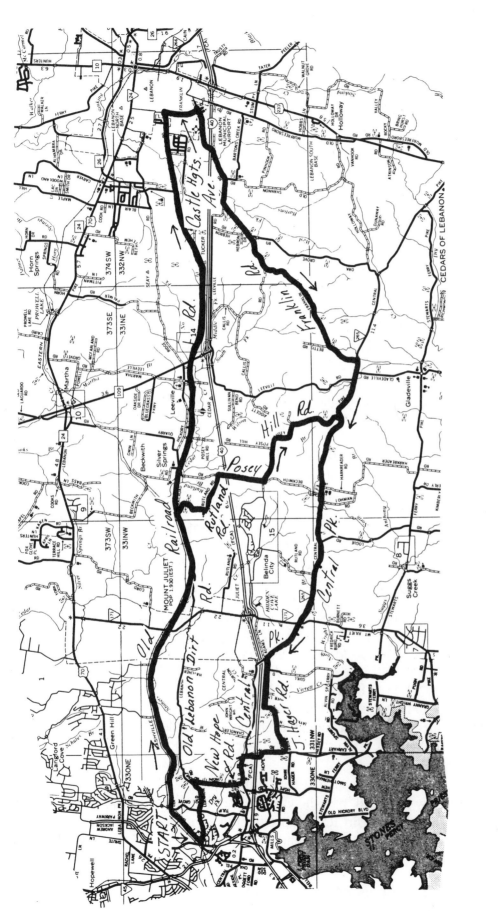

Ride # 25 PERCY PRIEST LAKE/MT. JULIET LOOP

Distance: 13 or 28 miles
Elevation Difference/Accumulated Climb: Option 1 - 170/670 ft., Option 2 - 190/1550 ft.
Terrain: Constant rolling terrain with no big hills.
Services: Option 1 has no services except near the beginning and end of the ride. Option 2 has markets at miles 8.0 and 17.6. Restaurant at mile 17.6.
Traffic: Light to moderate on Stewarts Ferry Pk. (Both Options) and Central Pk. (on Option 2 only). Light on all other roads. Traffic heavier on summer weekends near the lake.
Combining Ride: # 24 Old Railroad Road Loop.
Connector Route: 4.5 mi. to # 26 Long Hunter State Park/Lascassas Loop--From Beckwith Rd. and Central Pk. at mile 11.0 of Option 2, continue east on Central Pk. Turn right on Gladeville Rd.
Alternate Parking Sites: 1) Seven Point Recreation Area located at the corner of Stewarts Ferry Pk. and Earhart Rd. **2)** Mt. Juliet--Park at the shopping center at the corner of Hwy. 171 and Old Lebanon Dirt Rd.
Distance from Nashville: 13 miles

Every September hundreds of triathletes gather at the Cook Recreation Area for the annual Music City Triathlon. Since the bicycle course is very popular in this event, we mapped out two loop routes that incorporate this "out and back" triathlon route into two loop options. If you want to train by using the actual triathlon route, follow Option 2 to Hwy. 171 and turn around. On your return, go right on Earhart Rd. to the I-40 underpass and retrace your route back to the Cook Recreation Area. Our routes provide two nice loop options which are ideal for a hard training ride or an easy weekend cruise.

This tour begins along the shores of Percy Priest Lake, created in 1968 when 42 miles of the Stones River were dammed, forming a 14,000-acre lake. The 130-ft. dam generates 70 million kilowatts of hydroelectric power a year. The Cook Recreation Area offers camping, boating, fishing, and a shaded picnic area with barbecue grills and swimming beach, ideal for a refreshing post-ride picnic or swim.

Most of this tour wanders through sparse suburban areas intermingled with farmland. Occasional small, but often steep, hills are encountered in the first 6 miles, creating just enough of a workout to make the route interesting. The road occasionally dips down near the shores of the lake and offers glimpses of the water. Rocky cedar barrens are also common in this region of fairly unproductive soil.

Option 1 turns left on John Hager Rd. and travels past a new residential area before the fun downhill through a scenic wooded area. From here, our route runs south on Earhart Rd. to the lake and retraces its way home.

A long gradual descent on Central Pk. is in the store for the cyclists doing Option 2. It is, of course, followed by the inevitable uphill. The route crosses Hwy. 171 and follows Central Pk. for 3 more miles among a mix of old farm houses and new residences. A pleasant stretch on Beckwith Rd. and Posey Hill Rd. rolls among the green pastures.

After one mile on Old Railroad Rd., our trip turns onto Old Lebanon Dirt Rd. which was the stage route through the wilderness between Nashville and Lebanon. If you look to the north of Old Railroad Rd. at this intersection, it is possible to see where the old stage route continued. After passing a shopping center located on Hwy. 171 in Mt. Juliet, the road crosses Stoners Creek and climbs a substantial hill for which the "Mount" is derived in Mt. Juliet. The old town was located on top of this hill before it moved down to the railroad line.

After a minor descent, our route follows Chandler-Radford Rd. and Earhart Rd. through an appealing mix of urban, farmland, and forests before reaching the lake. From here, the route retraces itself 2.5 miles back to the start.

Basic Principles of Effective Cycling

- Drive on the right side of the roadway, never on the left and never on the sidewalk.
- When you reach a more important or larger road than the one you are on, yield to crossing traffic. Here, yielding means looking to each side and waiting until no traffic is coming.
- When you intend to change lanes or move laterally on the roadway, yield to traffic in the new lane of travel. Here, yielding means looking forward and backward until you see that no traffic is coming.
- When approaching an intersection, position yourself with respect to your destination direction--on the right near the curb if you want to turn right, on the left near the centerline if you want to turn left, and between those positions if you want to go straight.

25 PERCY PRIEST LAKE/MT. JULIET LOOP

HOW TO GET THERE: Take I-40 East to Old Hickory Blvd. South (Exit 221B). Turn right on Old Hickory Blvd., left on Bell Rd. at the stop sign, and then right on New Hope Rd. at the T-intersection. Turn right on Stewarts Ferry Pk. at the T-intersection and left on Old Hickory Blvd. After entering the Cook Recreation Area, turn right on the road to the Day Use Area/Swim Beach and park. (If this area is closed, park at the boat ramp.)

Mile

0.0 From the intersection of the Day Use road and Old Hickory Blvd., bike north (the direction from which you came) on Old Hickory Blvd.

0.8 **Right** on Stewarts Ferry Pk. (stop sign). Market.

2.4 Bear **left** on Alvin Sperry Rd. at a confusing 4-way intersection. Do not take a hard left onto Earhart Rd. Alvin Sperry Rd. becomes Gull Rd.
Go to Option 1 or Option 2

OPTION 1
13 miles

6.5 **Left** on John Hager Rd. (stop sign at the T-intersection).

8.8 **Left** on Earhart Rd. (stop sign at the T-intersection).
Go to Both Options

OPTION 2
28 miles

6.5 **Right** on John Hager Rd. (stop sign at the T-intersection).

6.7 **Right** on Central Pk./Hwy. 265 (stop sign).

8.0 Cross Mt. Juliet Rd./Hwy. 171 (stop sign). Market.

11.0 **Left** on Beckwith Rd. (easy to miss) immediately before a vacant market.

12.5 Continue straight at the 4-way intersection where Beckwith Rd. becomes Posey Hill Rd.

13.6 **Left** on Rutland Rd., the first street *after* crossing I-40. (Be careful not to turn onto the first Rutland Rd. at the 4-way intersection of Beckwith and Posey Hill Rd. before the interstate.)

15.3 **Left** on Old Railroad Rd. (stop sign at the T-intersection).

16.4 **Left** on Old Lebanon Dirt Rd. (first left).

17.6 Cross S. Mt. Juliet Rd./Hwy. 171. Market/restaurants.

20.0 **Left** on Chandler-Radford Rd. by the Chandler Baptist Church.

21.9 **Right** on Central Pk. (stop sign at the T-intersection).

22.3 **Left** on Earhart Rd. which is just after the Davidson County line.
Go to Both Options

BOTH OPTIONS

10.3, 25.0 **Right** on Stewarts Ferry Pk. You are now retracing your route back to the starting point.

12.0, 26.7 **Left** on Old Hickory Blvd. Market.

12.8, 27.5 End of Ride. Time to go soak in the lake if it's a hot day!

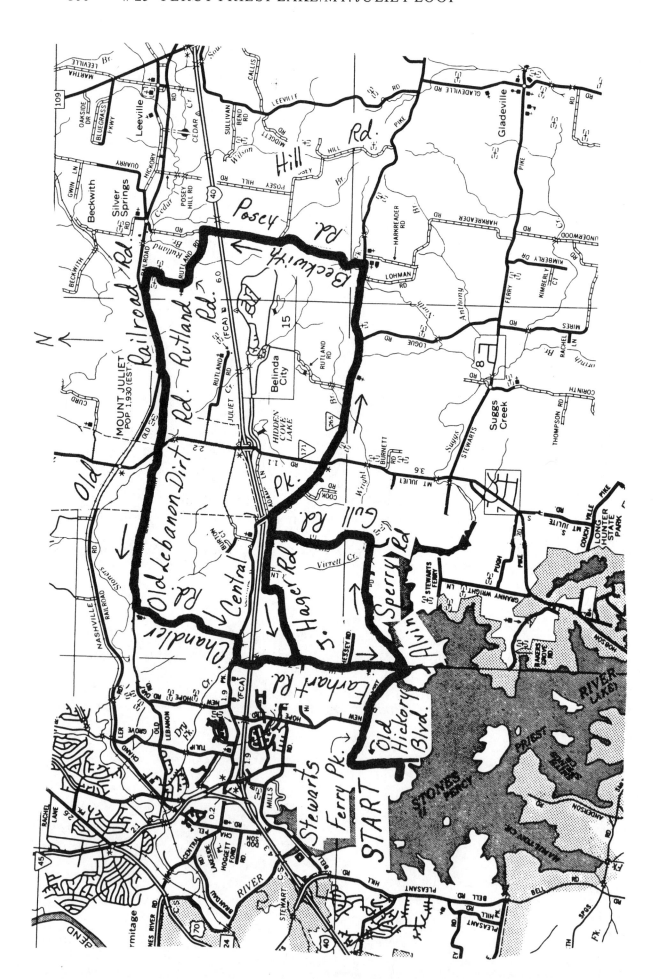

Ride #26   LONG HUNTER STATE PARK/GLADEVILLE LOOP

Distance: 57 miles
Elevation Difference/Accumulated Climb: 450/2400 ft.
Terrain: Moderately hilly with several flat sections. One big climb plus frequent large rolling hills.
Services: Markets at miles 9.6, 14.8, and 24.0. Camping/lodging at Cedars of Lebanon State Park at mile 14.8.
Traffic: Moderate traffic on Couchville Pk. Light on all other roads.
Combining Rides: *#20 Milton Loop, #27 Watertown Loop.*
Connector Routes: 1) 1.5 mi. to *#24 Old Railroad Road Loop*—From Gladeville, bike north on Gladeville Rd.
Alternate Parking Sites: 1) Cedars of Lebanon State Park **2)** Gladeville
Distance from Nashville: 23 miles

The *Long Hunter State Park/Lascassas Loop*, which follows portions of the Heart of Tennessee Bicycle Ride sponsored by the Murfreesboro Bicycle Club, encompasses Wilson and Rutherford Counties, two state parks, and a variety of terrain. If you desire a shorter tour (44 miles), begin in Gladeville and pick up the ride on Stewarts Ferry Pk., then continue straight on McCreary Rd. (Mona Rd.) when you get to Couchville Pk. near the end of the ride.

Bryant Grove Picnic Area, the starting point, is an ideal place for a post-ride swim and/or barbecue. You begin this tour by pedaling uphill to Couchville Pk. and heading east over rolling terrain. The land becomes mostly flat as Gladeville Rd. runs through unique thick cedar groves in shallow rocky soil with limestone outcrops. These evergreen cedars can survive in soil conditions where most hardwoods cannot, and the open rocky cedar glades host several rare, endemic plants and flowers which grow nowhere else in the world.

Our route rolls through the modest community of Gladeville which is situated on the edge of Cedars of Lebanon State Forest, a great mountain biking area. (See *Ride #43.*) You soon pass under the newly constructed I-840 (which hopefully will not change the peaceful ways of this region) and travel by dairy farms on Stewarts Ferry Pk. The entrance to Cedars of Lebanon State Park is .5 mile south off our route on Hwy. 231. The park has a Visitors' Center, several nature trails, picnic area, pool, camping and lodging. You may also decide to cut through the park to Norene (go through the park and continue on Cedar Forest Rd., then turn left on Norene Rd.) which will take two miles off your total trip. On our route, Chicken Rd./Hwy. 265 continues west from Hwy. 231 and soon encounters a series of moderate hills which provide scenic views of the surrounding landscape.

An 11-mile stretch on Cainsville Rd./Hwy. 266 runs up and down countless Tennessee rollers while traveling through charming countryside. The market with red benches in Norene has always been a favorite rest stop for us, and we have upon occasion exchanged information with the friendly locals on such matters as bicycling, farming, and weather. Hopefully this stop will give you the energy to get over the next gap near Grandfather's Knob past Cainsville. Next, our route briefly leaves Hwy. 266 and follows a narrow country lane through flat farmland at the foot of thickly-forested Casons and Rucker Knobs.

Originally, our route went into the town of Lascassas and picked up Hwy. 266 going west. The ever-growing urban sprawl along this route has brought an increasing number of impatient commuters in addition to the garbage trucks from Nashville using the local landfill. Our new route utilizes a series of scenic rural roads meandering among precipitous forested knobs and flat cedar glades. We think you will find that the challenging climb (200 ft. in .6 miles) on Pain Hill Rd. (this is not a joke) is better than "challenging" the high speed trucks and commuters on Hwy. 266! The terrain flattens as you pedal west among low rocky hills thick with cedars. Trailer homes and modest houses frequently dot the landscape of this region that is poorly suited for agriculture and occasionally shows signs of overgrazing.

#26   LONG HUNTER STATE PARK/LASCASSAS LOOP

HOW TO GET THERE: Take I-40 East and exit on Mt. Juliet Rd./Hwy. 171. (Exit 226A) going south. Turn left on South Mt. Juliet Rd. and left on Couchville Pk. Take the first right (Barnette Rd.) which leads to Bryant Grove Picnic Area of Long Hunter State Park.

Mile

0.0	Bike back toward Couchville Pk. from Bryant Grove Picnic Area.
1.4	**Right** on Couchville Pk.
6.3	**Left** on McCreary Rd. (Gladeville Rd.)(4-way stop).
9.6	**Right** on Stewarts Ferry Pk. (4-way intersection) in Gladeville. Market/restaurant.
13.6	**Right** on Central Pk./Hwy. 265 (stop sign at the T-intersection).
14.8	Cross Hwy. 231. Market.
20.2	**Right** on Hwy. 266/Cainsville Rd. (first stop sign).
24.0	Market in the town of Norene.
31.3	**Right** on Hoover Rd. (easy to miss)(first right after crossing the Rutherford County line).
32.7	**Right** on Barlow Ln. (Pain Hill Rd..) (stop sign at the T-intersection).
35.1	**Left** on Jordon Rd. after going downhill.
37.3	**Right** on Holly Grove Rd. (stop sign at the T-intersection).
40.1	**Right** on Rocky Hill Rd. where Holly Grove Rd. bends to the left.
42.6	**Left** on Alsup Mill Rd. (stop sign at the T-intersection).
43.3	Cross Hwy. 231 (stop sign).
43.4	**Left** on Old Lebanon Rd.
43.6	**Right** on Todd Rd. (first right).
45.1	**Right** on Claude Jones Rd. at the T-intersection.
45.9	**Right** on Powells Chapel Rd. (stop sign at the T-intersection).
46.8	Straight onto Dinky Ln. where Powells Chapel Rd. bends to the right.
47.6	**Right** on Mona Rd. (stop sign).
51.5	**Left** on Couchville Pk. (Vesta Rd.) (stop sign at the 4-way intersection). You are now retracing your route.
56.0	**Left** into Bryant Grove Picnic Area.
57.4	End of ride!

NOTE: State Route 840 (I-840) is not shown on this map.

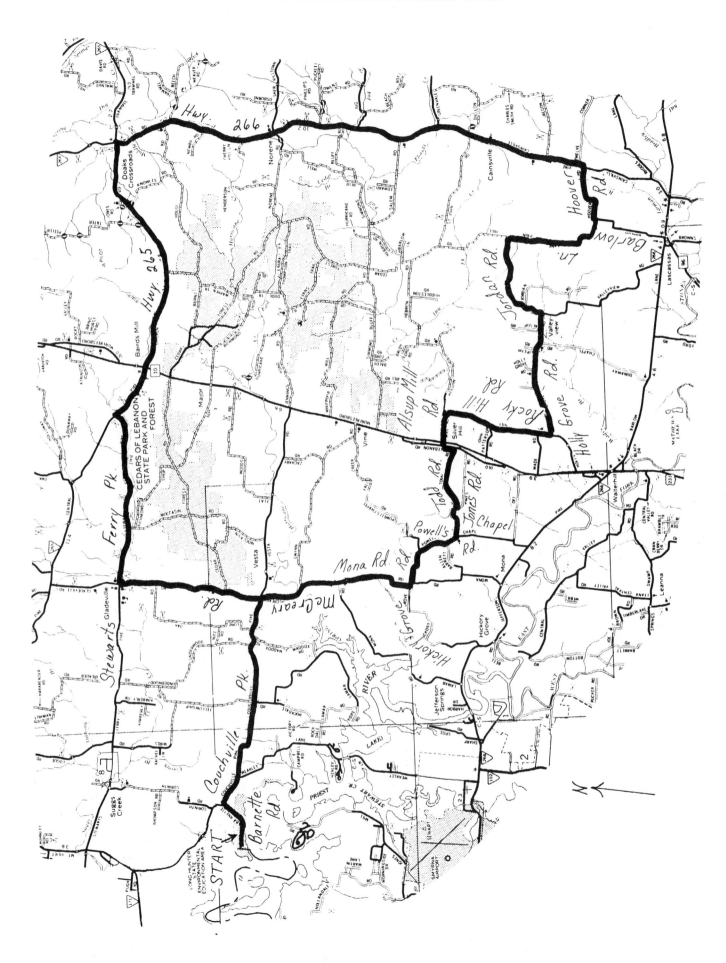

Ride #27   WATERTOWN LOOP

Distance: 38 or 50 miles
Elevation Difference/Accumulated Climb: Option 1 - 460/2430 ft., Option 2 - 460/2480 ft.
Terrain: Flat and rolling near Lebanon but becoming very hilly near the Watertown and
Statesville areas. Challenging rolling terrain on Hwy. 266 and Tater Peeler Rd.
Services: Option 1 has markets at miles 8.2, 15.8, 22.6, and a restaurant (1.5 mi. off the
loop) at mile 15.8. Option 2 has markets at miles 8.2, 15.8, 17.6, 23.6, 35.4, and a
restaurant at mile 17.5.
Traffic: Light on all roads.
Combining Rides: *#20 Milton Loop, #24 Old Railroad Road Loop, #26 Long Hunter State
Park Loop.*
Alternate Parking Site: Cedars of Lebanon State Park located south of Lebanon on Hwy.
231 (3.5 mi. to loop)—Bike north Hwy. 231 and east on Hwy. 265/Chicken Rd.
Distance from Nashville: 30 miles

Beginning in the busy town of Lebanon, the *Watertown Loop* cruises through rolling
countryside to the quaint town of Watertown before heading into the lush, green foothills of the
Cumberland Plateau.

The first part of our trip threads around short side streets of Lebanon, but it is well worth
this navigational effort to avoid the busier thoroughfares.

After the first mile, you will be leaving town on Bluebird Rd. and heading toward greener
(and bucolic) pastures. A nice stretch on Peyton Rd. cuts up to Trousdale Ferry Pk./Hwy. 141
which continues west, crossing open farmland and gently hilly terrain. After coming to the
junction at Tuckers Crossroads, the tour heads south, crosses I-40, and continues on Linwood
Rd., a winding cedar-lined lane rising and falling through sparsely populated hills with occasional
views of the Central Basin.

After reaching Hwy. 70 in the community of Cherry Valley, Option 1 turns onto Beech
Log Rd. Should you choose this option, consider taking a 3-mile roundtrip detour into Watertown
to experience a bit of the past and some good country cookin'. Don't eat too much pie though,
because Option 1 takes you up the slopes of Mt. Defiance (you can decide how it got its name)
with two consecutive 170-ft. climbs. In May, we cycled through a sea of colorful butterflies
congregating in this remote area of sloping pastures and hardwood forests.

Option 2 goes along W. Main St., passing nice old homes typical of small towns before
arriving at the Watertown square. The square, with old brick store fronts and a small park with
a gazebo in the center, fits ideally into the image of small town U.S.A., unfortunately a
diminishing part of our culture. While cycling through Watertown the first time, we couldn't
resist the temptation to indulge ourselves thoroughly at the Country Barn Restaurant on the
square. Little did we know that a few formidable hills awaited us on Statesville Rd. and Greenvale
Rd.!

Watertown was settled as early as 1780, but was not permanently established until 1799.
It was nothing more than a small farm community until 1889 when the Tennessee Central
Railroad began to come through town. With several freight trains and four passenger lines
daily, commerce grew, and the town doubled in size in ten years. Like so many small towns,
business declined after the trains no longer stopped at the depot (in 1955), and the station

was torn down. The Old Hotel (1893) still stands on Depot St. and has been converted into a charming bed and breakfast (see *Appendix*).

Leaving Watertown, Option 2 continues south on Statesville Rd. into a scenic hilly area with numerous steep knobs that border on being small mountains. A long broken 250-ft. pull reaches a gap on the east slope of Mt. Defiance, and then you get to fly down to Smith Fork Creek. A gradual broken descent continues to the community of Statesville located in a large grassy cove nestled in this range of steep hills. Our tour turns west on Greenvale Rd. which heads out to conquer another gap before departing this chain of hills.

The big knobs are replaced by rolling terrain as you cycle north to Norene and join Option 1. Norene is a pleasant little roadside town with a post office and two markets. We always enjoy stopping at the old market with cute red benches in front, and on a couple of occasions, have engaged in fascinating conversations with the local farmers who are amazed that anyone can ride a bicycle for more than 10 miles. (We wonder how far *we* could go on the original 1-speed bikes most of them rode in their youth.)

Both Options continue north over the rolling farmland before turning onto Hwy. 265. Be sure to save some strength for a few short, but substantial, grades on Tater Peeler Rd. Bet you're wondering about that name . . . Tater Peeler. This road used to be so bumpy, that it was said if you drove a wagon load of "taters" down it they would peel themselves. After crossing Hwy. 231, our route follows Old Murfreesboro Rd. to Lebanon where you pass a beautiful large cemetery on Maple St. before ending your ride. The town square, which can be reached by continuing north on Maple St., is well-known for its antique malls which offer a wide variety of unique and interesting items.

When you pull in behind another cyclist, always let her/him know of your presence by saying "on your wheel," "hello," etc. It is the decision of the front cyclist as to whether anyone may draft behind him or her.

#27 WATERTOWN LOOP

HOW TO GET THERE: Take I-40 East from Nashville and exit onto Hwy. 231 (Exit 238) going north toward Lebanon. Continue for 1.2 mi. and turn right on Leeville Pk./Tennessee Blvd. at the light. Turn right on Gulf Ave. immediately before the high school on the left and park at the municipal ball fields.

Mile

0.0	Begin ride by biking north (toward the high school) on Gulf St. from the intersection at Leeville Pk. Gulf St. becomes Harding Dr. as you go around the school.
0.5	**Left** on Park Ave. (stop sign at the T-intersection).
0.6	**Right** on Wheeler St. (first right).
0.7	**Right** on New Bell St. (Beard St.) (first right).
1.1	**Right** on C.L. Manier St. (stop sign).
1.2	Cross Baddour Pkwy./Hwy. 70/Hwy. 26 (stop sign) and continue on Blue Bird Rd.
2.5	**Left** on Peyton Rd. (4-way intersection).
3.1	**Right** on Hwy. 141 East/Trousdale Ferry Pk.
7.7	**Right** on Big Springs Rd. (4-way stop) at the town of Tuckers Crossroads.
8.2	Cross over I-40. Market.
8.5	**Right** on Blue Bird Rd. immediately after crossing over I-40.
8.6	**Left** on Linwood Rd. (first left).
10.8	**Right** on Poplar Hill Rd. (stop sign at the T-intersection).
11.0	**Left** on Linwood Rd. (first left).
15.8	**Left** on Hwy. 70 (stop sign at the T-intersection). Market.

Go to Option 1 or Option 2

OPTION 1
38 miles

16.0	**Right** on Beech Log Rd. (first right).
17.2	Stay **left** on the paved road which is now Sherrilltown Rd.
22.6	**Right** on Hwy. 266/Cainsville Rd. (stop sign). Market in the town of Norene.

Go to Both Options

OPTION 2
50 miles

16.2	**Left** on W. Main St. (first left).
17.5	**Right** on Depot Rd. at the town square in Watertown. Restaurant.
17.6	Cross Hwy. 70 and continue on Hwy. 267/Statesville Rd. Market.
23.6	**Right** on Greenvale Rd. just before the Missionary Baptist Church in Statesville. Stay right after crossing the creek. There is a market .5 mi. south on Hwy. 267.
31.4	**Right** on Hwy. 266 (stop sign at the T-intersection).
35.4	Market in the town of Norene.

Go to Both Options

BOTH OPTIONS

26.6, 39.3	**Left** on Hwy. 265/Chicken Rd. (4-way intersection).
28.6, 41.3	**Right** on Tater Peeler Rd. (easy to miss, .7 mi. past the Adams Grove Church of Christ).
32.0, 44.7	**Left** at the T-intersection. You are still on Tater Peeler Rd.
33.8, 46.5	Bear **left** at the "Y" in the road. You are now on Stumpy Ln.
34.5, 47.2	Cross Hwy. 231 (stop sign).

34.9, 47.6	**Right** on Old Murfreesboro Rd. (stop sign at the T-intersection).
35.9, 48.6	Cross over I-40 (road becomes S. Maple St.).
36.4, 49.1	Market.
37.3, 50.0	**Right** on Leeville Pk. (4-way stop).
37.5, 50.2	Cross Hwy. 231/S. Cumberland St. (traffic light).
37.7, 50.4	End of ride!

#27   WATERTOWN LOOP

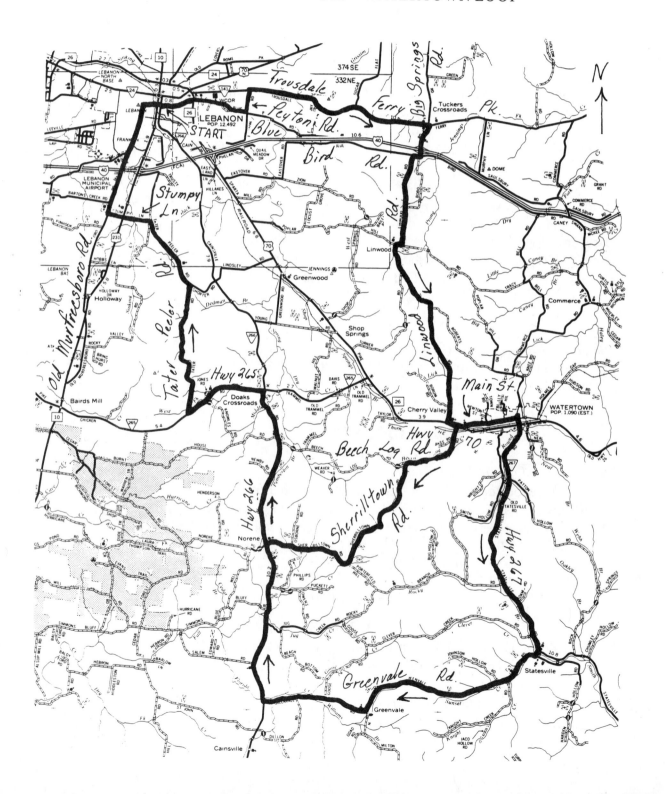

Ride # 28   LEBANON/HARTSVILLE RIDE

Distance: 38 miles
Elevation Difference/Accumulated Climb: 150/2,000 ft.
Terrain: Rolling
Services: Markets at mile 9.3 and 15.9. Markets/restaurant at mile 16.8 in Hartsville.
Traffic: Moderate on Hwy. 141 within 5 miles of the town of Lebanon and on 1.7 mi. of Hwy. 70N. Light traffic on all other roads.
Combining Rides: *#27 Watertown Loop.*
Connector Routes: 1) 1.2 mi. to *#24 Old Railroad Road Loop*—Bike west on Leeville Pk. **2)** 10.2 mi. to *#31 Bledsoe Creek Loop*—Bike west on Church St./Old Hwy. 25 from Hwy. 141 in Hartsville. Left on Hwy. 25.
Distance from Nashville: 30 miles

Originally an out-and back on Hwy. 141 in earlier editions of this book, the paving of Mitchell Rd. allows for a pleasurable loop trip using lightly-traveled roads. This excursion to Hartsville, the county seat of tiny Trousdale County, is our only trip than connects two county seats, and it's the only ride that crosses the Cumberland River. Once you pedal a few miles out of Lebanon, you will find Hwy. 141 to be a twisting rural highway with plenty of enticing scenery. Be forewarned that even though the traffic is not usually heavy (avoid commute hours and weekend afternoons), cars do travel fast on this narrow road. You can avoid most of Hwy. 141 by simply cycling the return leg as an out-and-back. Big Springs Rd. (see map) can be used instead of Goshen Rd. for a little variation.

Leaving the Lebanon High School, our route goes north on College St., passing within one block of the town square, a worthwhile detour if you are interested in antiques and curiosities.

Hwy. 141 heads north of Lebanon and, within a few miles, traffic diminishes. The route travels through wooded hills and rolling pastures, crosses Big Spring Creek and Cedar Creek, and runs the length of an unnamed bend of the Cumberland River before completing its journey to the town of Hartsville. Several minor climbs are encountered before the river crossing, and there are also occasional views of the precipitous knobs encompassing the Cumberland River. A fast descent brings you down to the fertile floodplain and across the river where another upgrade leads to Hartsville. This quiet town, with a block-long business district, makes an excellent rest stop. For additional miles of pedaling bliss, a wealth of paved rural roads offer endless exploration in this area.

The return trip begins by retracing your route on Hwy. 141 to Cedar Bluff Rd. The next 12 miles promises peaceful cycling over the rolling terrain covered by farms and forests. A moderately busy 1.7-mile stretch on US 70N is required before returning to Lebanon.

28 LEBANON/HARTSVILLE RIDE

HOW TO GET THERE: Take I-40 East from Nashville and exit at Hwy. 231 (Exit 238) going north toward Lebanon. Continue 1.2 mi. and turn right on Leeville Pk. at the light. Turn right on Gulf Ave. before the high school and park at the municipal ballfields.

Mile

0.0	Begin ride by biking west (toward Hwy. 231) on Leeville Pk.
0.1	**Right** on College St. (before Hwy. 231)
0.7	Cross Hwy. 70/Main St.
0.9	**Right** on High St./Hwy. 70 by-pass (stop sign at the T-intersection).
1.0	**Left** on Hwy. 141/Hartsville Pk.
9.3	Market
15.3	Cross Cumberland River.
15.9	Market.
16.8	Market/restaurant in the town of Hartsville. Return toward Lebanon on Hwy. 141.
20.4	**Left** on Cedar Bluff Rd. (easy to miss).
21.4	Bear **right** on Providence Rd. (first right) where Cedar Bluff Rd. bends to the left.
22.9	**Left** on Kittrell Rd. (Mitchell Rd.)
25.2	**Left** N.E. Young Rd. (stop sign at the T-intersection).
26.6	**Left** on Goshen Rd. (stop sign).
28.3	**Right** on Old Rome Pk. (stop sign at the T-intersection).
32.2	**Right** on Hwy. 70N (stop sign).
33.9	**Right** on Old Rome Pk. (easy to miss).
36.4	**Right** on High St./Hwy. 70N (markets, restaurants)
36.8	**Left** on College St.
37.5	**Left** on Tennessee Blvd.
37.7	End of ride!

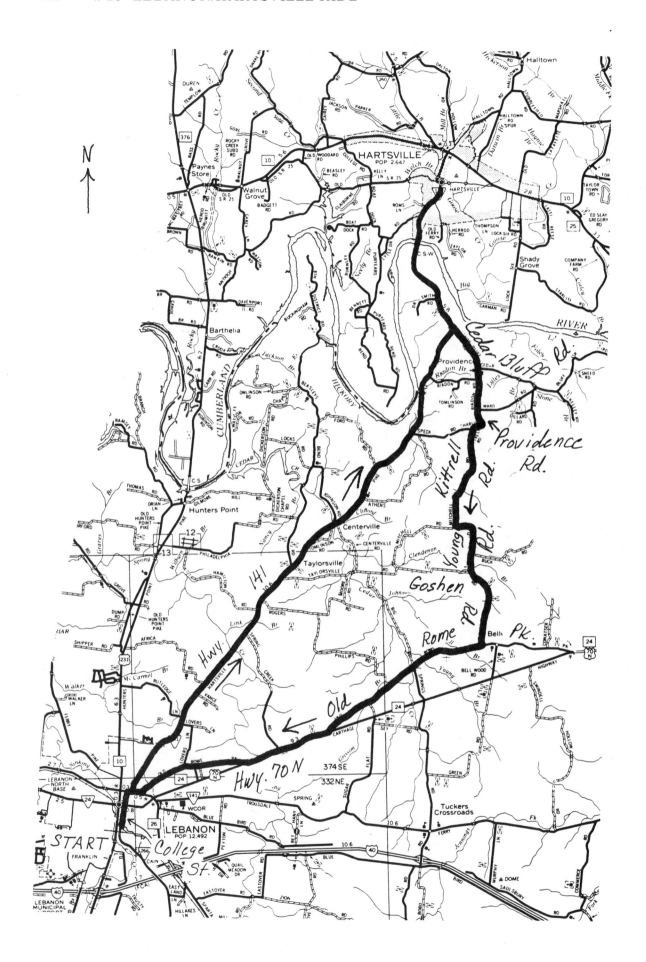

Ride #29   CAPPS GAP LOOP

Distance: 24 or 34 miles
Elevati on Difference/Accumulated Climb: Option 1 - 280/1300 ft., Option 2 - 430/2100 ft.
Terrain: Option 1 is moderately hilly with 2 big climbs. Option 2 is very challenging with 3 big climbs and several short steep pulls.
Services: Option 1 has a market at mile 13.5. Option 2 has a market at mile 22.8.
Traffic: 2 short stretches on Option 2 have moderate traffic. Light on all other roads.
Combining Ride: *#30 Station Camp Loop.*
Connector Routes: 1) 2.5 mi. to *#32 North Sumner County Loop*—From Capps Gap at mile 15.0 on Option 2, go left on Jones Rd. and right on Shun Pk., or take Upper Station Camp Rd. north from Garrison Branch to Hwy. 25. Each connector is 2.5 miles. **2)** 9 miles to *#34 Union Hill/Paradise Ridge Loop*—Go left on McMurtry Rd. from Hogan Branch Rd. Left on Hwy. 31W and right on Hwy. 257. Stay on Hwy. 257 through Ridge Top and continue straight on Greer Rd. where Hwy. 257 goes right.
Distance from Nashville: 16 miles

Cyclists in the Hendersonville area are lucky to have such a wonderful network of scenic rural roads through wide valleys, forested ridges, and narrow hollows. This quickly growing suburb was the site of one of the first settlements in Tennessee. Mansker Station, which can be reached via Center Point Rd. and Caldwell Dr., was built in 1779 and abandoned a year later due to increasing Indian hostilities. A reconstructed fort which is open to the public provides the backdrop for historical interpreters in pioneer dress to demonstrate interesting 18th century skills. The Bowen Campbell House (1787) sits next to the fort and is the oldest brick home in Middle Tennessee.

Our tour begins with a short, flat stretch on the paved shoulder of Long Hollow Pk. This will warm your legs up for a roundabout course through a rugged area of secluded hollows, lush forests, and crystal clear streams. Happy Hollow Rd. and Hogan Branch Rd. pass by an interesting mixture of simple country homes and suburban estates. The two tough climbs (175 ft. and 120 ft.) are merely preludes to wonderfully fun, speedy descents.

Upon arriving at Tyree Springs Rd./Hwy. 258, Option 1 heads south and soon turns onto Sandy Valley Rd. for another scenic climb (200 ft.) over the wooded hills to Station Camp Creek.

Option 2 travels north on Tyree Springs Rd. and turns onto New Hope Rd. for a delightful ride through a tranquil, pastoral valley. As this valley narrows, the grade gradually steepens until a seemingly vertical wall greets you just before the gap. (Total climb on New Hope Rd. is 330 ft.) This steep forested gap, known as Capps Gap, is also a 4-way junction with each road being excellent for cycling.

After barreling down a wooded hillside, you will be pedaling alongside gurgling Garrison Branch as it flows through a picturesque hollow down to Station Camp Creek. Upon arriving at Station Camp Creek Rd., you may opt to go right and connect up with Option 1 which enters this road from the south. Option 1 continues south on Station Camp Creek Rd., a very popular cycling route. (See *Ride # 30* for more information.)

For the hardy cyclists continuing on Option 2, our route climbs over the valley's east ridge and back again. The hills are challenging, but the views make it worthwhile. Cummings Ln. is a killer road, because when you reach the top of the initial 190-ft. climb, you dip down and immediately go up another steep pull--again and again. How many times? You'll find out! Liberty Pk. traverses rolling pastures and passes two stately antebellum homes before a modest rise (90 ft.) brings you back to the Station Camp Valley.

Both options continue on Lower Station Camp Creek Rd. as this shady lane runs along the wide creek. After crossing the creek and going over a double rise, our route runs through a mix of new residential areas and farmland as it heads west toward Center Point Rd. and back to your starting point.

"Looking behind" while riding is an invaluable technique that all cyclists should learn. In order not to dangerously swerve to the left as you are looking left, practice this skill in a deserted parking lot or on a quiet street. Rearview mirrors are useful but never rely on them entirely.

Ride #29 CAPPS GAP LOOP

HOW TO GET THERE: Take I-65 North and exit onto Long Hollow Pk./Hwy. 174 (Exit 97). Turn right (east) and go 5.5 miles and park at Hunter Middle School. There is also a church and fire station nearby if school is in session.

Mile

0.0	Begin ride by biking west (toward I-65) on Long Hollow Pk./Hwy 174.
0.7	**Right** on Happy Hollow Rd. (first right).
3.5	**Right** on Hogan Branch Rd. (stop sign at the T-intersection).

Go to Option 1 or Option 2

OPTION 1
24 miles

7.2	**Right** on Hwy. 258/Tyree Springs Rd. (stop sign at the T-intersection).
7.4	**Left** on Sandy Valley Rd. (first left).
9.5	Stay left at the top of the hill.
11.5	**Right** on Upper Station Camp Creek Rd. (stop sign at the 4-way intersection).

Go to Both Options

OPTION 2
34 miles

7.2	**Left** on Hwy. 258/Tyree Springs Rd. (stop sign at the T-intersection).
8.3	Go straight onto New Hope Rd. (Capps Gap Rd.) as Hwy. 258 goes to the left (flashing yellow light).
10.9	**Right** on Garrison Branch Rd. which immediately goes downhill at a confusing 4-way intersection. Do not take a hard right onto Weeping Willow Rd.
13.9	Cross Upper Station Camp Rd. and continue on Cummings Ln.
16.8	**Right** on Hwy. 25 (stop sign at the T-intersection).
17.6	**Right** on Liberty Ln. (first right).
22.0	**Left** on Upper Station Camp Rd. (stop sign at the T-intersection).

Go to Both Options

BOTH OPTIONS

13.3, 22.6	**Left** on Hwy. 174 (stop sign at the T-intersection). You may return to Hunter Middle School by going right on Hwy. 174 (paved shoulders) for 4 miles.
13.5, 22.8	**Right** on Lower Station Camp Creek Rd. (first right). Market.
14.6, 23.9	**Right** on Jenkins Ln. (first right).
15.9, 25.2	Bear **left** onto Anderson Rd. (Jenkins Ln.) (3-way intersection).
17.6, 26.9	Turn **right** (staying on Anderson Rd.) at the next intersection where Jones Rd. enters from the left.
18.1, 27.4	**Left** on Drakes Creek Rd. (stop sign at the T-intersection).
19.0, 28.3	**Right** on Stop Thirty Rd. (first right).
20.2, 29.5	Cross Hwy. 258 and continue on Old Shackle Island Rd.
20.3, 29.6	**Right** on Goshentown Rd. (first right).
22.2, 31.5	**Right** on Center Point Rd. (stop sign at the T-intersection).
23.6, 32.9	**Right** on Long Hollow Pk./Hwy. 174 (stop sign).
24.3, 33.6	End of Ride!

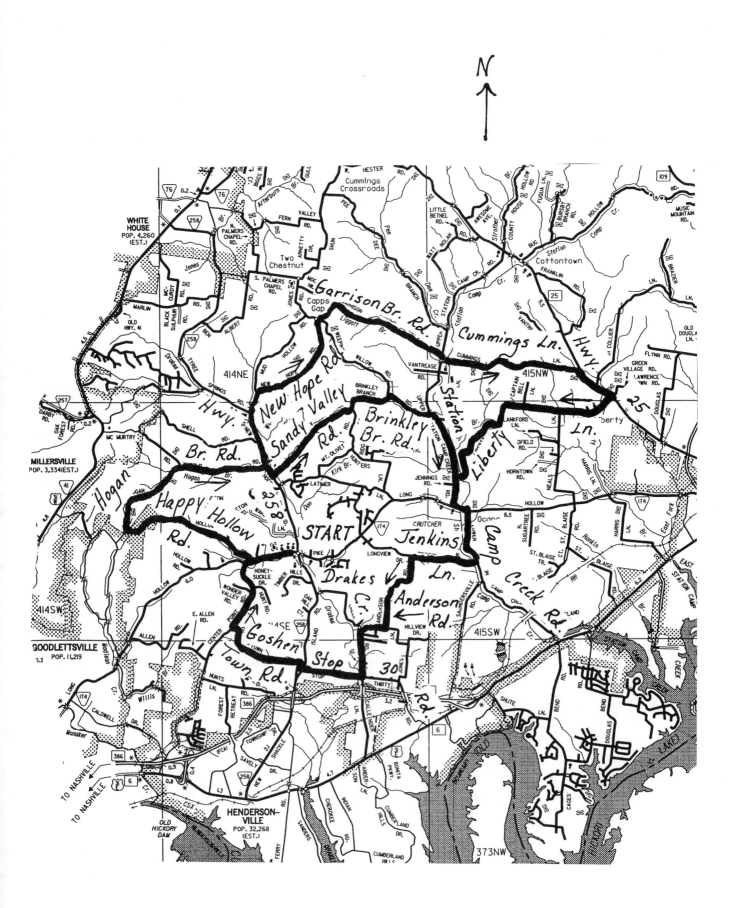

Ride # 30   STATION CAMP LOOP

Distance: 27 or 49 miles
Elevation Difference/Accumulated Climb: Option 1 - 480/720 ft. Option 2 - 550/1730 ft.
Terrain: Moderately hilly with 1 substantial climb up the Highland Rim on each option.
Services: Option 1 has markets at miles 3.4, 10.6, 18.0 and 23.6. Option 2 has markets at
  mile 3.4, 16.5, 26.5, 38.2, and 45.3.
Traffic: Moderate on Hwy. 76 on Option 2. Light on all other roads.
Combining Rides: *# 29 Capps Gap Loop, # 31 Bledsoe Creek Loop, # 32 North Sumner
  County Loop.*
Distance from Nashville: 22 miles

This tour begins along Station Camp Creek on a 9-mile stretch that is, for good reasons, the most popular area to ride north of Nashville. Station Camp Creek Rd. provides a moderately easy cruise for the casual cyclist and a good time-trial route for racers. Our tour encompasses many miles of fine cycling territory beyond Station Camp Creek for those who wish to explore the Highland Rim.

Beginning from the Gallatin soccer field, our route travels along a tree-canopied road next to beautiful Station Camp Creek as it peacefully cascades down to the Cumberland River. The creek is named after the station or post established here from May to August, 1772 by the long hunters. This whole area, which was abundant in game (including buffalo), was one of the most popular and productive hunting grounds in Middle Tennessee. Kasper Mansker and Isaac Bledsoe (see *Rides # 29* and *# 31* for more historical information) were among these hunters who, after months of hunting, had their camp plundered by Indians who stole all their pelts.

The antebellum Clark Brothers House sits on the bluff above the creek at Long Hollow Pk./Hwy. 174. Upper Station Camp Creek Rd. proceeds up this fertile valley of open pastures and corn fields. The terrain is increasing hilly as the road rolls up and down the small hills along the west side of the valley. Station Camp Creek Rd. ends at Cottontown, a community named after Thomas Cotton who settled here in 1795. An unusual historic home built by Moore Cotton and called The Bridal House, was built in the Elizabethan style and constructed of unusually large logs.

Option 1 heads west on Hwy. 25 from Cottontown and soon begins to ascend a mile-long hill (310 ft.) up the Highland Rim. Option 2 proceeds through a quaint little hollow with the not-so-quaint name of Bug Hollow. As the hollow narrows, the route enters a lush forested area before a final steep ascent completes the 330-ft. climb up to the Highland Rim where you cross Hwy. 109.

Option 2 soon passes several well-maintained old homes in the community of South Tunnel, named for a nearby tunnel constructed by the L & N Railroad in the 1850s. Some of our other rides follow a network of excellent bicycling roads which crisscross this area. (See maps of *Ride # 31* if you wish to shorten/extend your trip or experience different scenery.) Our route follows South Tunnel Rd. as it climbs to a high point of the Rim, a dizzying 1,000 ft. above sea level (pretty high for Middle Tennessee).

After reaching the community of Graball, our tour continues to climb a broken ascent on Hwy. 174 and, after cresting a hill, heads west on Fowler Ford Rd. Here a nice winding stretch of smooth pavement with little traffic and a fun descent await the cyclist. After crossing Hwy. 109 just south of Portland, you have two choices: You can follow our directions which take Hwy. 76 for 1.5 miles and then follow a chain of scenic quiet backroads to Shun Pk., or you can simply stay on Hwy. 76 to Shun Pk. which is the first left past Hwy. 25. Hwy. 76 is often moderately busy with no shoulders, but we find it tolerable to ride. Our original route requires more navigation and encounters two fairly challenging 100+ ft. climbs.

Both options come together on Shun Pk. and travel among a mix of new homes and farmland along the west ridge above Station Camp Creek. Soon you will roll down to a forested pass in the ridge known as Capps Gap where there is a somewhat confusing intersection. Our route takes Weeping Willow Rd., the only road that does not go downhill, but don't worry--you do get an exhilarating drop down to Brinkley Branch which lets out at Station Camp Creek. The views along this wonderful valley are just as nice the second time as you retrace the first 5.5 miles of your trip.

30 STATION CAMP LOOP

HOW TO GET THERE: Take I-65 North and exit at Vietnam Veterans Blvd./Hwy. 386 (Exit 95) toward Hendersonville. Continue on Hwy. 386 until it empties onto the Nashville Pike (Hwy. 31E) going west toward Gallatin. Go 1.8 miles and turn left on Station Camp Creek Rd. which is opposite the sign for the Cages Bend Recreation Area. Park at the soccer field on the left.

Mile

0.0   Bike north (away from Hwy. 31E) on Lower Station Camp Creek Rd.
3.4   **Left** on Long Hollow Pk./Hwy. 174 (stop at the T-intersection). Market.
3.6   **Right** on Upper Station Camp Creek Rd. (first right).
Go to Option 1 or Option 2

OPTION 1
27 miles

9.3   **Left** on Hwy. 25 (stop sign at 4-way intersection).
10.6   Market.
12.8   **Left** on W. Hester Rd. (4-way intersection after climbing a long hill).
14.3   **Left** on Shun Pk. (stop sign at the 4-way intersection).
Go to Both Options

OPTION 2
49 miles

9.2   **Right** on Hwy. 25 (stop sign at the 4-way intersection).
9.6   **Left** on Bug Hollow Rd. (first left) in the community of Cottontown.
13.8   **Right** on Hwy. 109 (stop sign at the T-intersection).
13.85   **Left** *immediately* on South Tunnel Rd. which goes down a small hill.
14.8   **Right** on Old Gallatin Rd. (South Tunnel Rd.) Follow the sign for Bush's Chapel. Descend and cross RR in the community of South Tunnel.
16.5   **Left** on Hwy. 174/Dobbins Pk. (stop sign at the T-intersection). Market.
20.7   **Left** on Fowler Ford Rd. at the top of a hill (easy to miss).
23.6   **Left** on Butler Bridge Rd. (first 4-way intersection).
25.3   Cross Old Gallatin Rd. (4-way stop).
26.5   Cross Hwy. 109 (stop sign) and continue on Hwy. 76 West. Market.
28.1   **Left** on Brandy Hollow Rd. (easy to miss) in the community of Chestnut Grove.
29.5   **Right** on Wilson Rd. (first right).
29.8   Bear **left** (staying on Wilson Rd.) where Penny Morris Rd. continues straight. You may wish to continue straight for a short cut that also bypasses a hill if you don't mind a one mile gravel stretch on Penny Morris Rd.
30.9   Continue straight at the stop sign onto Hollis Chapel Rd.
32.0   Bear **left** at the next intersection onto Penny Morris Rd. The gravel road going to the right is also Penny Morris Rd.
32.3   **Left** on Hall Town Rd. (stop sign at the T-intersection).
35.7   Cross Hwy. 25 and continue onto W. Hester Rd. (stop sign).
37.2   **Left** on Shun Pk. (stop sign at the 4-way intersection).
Go to Both Options

BOTH OPTIONS

17.0, 38.7   **Left** on Jones Rd. (easy to miss).

18.0, 39.7   Bear **right** onto Weeping Willow Rd. (Brinkley Branch Rd.) which goes uphill at the confusing 4-way intersection. Do not take a hard right on New Hope Rd. Market.

20.5, 42.2   **Left** on Brinkley Branch Rd. (first left).

21.6, 43.3   **Right** on Upper Station Camp Creek Rd. (stop sign the 4-way intersection). Retrace the rest of the route to the starting point.

27.0, 48.7   End of Ride!

30 STATION CAMP LOOP

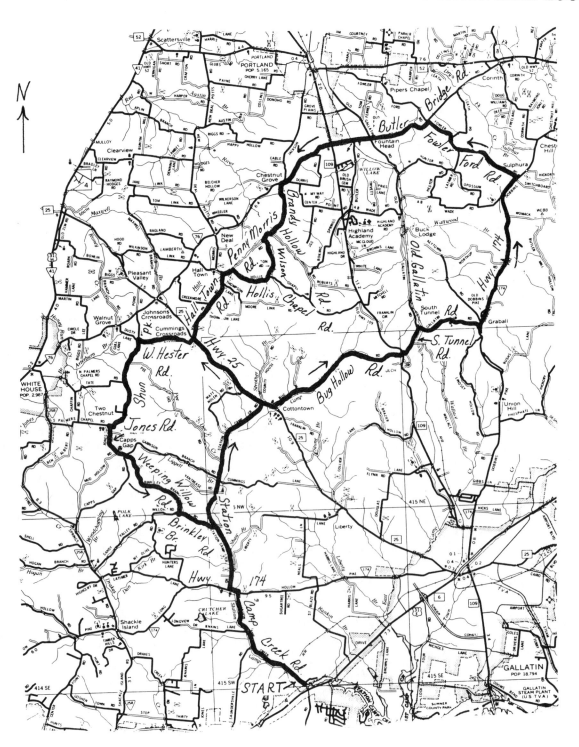

Ride # 31   BLEDSOE CREEK LOOP

Distance: 38 or 60 miles
Elevation Difference/Accumulated Climb: Option 1 - 550/2050 ft., Option 2 - 540/2900 ft.
Terrain: Mostly moderate rolling terrain. Both options have a major climb. Option 2 has an additional climb.
Services: Option 1 has markets at miles 8.6, 21.3, 30.1. Option 2 has markets at miles 8.6, 16.3, 18.5, 23.6, 27.3, 32.2, 36.8, 51.2. Restaurants at mile 16.3.
Traffic: Moderate on Main St. and Hwy. 25. Light to moderate on Hwy. 174 near Gallatin. Light on all other roads.
Combining Rides: # *30 Station Camp Loop*, # *32 North Sumner County Loop*.
Connector Route: 10.2 mi. to # *28 Lebanon/Hartsville Ride*--Continue east on Hwy. 25. Right on Old Hwy. 25 *after* crossing Hwy. 231. Old Hwy. 25 becomes Church St. as it enters Hartsville.
Alternate Parking Site: Bledsoe Creek State Park.
Distance from Nashville: 28 miles

This tour of eastern Sumner County stretches from the shores of the Cumberland River to the rolling pastures of the Highland Rim near Kentucky, and passes several important historic sites along the way. We begin near the old district of Gallatin and travel through flat-to-rolling farmland to Cairo (pronounced "Kay-ro") on the shores of Old Hickory Lake. This quiet community established in 1800 no longer has stores and businesses, but at one time was a thriving port on the Cumberland River where cotton, tobacco, horses, and slaves were bartered, and local produce was shipped to New Orleans. Heading north from Cairo, our route passes Bledsoe Creek State Park (mile 6.5) which offers camping, hiking, bird watching, swimming, boating, and fishing. The next few miles take you through a land rich in history, including the site of Zeigler Station, a fort built in 1790 and later destroyed by Indians. At mile 9.0 is General Winchester's home, Cragfont (open to the public). This unique mansion, believed to be the first rock house in Middle Tennessee (1802), was constructed of gray, rough finished Tennessee limestone quarried on the place, and poplar, walnut, cherry and ash, hand hewn and cut from the surrounding virgin forest. Wynnewood (tours available), a restored sulphur springs resort and the largest log structure in the state, lies 2 miles east from where our route turns onto Greenfield Ln. This home was built in 1828 on the site of Bledsoe's Lick, one of the first permanent Middle Tennessee settlements (1779). It is here that the legendary Thomas Spencer is reputed to have wintered in the hollow of a 9-foot wide sycamore tree.

Greenfield Ln. rises and falls over a series of substantial rolling hills, displaying views of the Central Basin and the Highland Rim. Options 1 and 2 split and follow equally scenic and challenging routes up the Highland Rim.

Option 1 gradually ascends along a lovely section of Dry Creek before encountering a challenging 180-ft. climb to the Rim. Relief to the leg muscles is given during the gradual downgrade through a picturesque, shallow valley before another hill is crested. (At Hwy. 174, where Option 1 temporarily joins Option 2, you can extend your trip 6 miles by taking Option 2 where it turns onto Fowler Ford Rd.)

From Greenfield Ln., Option 2 travels north to the town of Bethpage and soon follows Bledsoe Creek into a narrow hollow with small, but striking rock cliffs. The grade up to the town of Westmoreland on the Highland Rim (420 ft. total) is surprisingly gentle although it lasts over 2 miles. Our route continues north on Old Hwy. 31, following a slight downgrade next to the abandoned L & N rail bed, before turning west onto Hwy. 174, the historic Nashville-Bardstown Stage Route. Little traffic goes by as this winding road traverses consistently rolling countryside for the next 12 miles.

On a challenging detour from Hwy. 174, Option 2 spins along wonderful backroads, then gives you two tough hills (200 ft. and 170 ft.) to conquer on remote Keytown Rd. (Option 2 can be shortened 6 miles by simply staying on Hwy. 174.)

Leaving the community of Graball, Options 1 and 2 begin a long broken descent (something to look forward to during the entire ride) into the Cumberland Valley. After a final rural stretch on Gibbs Ln., Main St. East leads through a residential neighborhood to the starting point.

Communication is important when riding in a group, even if there are only two cyclists. Accidents involving two or more cyclists are much more common than accidents involving cyclists and motorists. Call out loudly information such as:

- Car back
- Car up
- Stopping (or slowing)
- Gravel, glass, bump, etc.
- Left turn, right turn

Also, use hand signals for turns and for pointing out hazards in the road.

31 BLEDSOE CREEK LOOP

HOW TO GET THERE: Take I-65 North and exit onto Vietnam Veterans Blvd./Hwy. 386 (Exit 95) toward Hendersonville. Stay on Vietnam Veteran Blvd. until it terminates on Hwy. 31E/Nashville Pk. going toward Gallatin. Continue into Gallatin and turn right on Main St./Hwy. 25 East. Turn left on Main St. East (easy to miss). If you get to the Sumner County Hospital, you've gone too far. Continue for .3 mi. and park at the Gallatin Middle School on the right.

Mile

0.0	Begin ride by cycling toward Hwy. 25 on Main St. East.
0.3	**Left** on Hwy. 25 going east (stop sign).
1.0	**Right** on Cairo Rd. immediately past the 7th Day Adventists Church. Market.
5.1	**Left** on Zeiglers Fort Rd. in the town of Cairo.
6.5	Bledsoe Creek State Park. Water/restrooms.
7.9	**Right** on Hwy. 25 (stop sign at the 4-way intersection).
8.6	Market.
9.4	**Left** on Greenfield Ln. (second left after crossing Bledsoe Cr.).

Go to Option 1 or Option 2

OPTION 1
38 miles

13.2	**Left** on Rogana Rd.
15.3	**Left** on Hwy. 31E (stop sign at the T-intersection).
16.2	**Right** on Bill Reese Rd. (second right) which becomes Rock Bridge Rd.
21.3	Market.
24.6	**Left** on Hwy. 174/Dobbins Pk. (stop sign at the T-intersection).
30.1	Markets in the community of Graball.

Go to Both Options

OPTION 2
60 miles

13.2	Bear **right** (staying on Greenfield Ln.) as Rogana Rd. goes to the left.
13.3	**Left** on Rock Springs Rd. (stop sign at the T-intersection).
15.8	**Right** on Old Hwy. 31E # 3 (stop sign at the T-intersection).
16.3	Markets in the town of Bethpage.
17.3	**Right** on Hwy. 31E (stop sign at the T-intersection).
17.6	**Left** on Old Hwy. 31 (second left).
18.5	Market.
23.2	Bear **left** at the "Y" (staying on Old Hwy. 31) after you enter the town of Westmoreland.
23.5	Cross Hwy. 52 (stop sign).
23.6	Cross Austin Peay Hwy. (Old Hwy. 52). Market/restaurant.
27.3	Market.
28.2	**Left** on Hwy. 174.
32.2	Market.
32.8	Hwy. 174 bends to left near a cemetery. Don't go straight on Nubia Rd.
36.8	Cross Hwy. 52 (stop sign). Market in the town of Oak Grove.
40.1	**Right** on Fowler Ford Rd. (easy to miss) just before Hwy. 174 descends. Look for the sign for the Pipers Chapel Baptist Church.

43.2   **Left** on Butler Bridge Rd. (first 4-way intersection).

44.9   **Left** on Old Gallatin Rd. (4-way stop).

46.1   Bear **right** and cross the RR tracks.

47.5   **Left** on Keytown Rd. (very easy to miss) after going up and down a small but steep hill. Immediately cross a wood bridge after this turn.

51.1   **Right** on Hwy. 174/Dobbins Pk. (stop sign at the T-intersection).

51.2   Market in the community of Graball.

Go to Both Options

BOTH OPTIONS

34.5, 55.6   **Left** on Gibbs Ln. (first 4-way intersection).

36.0, 57.1   **Right** on Greystone Dr. (first right).

36.9, 58.0   **Right** on Hwy. 31E (stop sign at the T-intersection).

37.0, 58.1   **Left** on Main St. East (first left).

38.4, 59.5   End of Ride!

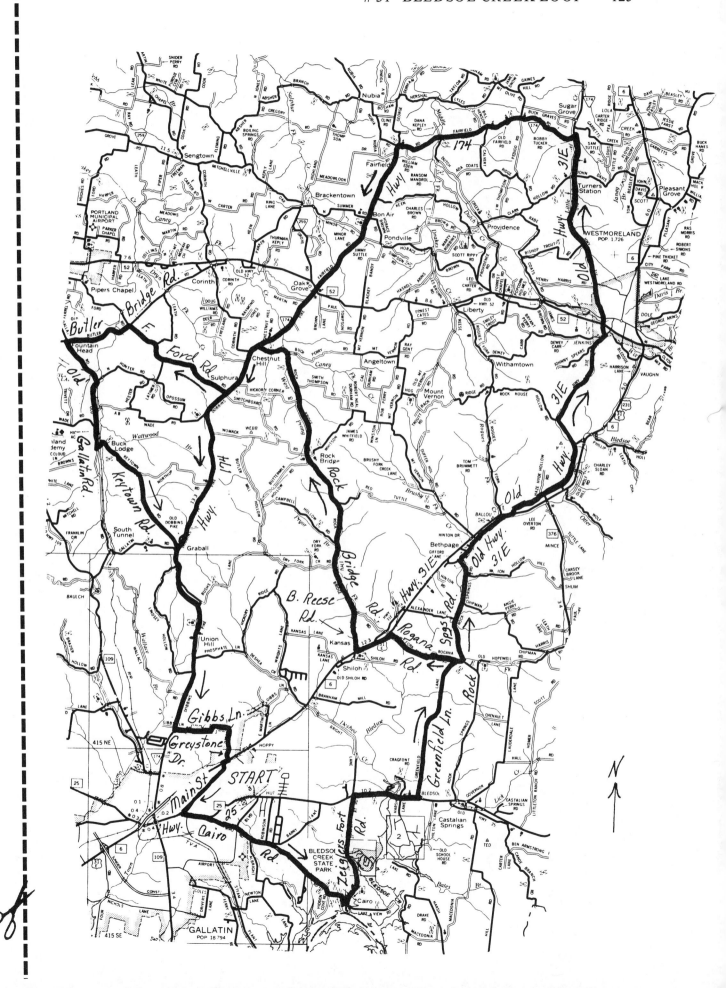

Ride # 32   NORTH SUMNER COUNTY LOOP

Distance: 30 or 37 miles
Elevation Difference/Accumulated Climb: Option 1 - 150/750 ft., Option 2 - 360/1,580 ft.
Terrain: Option 2 has 1 big climb on Hwy. 25. Otherwise mostly gentle, rolling terrain with a few minor hills.
Services: Both options have a market at miles 4.1 and markets and restaurants near mile 16. Option 3 has a market at mile 30.6. Restaurant at mile 15.5.
Traffic: Light to moderate on Hwy. 76 and Hwy. 25. Light on all other roads.
Combining Rides: #30 Station Camp Loop, #31 Bledsoe Creek Loop.
Connector Routes: 1) 2.5 mi. to #29 Capps Gap Loop—Continue south on Shun Pk. at mile 34.3, then left on Jones Rd. to Capps Gap or at mile 29.0 take Upper Station Camp Rd. to Garrison Branch Rd. Each connector is 2.5 mi. **2)** 11.2 mi. to #38 Cross Plains Loop and #39 Upper Red River Loop—From Portland, bike west on Hwy. 52.
Distance from Nashville: 25 miles

Our other Sumner County rides start near the Cumberland River and travel up onto the Highland Rim. However, the *North Sumner County Loop* begins on the rim and tours the relatively flat farmland of northern Sumner County. While Option 1 avoids any major climbs, Option 2 descends briefly to Station Camp Creek and climbs back up the Rim. This tour combines nicely with the *Station Camp Loop,* the *Bledsoe Creek Loop*, and the *Capps Gap Loop* providing numerous route possibilities, and we know there are other excellent roads out there waiting to be discovered!

Our bicycle journey begins in the town of White House, a growing bedroom community of Nashville which was named after an inn on the Nashville & Louisville stage route (now Hwy. 31W). This stately two story building, built in 1796, was painted white (one of the few painted homes in this region at the time) and became known as the White House. Unfortunately, it was torn down in the 1950s, but a replica was constructed and is located on Hwy. 76 one mile east of I-65. This new building houses both a library and an interesting museum featuring local history, antique tools, and old farm implements. When complete, a 7-mile greenway loop (with a trailhead across the highway from the white house) will provide an excellent way to begin and end this ride while avoiding a busy portion of Hwy. 76.

From White House our journey heads northeast on the sometimes busy Hwy. 76 for 4 miles before taking a peaceful roundabout course toward Portland. Maxwell Branch Rd. runs through a remote, shallow valley with patches of thick forests before climbing up to the aptly named community of Clearview. We always enjoy cycling the virtually traffic-free roads that wind through expansive rolling fields of corn, tobacco, and soybeans. A moderate climb is in store after you cross the upper reaches of the Red River. Then you travel through a sparse residential area before another flat open stretch leads into Portland.

The town of Portland (originally called Richland) dates back to the 1820s, but the town came into prominence as a railroad stop along the Louisville and Nashville Railroad line which opened in 1858. A restored 19th century school house known as the Cold Springs School is located on Portland St. one block north of Russell St. and currently houses a museum (open Sunday afternoons in the summer). Today, Portland is famous for its week long Strawberry Festival held every May.

Option 1 leaves Portland on Jackson Rd., a mostly flat rural short-cut to Hwy. 76. The cycling only gets better after crossing Hwy. 76, especially the short stint on the one lane Penny Morris Rd.

Option 2 leaves Portland on Old Gallatin Rd., heading south over the open rolling plains before dropping down to Drakes Creek. Old Gallatin Rd. continues up a pleasant valley through which the CSX Railroad (formerly L & N) line runs.

After crossing Hwy. 109, the cyclist is treated to an adrenaline rush on a speedy descent into a narrow and shady hollow which eventually leads to Cottontown on the upper end of Station Camp Creek. This peaceful community is named after Thomas Cotton who settled here in 1795. The Bridal House, a unique historic home constructed of unusually large logs, was built by his son, Moore Cotton, and is remarkably well-preserved today.

Heading west on Hwy. 25 from Cottontown, our journey ascends a mile-long moderate grade (310 ft.) up to the Highland Rim where series of scenic backroads lead into White House.

32 NORTH SUMNER COUNTY LOOP

HOW TO GET THERE: Take I-65 North and exit at Hwy. 76 (Exit 108). Turn right on Hwy. 76 going east toward White House. Turn right on Hwy. 31W (traffic light) and immediately left into the parking area for the Municipal Center, police station, and ballfields.

Mile

0.0	Begin ride by going **right** (north) on Hwy. 31W from the parking lot.
0.2	**Right** on Hwy. 76 East.
4.1	Cross Hwy. 25 at the community of Johnsons Crossroads. Market.
4.2	**Left** on Maxwell Branch Rd. (first left).
5.4	Bear **left**, staying on Maxwell Branch Rd.
7.4	Go straight at the stop sign where Jake Link Rd. enters from the right.
7.6	Bear **left** (staying on Maxwell Branch Rd) where Tom Link Rd. enters from the right.
8.4	Continue straight onto Clearview Rd. (stop sign at the 3-way intersection) by the Clearview Church of Christ.
10.1	**Left** on New Deal Potts Rd. (stop sign at the T-intersection).
12.4	**Right** on Payne Rd. (easy to miss).
13.9	Stay on Payne Rd. which bends to the left as Collins Rd. enters from the right.

Go to Option 1 or Option 2

OPTION 1
30 miles

15.6	**Right** on Jackson Rd. Markets/restaurants just ahead along Hwy. 109
18.6	**Right** on Hwy. 76 (stop sign).
18.7	**Left** on Brandy Hollow Rd.
20.2	**Right** on Wilson Rd.
20.5	**Right** on Penny Morris Rd.
21.7	**Right** on Hollis Chapel Rd. (stop sign at the T-intersection).
22.0	**Left** on Hall Town Rd. (stop sign).
23.9	Cross Hwy. 25 (stop sign) and continue on W. Hester Rd.\

Go to Both Options

Option 2
37 miles

15.0	Cross Hwy. 52 (stop sign) and continue on Market St.
15.9	Cross Hwy. 109/S. Broadway (traffic light) in the town of Portland. Market/restaurants.
16.0	Bear **right** on S. Russell St. after crossing the RR tracks.
16.4	Cross Hwy. 52 (flashing light). Russell St. becomes Old Gallatin Rd.
18.5	Cross Butler Bridge Rd. (4-way stop) in the town of Fountain Head.
19.8	Bear **right** and cross the RR tracks.
20.8	Stay left along the RR tracks at the "Y".
23.8	Continue straight on South Tunnel Rd. (stop sign). Don't go left to the railroad tracks.
24.65	**Right** on Hwy. 109 (stop sign at the T-intersection).
24.7	**Left** *immediately* on Bug Hollow Rd. which goes down the other side of the ridge.
28.9	**Right** on Hwy. 25 in the community of Cottontown (stop sign at the T-intersection).
30.6	Market.
31.8	**Left** on W. Hester Rd. (4-way intersection after a long climb).

Go To Both Options

BOTH OPTIONS

25.4, 33.3	**Left** on Shun Pk. (stop sign at the 4-way intersection).
26.6, 34.5	**Right** on Fern Valley Rd. (Tate Rd.) (first right).
28.2, 36.1	**Right** on N. Palmers Chapel Rd. (Chaffin Rd.) (first right)
29.2, 37.1	**Right** on Hwy. 258/Tyree Springs Rd. (stop sign).
29.5, 37.4	End of ride!

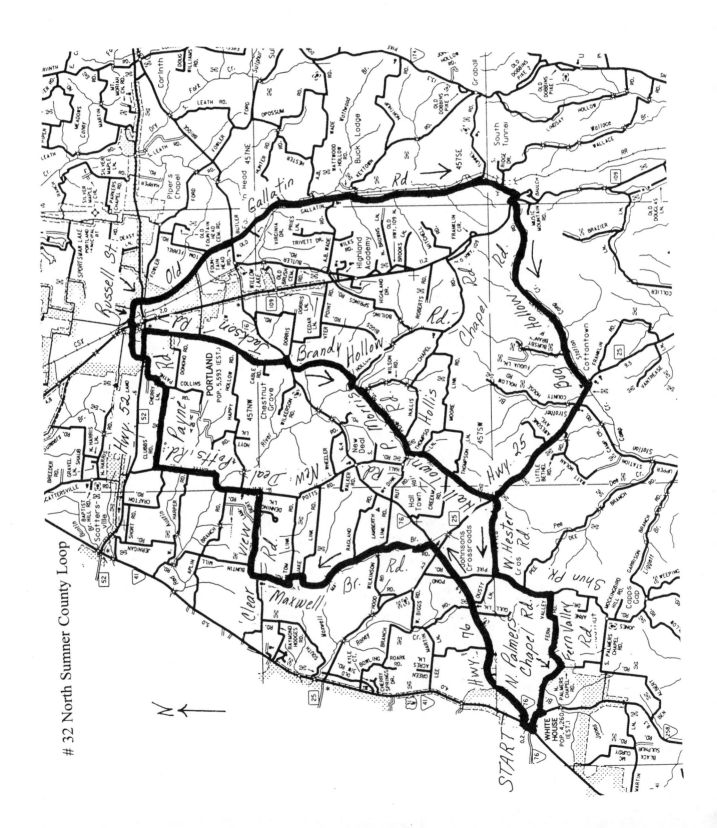

32 North Sumner County Loop

Ride # 33A   BELLS BEND, BULL RUN,
and LITTLE MARROWBONE CREEK RIDES

Distance: 11, 13, or 20 miles
Elevation Difference/Accumulated Climb: *Bells Bend Ride - 200/700 ft., Bull Run Loop - 250/520 ft., Little Marrowbone Creek Loop - 440/910 ft.*
Terrain: Moderately hilly on the *Bells Bend Ride*. One big hill on each the *Little Marrowbone Creek Loop* and the *Bull Run Loop*.
Services: Market near the starting point. *Little Marrowbone Creek Loop* has a market at mile 4.7.
Traffic: Heavy on Hwy. 12 (wide paved shoulders). Light to moderate on Old Hickory Blvd. north of Hwy. 12 and Little Marrowbone Rd. Light on all other roads.
Connector Routes: 1) 4 mi. to *#35 Lower Sycamore Creek Loop*—Continue north on Eatons Creek Rd. at mile 4.9. Left on Clarksville Pk, and right on Eatons Creek Rd. to Old Clarksville Pk. **2)** 5 mi. to *#34 Union Hill/Paradise Ridge Loop*—Continue north on Eatons Creek Rd. Go left on Clarksville Pk, right on Eatons Creek Rd., and right on Old Clarksville Pk. Turn left on Hwy. 431/Whites Creek Pk., and right on Union Hill Rd. **3)** 8.4 mi. to *#35 & #36 Lower and Upper Sycamore Creek Loops*—From Little Marrowbone Rd., go north on Higdon Rd. Turn left on Ridge Rd., right on Abernathy Rd., and then right on Bear Wallow Rd./Hwy 249.
Alternate Parking Site: The market at Old Hickory Blvd. and Eatons Creek Rd. (Ask permission). Beaman Park on Little Marrowbone Rd.
Distance from Nashville: 8 miles

Northwest Davidson County has traditionally been characterized as a rugged and tough region, not only for its terrain but because of the colorful history of its inhabitants. In this choice area for bicycling, we've put together two enjoyable loops and one "out-and-back" which all start from the same location. The *Bells Bend Ride*, excellent for beginners, is more gentle, whereas the other two make challenging excursions over rugged terrain.

This wonderful cycling territory has gotten even better with two new parks and wide shoulders on the new Ashland City Highway which replaced what was a cyclist's nighmare—narrow lanes, fast traffic, and lots of trucks. While not a peaceful country lane, cyclists can at least comfortably use this road to create loop rides with the described routes. A portion of the old highway is now a quiet scenic road along the Cumberland River.

The remote hollows of this region were ideal hideouts for thieves and bandits such as the notorious Jesse James and his famous gang of outlaws. While posing as a respectable farmer along Whites Creek in 1868, James robbed a bank up in Russellville, Kentucky and got away with $17,000! Moonshine stills were extremely numerous in this area during prohibition (and perhaps even today!) It was estimated that bootleggers from all over the mid-South were operating about 1,000 illegal stills in northwest Davidson County alone during the 1920s.

The *Bells Bend Ride* is a delightful excursion through the serene farmland of this bend in the Cumberland River. After the initial moderate hill (180 ft.), the road meanders through the forested knobs and grassy pastures to the site of the former little 8-car Clees Ferry which ceased operating here in 1990. In the future, Bell's Bend Park will provide a wonderful rest stop with views of the river and maybe even biking trails.

The *Bull Run Loop* is a pleasant little trip that travels through a rural but moderately populated valley along Old Hickory Blvd. before turning onto Bull Run Rd. for a steep pull (170 ft.) over a wooded gap. You'll find the next segment through this quaint hollow along Bull Run Creek to be very scenic and enjoyable. The Bull Run Recreation Area, complete with picnic tables, a small lake, and trails along the river bank, is a very short distance to the right on Ashland City Highway.

Cyclists choosing the *Little Marrowbone Creek Loop* will be rewarded with wonderful scenery including a beautiful, clear creek, intermittent waterfalls, and tall limestone bluffs sticking out among the clinging cedar trees. The trash left by thoughtless individuals is unfortunately a reality along the roadside, but we think that the beauty of nature still overcomes this occasional eyesore.

This trip includes a long challenging climb (240 ft.) on Old Hickory Blvd. Be sure to stop at "Z" Store, a most unusual country market with the front, outside wall brightly painted with skeleton musicians having a jam session. Beaman Park, along Little Marrowbone Rd., will open in the summer of 2003. Here you will discover delightful hiking trails in a rugged and pristine habitat puntuated by steep hollows carved by clear cascading creeks. Upon reaching Ashland City Hwy., hungry cyclists may find nourishment three miles off the loop in Ashland City.

Ride # 33B CUMBERLAND RIVER BICENTENNIAL TRAIL

Distance: 8-15 miles roundtrip
Terrain: Flat
Distance from Nashville: 20 miles

This multi-use trail is the result of volunteers and government officials from Nashville, Ashland City, and Clarksville who realize the recreational and economic potential of a rail-to-trail greenway along the Cumberland River. This project began when a few local citizens envisioned an approximately 100-mile trail to link Nashville with Land Between the Lakes Recreation Area. If completed, this rail-trail would be one of the best in the country. But little will happen if citizens don't make it happen. At the time of this printing, the original 4 miles starting at the Marks Creek Trailhead will soon be paved. The next 2.5 miles, known as Eagle Pass for a nesting pair of Bald Eagles, is gravel and can be a bit rough at times. Call the Parks Department in Ashland City at (615) 792-2655 for updated information and to volunteer for trail maintenance.

The trail follows the old Tennessee Central railbed as it hugs the base of limestone cliffs. The hardwood forest often forms a canopy over the trail, but occasional clearings reveal views wetlands and cornfields. This portion of the rail line ceased operations in the 1970s. You will no doubt relish the Sycamore Creek Trestle which was built in 1903 and refurbished to accomodate cyclists, hikers, and equestrians. Upon arriving at the Sycamore Harbour Trailhead on Chapmansboro Rd., you may opt to take this road back (go left) for an 8.5-mile rountrip. Chapmansboro Rd. offers wonderful views of the river and gives cyclists the opportunity to take a break at a picnic area (water and restrooms) and a market. Those on mountain or hybrid bikes won't want to miss the wonderful scenery on the Eagle Pass segment. The railbed is directly above the river with sheer 200 ft. cliffs rising above. This trail ends at the Cheatham Dam Recreation Area complete with campgound, picnic facilities, swim beach, and playground—a great family destination. You may continue to pedal on Cheatham Dam Rd. for another mile or so.

> When it is necessary to ride over any type of bump such as a pothole or a railroad track, slow down to a safe speed and stand with your knees and arms slightly bent, and put your weight toward the back of the bike. This will lessen the impact on you and your bike.

33A BELLS BEND, BULL RUN, and LITTLE MARROWBONE CREEK RIDES

HOW TO GET THERE: Take I-40 West and exit at Robertson Ave./White Bridge Rd./Hwy. 155 (Exit 204). Go right at the end of the ramp and continue on Briley Pkwy 4.3 mi. to Ashland City Hwy./Hwy. 12 (Hydes Ferry Pk.). Go left on Hwy. 12 toward Ashland City then left on Old Hickory Blvd. (flashing yellow light). Take the first right which is Old Hydes Ferry Pk. Continue for .5 mi. and park at the Scottsboro Community Center or park at Wade Elementary School if not in session.

BELLS BEND RIDE
13 miles

Mile

0.0	From the community center, turn **left** (going toward Old Hickory Blvd.) on Old Hydes Ferry Pk.
0.5	**Right** on Old Hickory Blvd. (stop sign).
6.7	Turn around when the road goes into the Cumberland River. (Do not go on or you will get very wet!) Retrace your route to the starting point.
13.4	End of ride!

BULL RUN LOOP
11 miles

0.0	From the community center, turn **left** (going toward Old Hickory Blvd.) on Old Hydes Ferry Pk.
0.5	**Left** on Old Hickory Blvd. (stop sign).
0.6	Cross Hwy. 12/Ashland City Hwy. (flashing red light). Market.
2.1	**Left** on Bull Run Rd. (second left).
7.1	**Right** on Hwy. 12/Ashland City Hwy. (stop sign).
7.5	**Left** on River Trail Rd. (Old Ashland City Hwy.).
7.6	**Left** staying on River Trail at the T-intersection.
9.3	**Right** on Hwy. 12 (stop sign).
10.3	**Right** on Old Hydes Ferry Pk. (first right).
10.7	End of ride!

LITTLE MARROWBONE LOOP
20 miles

0.0	From the community center, turn **left** (going toward Old Hickory Blvd.) on Old Hydes Ferry Pk.
0.5	**Left** on Old Hickory Blvd. (stop sign).
0.6	Cross Hwy. 12/Ashland City Hwy. (flashing red light). Market.
4.7	**Left** on Eatons Creek Rd. (4-way intersection). Market.
5.5	**Left** on Little Marrowbone Rd. at the bottom of a hill.
13.8	**Left** on Hwy. 12/Ashland City Hwy. (stop sign).
16.9	**Right** on River Trail Rd. (Old Ashland City Hwy.).
17.0	**Left** staying on River Trail at the T-intersection.
18.7	**Right** on Hwy. 12 (stop sign).
19.7	**Right** on Old Hydes Ferry Pk. (first right).
20.2	En d of ride!

33B CUMBERLAND RIVER BICENTENNIAL TRAIL
(not shown on map)

HOW TO GET THERE: Same as above except continue north on Ashland City Hwy./Hwy. 12. Go 1 mi. past the Ashland City courthouse and turn left on Chapmansboro Rd. after crossing a creek. The Marks Creek Trailhead is immediately on the right.

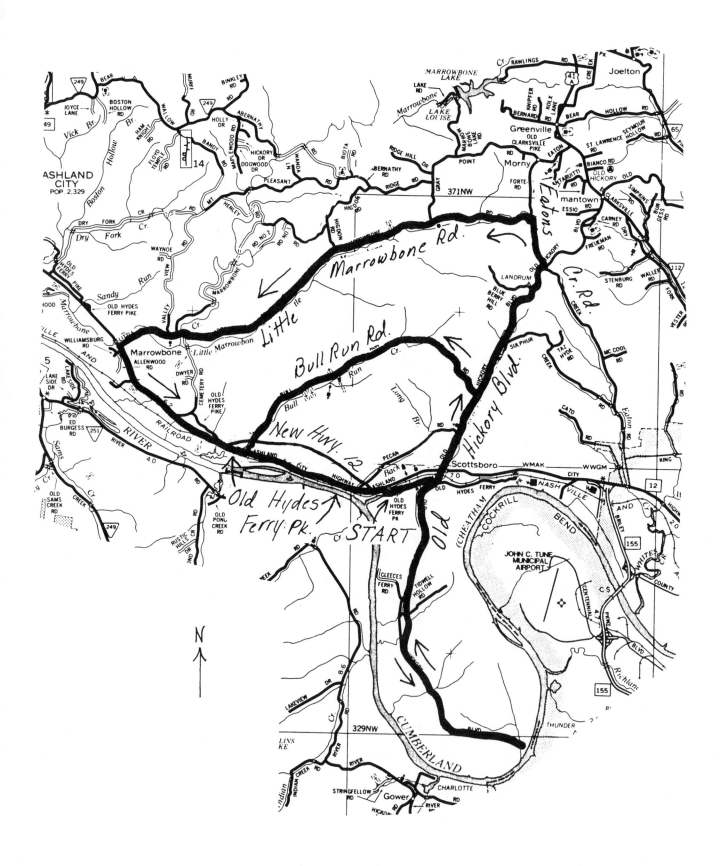

Ride # 34 UNION HILL/PARADISE RIDGE LOOP

Distance: 18 or 25 miles
Elevation Difference/Accumulated Climb: Option 1 - 450/600 ft., Option 2 - 480/1050 ft.
Terrain: Very hilly with at least 2 good climbs but some long level stretches in between.
Services: Option 1 has a market at mile 6.1 and a market/restaurant at mile 12.5 (.3 mi. off loop). Option 2 has a market at mile 6.1 and a market/restaurant at mile 19.5 (.3 mi. off the loop).
Traffic: Light to moderate on all roads.
Connector Routes: 1) 5 mi. to # *33 Bells Bend/Bull Run/Little Marrowbone Creek Rides*--From Joelton, go west on Old Clarksville Pk., left on Eatons Creek Rd., left on Clarksville Pk., and right on Eatons Creek Rd. **2)** .3 mi. to start of # *35 Lower Sycamore Creek Loop*--From Union Hill Rd., bike west on Clay Lick Rd. to the town of Joelton.
Alternate Parking Sites: 1) Goodlettsville City Hall (3.8 mi. to loop)--Bike north for 2 blocks on Dickerson Rd, left on Old Brick Church Pk. and left on Brick Church Pk. **2)** Hunters Lane High School near the intersection of Old Hickory Blvd. and Dickerson Pk.(3.9 mi. to loop)--Bike west on Hunters Ln. and right on Brick Church Pk. **3)** Joelton High School (.3 mi. to loop)--Bike east on Union Hill Rd.
Distance from Nashville: 8 miles

The northwest region of Davidson County boasts of some of the most remote, rugged, and scenic areas in the Metropolitan County. When pedaling this route, you are approximately 15 miles from downtown Nashville (as the crow flies), but could just as easily be up on the Cumberland Plateau. Although newer residences are numerous along the ridges and wide valleys, one doesn't have to look hard to see thick forests and near-vertical hillsides beyond.

The first part of this ride on Lickton Pike follows Whites Creek to its headwaters, passing through a peaceful valley dotted with old farms and newer homes. Shortly after the road goes under I-24, four tributaries converge near the community of Lickton to form Whites Creek. Good roads for bicycling follow all four hollows up to the ridge; we have opted to take Shaw Branch/Brick Church Pike up to the community of Union Hill. Before arriving, though, there is a steep pull (150 ft. in .4 mile) through shady woods to the top. Union Hill, a town which predates the Civil War, was given its name because at least eight roads intersect in the area. This can, of course, be confusing to a bicyclist and would be dismaying if he or she dropped down the wrong side of the hill and had to ride back up it again! Follow our directions carefully and keep in mind that you will not come off the ridge for several more miles.

On Union Hill Rd, there is a small park with a picnic shelter that makes a nice rest/lunch stop. (There is also a market at Lickton Pike and Union Hill Rd. .8 mi. past the park.) From the market, another climb (140 ft. in .4 mile) awaits as you go from the "hill" to the "ridge" as locals call it.

After conquering this hill, you are now up on Paradise Ridge, named after the Paradise brothers who settled here in the early 1800s. The ridge, at one time a haven for bandits and outcasts, has a colorful history of both romance and violence. Far from Nashville's law enforcers and legal courts, the region was governed by its own laws (or lack thereof!), and family feuds resulting in murder were not uncommon. The people who settled the ridge were of a rugged and individualistic nature; you can still sense these qualities as you ride through this area today.

Option 1 travels west along the ridge on Union Hill Rd. which is lined by several residential homes interspersed among the pastures. As you enter the outskirts of Joelton, Option 1 joins Option 2 for a fun drop down Clay Lick Rd.

Option 2 runs north along Paradise Ridge through pleasant patches of scenic fields and forests mixed with small modest residential areas. Soon you go left on Dividing Ridge, a peaceful road following one of the arms of the ridge. According to some map publications, Dividing Ridge Rd. is also known as Seedtick Rd. (So you might want to keep this in mind if you need to use the bushes!) We wonder if the residents perhaps did not like having the name "Seedtick" in their mailing addresses. Regardless of its name, this road offers several scenic glimpses through the trees of this interesting land of ridges.

Paradise Ridge is actually an extension of the Cumberland Plateau and has many similar plant and soil characteristics. Although the soil is not suitable for leguminous crops, tobacco grows well and is seen hanging inside the barns in late fall. We cycled this trip on a warm clear day in late October and enjoyed the activity of the harvest and the spectacular autumn foliage.

Greer Rd. sends you down from the ridge, across the South Fork of Sycamore Creek, and then back up again. According to popular legend, an Indian chief and his wife are buried facing each other on either side of this creek. Shortly after the route turns left onto Wilkinson Rd., a fun descent brings you into a charming, wooded hollow. The route then gradually ascends to the ridge along Sulphur Branch.

At Clay Lick Rd. you may choose to turn right (leaving the loop) and cycle into the small community of Joelton for refreshments. Starting in the mid-1800s, many German and Italian immigrants settled in Joelton and in Germantown to the south along Paradise Ridge. However, don't expect to find any knockwurst and sauerkraut here, because the cuisine today is typical of small Tennessee towns.

Both Options continue on Clay Lick Rd. going east (away from Joelton) where your long awaited descent plummets into the thickly forested hills. It's all downhill from here! After you cross I-24, the road follows Clay Lick Creek down to Lickton Pike and back to the starting point.

34 UNION HILL/PARADISE RIDGE LOOP

HOW TO GET THERE: Take I-24 West and exit at Old Hickory Blvd./Hwy. 45 (Exit 40). Turn left (west) on Old Hickory Blvd. and continue to Whites Creek Park adjacent to Whites Creek High School. Park next to the baseball diamond.

Mile

0.0	Begin ride by biking north on Lickton Pk. from Old Hickory Blvd.
2.5	**Right** on Shaw Rd. after going under I-24.
3.3	**Left** on Brick Church Pk. (first left).
5.2	**Left** on Union Hill Rd. (stop sign).
6.1	**Right** on Lickton Pk. (stop sign). Market in the town of Union Hill.
6.2	Bear **left** on Union Hill Rd.

Go to Option 1 or Option 2

OPTION 1
18 miles

6.8   **Left** on Union Hill Rd. at the top of a hill where Greer Rd. goes straight.

Go to Both Options

OPTION 2
25 miles

6.8	Go straight on Greer Rd. at the top of the hill where Union Hill Rd. goes left.
9.7	**Left** on Dividing Ridge Rd. (Seedtick Rd.).
10.9	Dividing Ridge Rd. bears right at Spring Valley Baptist Church.
14.3	**Left** on Greenbrier Rd. (Edgar Dillard Rd.) (4-way stop).
15.9	**Left** on Wilkinson Rd. (second left).
18.3	**Right** on Union Hill Rd. (stop sign at the T-intersection).

Go to Both Options

BOTH OPTIONS

12.5, 19.5	**Left** on Clay Lick Rd. Market/restaurant (.3 mi. off the route) to the right on Union Hill Rd. in the town of Joelton.
15.8, 22.8	**Right** on Lickton Pk. (stop sign at the T-intersection). Retrace your route back to the starting point.
17.6, 24.6	End of ride!

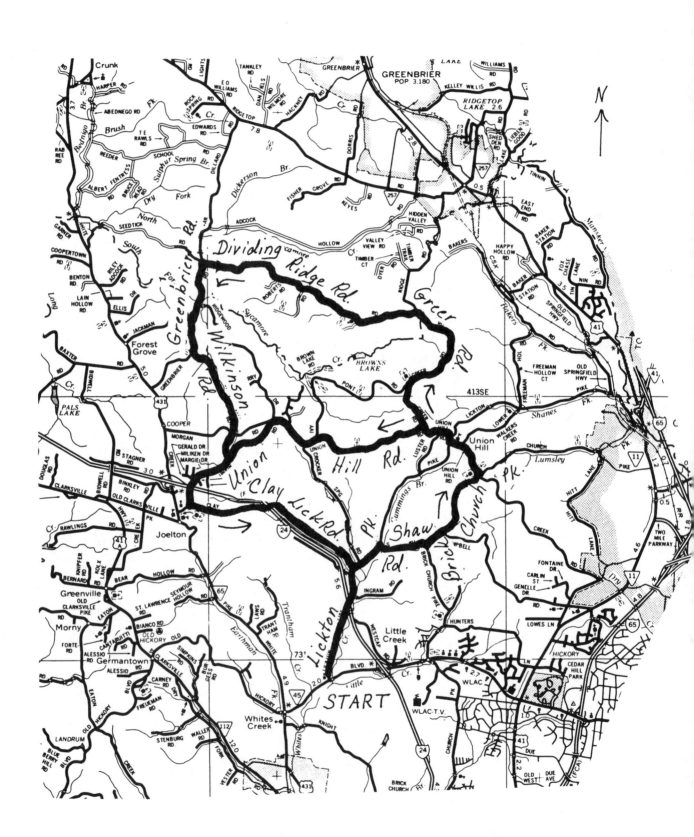

Ride #35   LOWER SYCAMORE CREEK LOOP

Distance: 37, 43, or 45 miles

Elevation Difference/Accumulated Climb: Option 1- 440/1785 ft., Option 2 - 440/2365 ft., Option 3 - 450/2120 ft.

Terrain: Moderate to very hilly with plenty of pleasant, flat stretches. Mostly gradual (but sometimes long) climbs plus a real tough climb on Peter Pond Rd. Option 3 has a steep climb on Marks Creek Hill Rd.

Services: Option 1 has markets at miles 6.6, 11.7, 24.4, and 31.2. Option 2 has markets at miles 6.6, 11.7, 30.4, and 37.0. Option 3 has markets at miles 6.6, 11.7, 25.4, 31.8, and 38.4.

Traffic: Light to moderate on Clarksville Pk., Old Clarksville Pk., and Hwy. 249. Light on all other roads. On Option 3, Hwy. 12 has moderate to heavy traffic for a total of 1.5 mi.

Combining Ride: *#36 Upper Sycamore Creek Loop.*

Connector Routes: 1) .3 mi. to *#34 Union Hill/Paradise Ridge Loop*--From the high school in Joelton at the start, bike east on Union Hill Rd. **2)** 2.1 mi. to *#22 Narrows of the Harpeth Loop* from mile 27.8 on Option 3--Take Hwy. 12 into Ashland City and go right on Hwy. 49 across the Cumberland River. (Moderate to heavy traffic, plus a long bridge crossing. Use caution!) **3)** 4 mi. to *#33 Little Marrowbone Creek Ride*--Bike south on Eatons Creek Rd. (which is .6 mi. from the start of the ride) from Old Clarksville Pk., turn left on Clarksville Pk., then right on Eatons Creek Rd. You can also connect with this ride by continuing on Hwy. 249 at Carney Winters Rd., turning right on Bandy Rd. by the market, and right on Valley View Rd. (*extremely* steep hill with stop sign at the bottom. Use caution!)

Alternate Parking Sites: 1) The Park and Ride Lot at I-24 and Hwy. 249/Exit 31 (1.4 mi. to loop)--Take Hwy. 249 south to Old Clarksville Pk. **2)** Ashland City--Park on Chapmansboro Rd. near its intersection with Hwy. 12 (1.1 miles north of Ashland City).

Distance from Nashville: 15 miles

This tour follows the edge of the Highland Rim on Old Clarksville Pk. as it occasionally drops and rises among the hollows leading to the Cumberland River. This road, once a narrow dirt road dating back to the early 1800s, was the major thoroughfare between Nashville and Clarksville before the new Clarksville Highway and later, the interstate were constructed. The road is now paved and makes a good workout excursion among tobacco and corn fields mixed with patches of forests. Many new homes now dot the route, but much of the scenery has changed little over the years.

A long, steady drop to Sycamore Creek (mile 10.0) brings the first excitement of the day and is followed by a 1.5-mile gradual, but practically relentless, grade (250 ft.) back up to the ridge where a market and restaurant are conveniently located. (The next market is 13-20 miles later.)

After crossing Hwy. 49, a network of lightly traveled roads meander along the ridges and hollows, allowing for numerous route possibilities. Our three options can be combined to create a variety of routes, and the *Upper Sycamore Creek Loop* also combines nicely with this ride. Cycling the northwest corner of Cheatham County, with its old tobacco barns, tumbling creeks, woods, and pastures is always worth the climbs.

An exhilarating drop on Sweet Home Rd. on Option 1 takes you down to Spring Creek and up a lovely hollow to Lockertsville Rd. Option 2 continues on Old Clarksville Pk. as it descends and climbs out of two hollows before reaching the abandoned store in Thomasville. This route turns south on Thomasville Rd. and meanders up and down the rolling hills of this picturesque area. We biked here on a cold day in late November when the crisp autumn air was filled with the earthy aroma of the tobacco smoking in the barns. Option 3 leaves Old Clarksville Pk. on Poplar Ridge Rd., providing a mostly-flat shortcut to Thomasville Rd.

All options come together at the intersection of Sweet Home Rd. and Lockertsville Rd. where we have devised two routes to take you back. Options 1 and 2 travel the shorter route on Lockertsville Rd. After a mild upgrade (200 ft.) to a ridge above Sycamore Creek, this road twists and turns among the picturesque farms before descending a forested hillside to a small flat valley at the confluence of Sycamore and Spring Creeks. After a short stretch through the corn fields and across Sycamore Creek, a gradual climb (225 ft.) through a small hollow takes you up to another ridge where Option 3 is joined.

A more extended tour down to the banks of the Cumberland River (and the inevitable climb back up!) is in store for those who choose Option 3. Riding two stretches (.7-mi. and .8-mi.) on busy Hwy. 12 is required in order to reach this premier segment on Chapmansboro Rd., a delightful road which winds through lush forests as it descends to the Cumberland River floodplain. After passing interesting stilted fishing cottages, the route crosses the mouth of Sycamore Creek and transits a flat, open area with unobstructed views of the river. A very steep hill (225 ft.) on Marks Creek Hill Rd. quickly takes you out of the Cumberland Valley.

All options meet at Ed Harris Rd. and continue through a flat section to Hwy. 249, a highway which often has fast traffic. The very steep descent (with a nasty hairpin turn on Carney Winters Rd.) takes you down to Blue Springs Creek where an old cemetery sits under large cedar trees. You must, unfortunately, slow down on your descent in order to turn onto Peter Pond Rd. Here a short, but seemingly vertical, hill awaits. The route drops down to the creek once again and, of course, climbs back out where it joins Old Clarksville Pk. From here, you are retracing your route for 7 miles back to Joelton.

Intersections are one of the most common locations for cycling accidents, and many are the fault of cyclists. Obey all traffic rules just like any other vehicle and be watchful for motorists who don't see you.
Beware of the three most common driver errors:

- Turning left in front of an oncoming cyclist.
- Proceeding through a stop sign and pulling in front of an oncoming cyclist who has the right of way.
- Passing a cyclist and immediately turning right into his/her path.

Use hand signals (except when you need both hands for steering or braking) and establish eye contact with motorists. If you cannot safely reach the left lane when turning left, dismount and use the crosswalks.

#35 LOWER SYCAMORE CREEK LOOP

HOW TO GET THERE: Take I-24 West from Nashville and exit at Hwy. 431 (Exit 35). Go left on Hwy. 431, continue for 1 mi. and park at the middle school in Joelton.

Mile

0.0   Begin ride by cycling west on Old Clarksville Pk. from Whites Creek Pk./Hwy. 431 which is the main intersection near the high school.

1.6   **Right** on Clarksville Pk./Hwy. 41A (stop sign at the T-intersection).

2.6   **Left** on Old Clarksville Pk. near the top of a gradual incline. This is the *third* Old Clarksville Pk. on the left (easy to miss).

4.7   Continue straight onto Hwy. 249 (still Old Clarksville Pk.).

5.4   Continue straight (staying on Old Clarksville Pk.) as Hwy. 249 goes to the left.

6.5   Market.

11.7   Cross Hwy. 49. Market/restaurant.
Go to Option 1, Option 2, or Option 3

OPTION 1
37 miles

12.6   **Left** on Shahan Rd. (first left).

13.5   **Right** on Sweet Home Rd. (stop sign at the T-intersection).

16.8   **Left** on Lockertsville Rd. (4-way intersection). You can extend the ride for a 43-mi. total trip by continuing straight on Sweet Home Rd. and doing the remainder of the Option 3 ride.

20.2   Bear **right** on Lockertsville Rd. after descending into a valley where Harris Town Rd. goes straight. Cross Sycamore Creek.

21.9   **Left** on Ed Harris Rd. after climbing out of a hollow.
Go to All Options

OPTION 2
43 miles

18.4   **Left** on Thomasville Rd. in Thomasville immediately before an old abandoned store.

20.3   Cross Mosley Ferry Rd. (stop sign at the 4-way intersection).

22.8   Cross Sweet Home Rd. and continue on Lockertsville Rd. (stop sign at the 4-way intersection). Extend your ride for a 49-mi. total trip by going right on Sweet Home Rd. and riding the remainder of the Option 3.

26.2   Bear **right** on Lockertsville Rd. after descending into a valley where Harris Town Rd. goes straight. Cross Sycamore Creek.

28.0   **Left** on Ed Harris Rd. after climbing out of a hollow.
Go to All Options

OPTION 3
45 miles

14.1   **Left** on Poplar Ridge Rd. (easy to miss).

16.9   **Left** on Thomasville Rd. (stop sign).

18.5   **Right** on Sweet Home Rd. (stop sign at the 4-way intersection). You can choose to follow Options 1 and 2 for a 40-mi. total trip by going straight onto Lockertsville Rd.

21.4   **Left** on Hwy. 12 (stop sign) at the Chapmansboro Post Office.

22.1   **Right** on Chapmansboro Rd. (first right).

24.3   **Left** (stop sign at the 3-way intersection) and go over a bridge. This is still Chapmansboro Rd. although the street sign may indicate Matlock Rd.

24.4   Sycamore Creek Recreation Area. Water/restrooms.

25.4   Market.

27.8   Cross Hwy. 12 (stop sign at the 4-way intersection) and continue on Marks Creek Hill Rd. (Fields Rd.)

28.3   **Right** on Hwy. 12 (stop sign at the T-intersection).

29.1   **Right** (or straight) on Lockertsville Rd. as Hwy. 12 bends to the left near a used car lot.

29.3   **Right** on Ed Harris Rd. (first right).

Go to All Options

ALL OPTIONS

24.1, 30.1, 31.5   **Right** on Hwy. 49 (stop sign at the T-intersection).

24.4, 30.4, 31.8   **Left** on Hwy. 249 (first left). Market. (Market/restaurants .2 miles off the route to the south on Hwy. 49.)

26.0, 32.0, 33.4   **Left** on Carney Winters Rd. (first left after passing the Bearwaller Church of Christ).

27.6, 33.6, 35.0   **Right** on Peter Pond Rd. (first right).

28.4, 34.4, 35.8   **Left** on Bennet Rd. (Blue Springs Rd.)(first left).

29.9, 35.9, 37.3   **Left** on Blue Springs Rd. (stop sign at the T-intersection).

31.0, 37.0, 38.4   **Right** on Old Clarksville Pk. (stop sign at the 4-way intersection). Market. You are now retracing your route back to the starting point.

32.0, 38.0, 39.4   Straight onto Hwy. 249 (stop sign), still Old Clarksville Pk.)

32.7, 38.7, 40.1   Continue straight on Old Clarksville Pk. as Hwy. 249 goes to the left.

34.8, 40.8, 42.2   **Right** on Clarksville Pk./Hwy 41A (stop sign at the T-intersection).

35.8, 41.8, 43.2   **Left** on Old Clarksville Pk. (easy to miss).

37.4, 43.4, 44.8   End of ride!

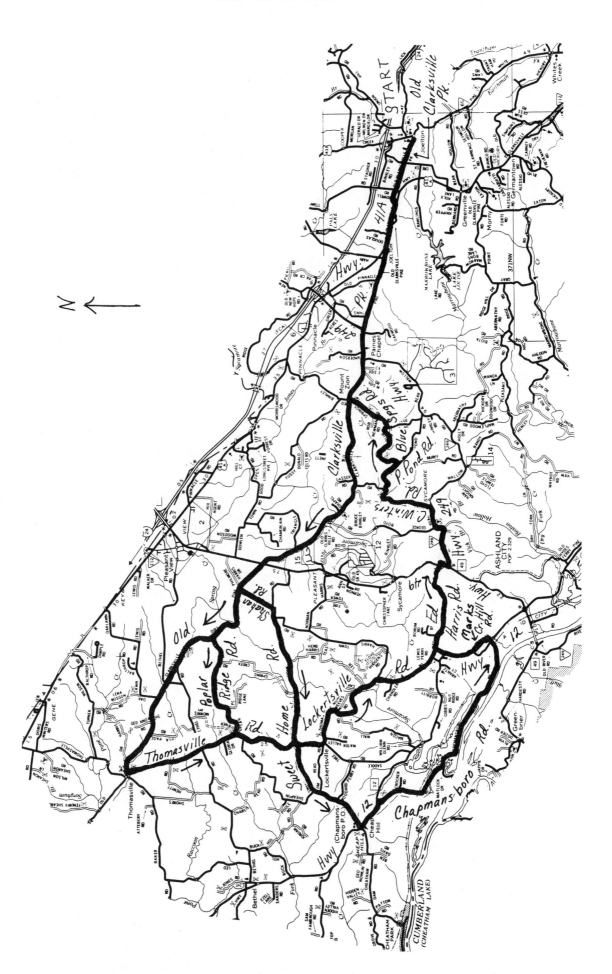

Ride # 36   UPPER SYCAMORE CREEK LOOP

Distance: 26 or 45 miles
Elevation Difference/Accumulated Climb: Option 1 - 330/1335 ft., Option 2 - 330/2575 ft.
Terrain: Moderately hilly on both options.
Services: Option 1 has markets at miles 3.1, 9.9, 17.5 and 23.7. Restaurant at mile 17.5.
 Option 2 has markets at miles 3.1, 26.7, 36.3, and 43.3. Restaurant at mile 36.3.
Traffic: Moderate on Hwy. 249 at the start and end of ride. Moderate to heavy for .7 mi. on
 Hwy. 49 on Option 1. Light to moderate on Old Clarksville Pk. east of Hwy. 49. Light on
 all other roads.
Combining Rides: # 35 Lower Sycamore Creek Loop, # 37 Lower Red River Loop.
Distance from Nashville: 20 miles

This tour of the broken escarpment of the Highland Rim travels through picturesque farmland of Cheatham and Robertson Counties and follows portions of the *Lower Red River Loop* and the *Lower Sycamore Creek Loop*. Ambitious cyclists can combine all three tours to create trips of 100+ miles covering the area from the Cumberland River near Ashland City to the open plains of Kentucky.

Our tour begins on the sometimes busy Hwy. 249, but soon escapes onto Old Clarksville Pk. and heads north on Mt. Zion Rd. This delightful country road takes you over rolling pastures before plummeting down to an old truss bridge at Sycamore Creek. A seemingly vertical climb (215 ft.) through a dense forest takes you back up to the rim.

Option 1 travels to the town of Pleasant View before continuing the journey through more scenic rolling countryside on lightly traveled Pleasant View Rd.

Option 2 runs west a short distance on Good Springs Rd. and immediately crests a small rise, giving a panoramic view of the hills and hollows to the west. The wonderful vista disappears as a hair-raising descent (watch for gravel!) is followed by a climb and another roller coaster plunge. Next the route travels north on McMahan Hollow Rd., the premier segment of this trip. Cycling this narrow country lane as it follows a clear, bubbling creek through a shallow, forested hollow is absolutely delightful. After a short climb, the road meets Battle Creek Rd. near the site of the Battle Creek Massacre (1780) where settlers fleeing from Renfro Station were killed by Indians. Only one person, a widow, survived.

After reaching Coopertown Rd., you will be riding the *Lower Red River Loop* to the community of Turnersville after which a long gradual rise (180 ft.) takes you up to Hwy. 256. Our tour crosses the highway and continues on Stroudsville Rd., passing through wooded areas while dipping down to Brush Creek. Leaving the community of Stroudsville, this road turns south and rolls along level farmland.

A much-needed market is finally reached at the intersection of Clarksville Pk. Here our tour picks up Thomasville Rd. which soon traverses increasingly hilly terrain including two short steep pulls en route to Thomasville. The remaining part of this tour follows the *Lower Sycamore Creek Loop* (in the opposite direction) on Old Clarksville Pk. where Option 1 soon joins. At least four climbs (including a tough 270-ft. pull after Sycamore Creek) await the cyclist as she or he travels this old stage route between Nashville and Clarksville.

36 UPPER SYCAMORE CREEK LOOP

HOW TO GET THERE: Take I-24 West from Nashville, exit onto Hwy. 249/New Hope Rd. (Exit 31), and go left toward Ashland City. Park at the Park and Ride Lot at the intersection of Clarksville Pk./Hwy. 41A and Hwy. 249.

Mile

0.0	Begin by biking south (away from I-24) on Hwy. 249/Jackson Felts Rd.
1.4	**Right** on Old Clarksville Pk. (still Hwy. 249).
2.1	Straight on Old Clarksville Pk. as Hwy. 249 goes left.
3.1	**Right** on Red Binkley Rd. (4-way intersection). Market.
3.4	**Left** on Mt. Zion Rd. (Fussy Rd.) (first left).
6.2	Cross Sycamore Creek.

Go to Option 1 or Option 2

OPTION 1
26 miles

7.9	**Left** on Good Springs Rd. (Dowlen Town Rd.) (stop sign at the T-intersection).
8.4	**Right** on Hwy. 49 (stop sign at the T-intersection).
9.1	**Right** on Pleasant View Main St. immediately past the cemetery.
9.8	Cross Hwy. 49 (stop sign).
9.9	**Left** on Pleasant View Rd. (Cherry St.) (Bethel Rd.) (4-way stop in the town of Pleasant View). Market short distance off the loop to the right at this intersection.
13.4	**Left** on Old Clarksville Pk. (stop sign).

Go to Both Options

OPTION 2
45 miles

6.9	**Right** on Good Springs Rd. (stop sign at the T-intersection).
8.1	**Right** on Lee Rd. across from church on the left.
8.3	Bear **left** at the "Y".
8.7	**Right** on Clarksville Pk./Hwy. 41A. (stop sign).
9.1	**Left** on McMahan Hollow Rd. (first left).
9.5	Go under I-24.
9.8	Straight at the 4-way intersection.
12.0	**Left** on Battle Creek Rd. (stop sign at the T-intersection).
14.0	**Left** on Coopertown Rd. (stop sign).
14.6	Cross Hwy. 49 (stop sign) in Coopertown.
16.0	Cross Sandy Springs Rd. (4-way stop).
19.6	**Left** on Maxie Rd. (3-way intersection).
20.3	Bear **left** at the "Y" (staying on Maxie Rd.) after crossing Millers Creek.
22.2	Cross Hwy. 256 (stop sign) and continue onto Stroudsville Rd.
24.2	**Left** (staying on Stroudsville Rd.) by the Stroudsville Church of Christ.
25.8	Cross I-24.
26.7	Cross Clarksville Pk./Hwy.41A and continue on Thomasville Rd. Market.
29.7	**Left** on Old Clarksville Pk. (stop sign at the 4-way intersection).

Go to Both Options

BOTH OPTIONS

17.5 36.3   Cross Hwy. 49 (stop sign). Market/restaurant.
22.7 41.5   Market.
23.7 42.5   Straight onto Hwy. 249.
24.5 43.3   **Left** on Jackson Felts Rd./Hwy. 249.
25.8 44.6   End of Ride!

36 UPPER SYCAMORE CREEK LOOP

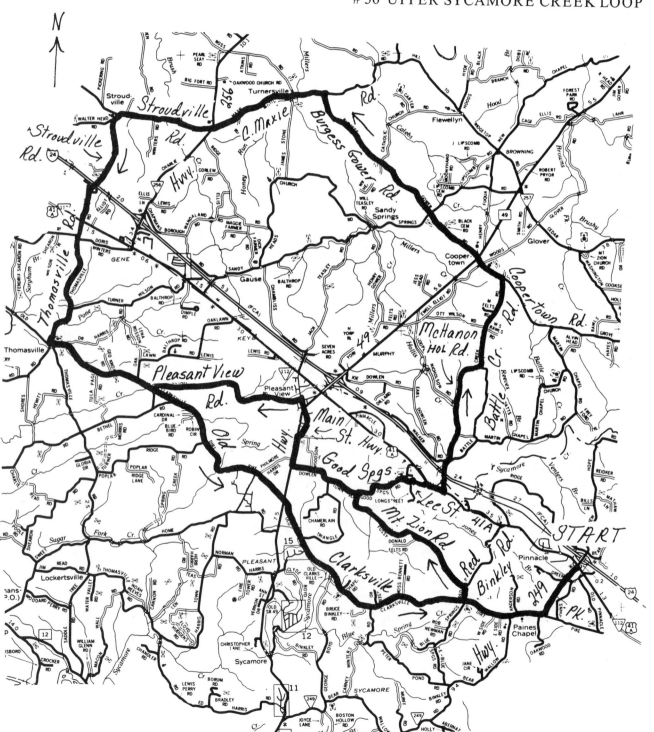

Ride #37   LOWER RED RIVER LOOP

Distance: 33, 48, or 65 miles
Elevation Difference/Accumulated Climb: Option 1 - 380/1575 ft., Option 2 - 400/2065 ft., Option 3 - 420/2435 ft.
Terrain: Mostly rolling with a few moderate climbs. Several long, flat stretches, especially on Option 3.
Services: Option 1 has markets at miles 25.5 and markets/restaurants at 26.5. Option 2 has markets at miles 18.6, 29.5, 36.9, 42.2, and markets/restaurants at 44.0. Option 3 has markets at miles 16.7 (.4 mi. off the loop), 22.2, 25.3, 32.2, 46.5, 53.9, 59.2 and markets/restaurants at 61.0.
Traffic: Light on all roads except moderate near the town of Springfield.
Combining Rides: #36 *Upper Sycamore Creek Loop*, #38 *Cross Plains Loop*, #39 *Upper Red River Loop*.
Alternate Parking Sites: 1) Springfield. **2)** Port Royal State Park.
Distance from Nashville: 21 miles

We love this ride! The scenery is excellent, the traffic light, and the mood is one of expansiveness. The sky often seems to be just a little bigger up here. (Okay, it's not Montana but it's nice.)

Our tour begins by heading west on Coopertown Rd. which travels over gently rolling farmland with occasional views into the Middle Tennessee Basin.

Robertson County is famous for its tobacco (especially the dark-fired) which grows in the fields in the summertime. In the fall, it is cut, hung on racks in barns which are sealed, and dried by smoke from fires, creating an earthy aroma and a startling sight. (You need not report to the farmer that his/her barn is on fire!)

After crossing Hwy. 49 in Coopertown, you will see a sign that marks the historic Trail of Tears route. During this tragic episode of our history in 1838-39, 20,000 Cherokee Indians were forced to leave their Appalachian homes and travel through this region on their way to Oklahoma. It is sad to think of the approximately 4,000 natives, mostly women and children, who died of hunger, cold, and disease during the long, arduous journey upon the very roads we enjoy bicycling today. After much level-to-rolling cycling, a short descent takes you across Millers Creek where a few old clapboard-covered log homes still stand. Keep your momentum going, because a steep 160-ft. climb up a forested hillside is soon to be conquered.

Hwy. 256 plunges down into a shady hollow, crosses Sulphur Fork Creek, and gently leads up to Kenney Rd. Here, Option 1 heads east while traversing flat, open farmland interspersed with small dips and rises across the creeks before the long steady rise into the town of Springfield.

Options 2 and 3 continue uphill on Hwy. 256 and soon pass the magnificent Glen Raven Home (1897), barely visible through the mature hardwood trees that shade the grounds. This elaborate well-preserved home with a ballroom on the third floor, was modeled after a French country estate and was the site of many parties attended by Nashville's elite. Its original owner, Felix Ewing, unfortunately lost his entire estate during the depression.

Option 2 heads to the town of Adams and passes the Red River Baptist Church (founded in 1791) which is believed to be the first church established in Middle Tennessee. It was originally located at Port Royal and moved to Adams in the 1860s. Next, this option crosses the Red River not far from the mouth of the Bell Witch Cave on Keysburg/Adams Rd. The legendary Bell Witch is reputed to have haunted John Bell and his family in the 1820s. She was frequently seen and heard in this vicinity, not only by the Bells, but by many reputable people including the skeptical Andrew Jackson who was actually harassed by the spirit when he came to investigate this phenomenon. He later said, "I'd rather fight the British than deal with this torment they call the Bell Witch!" Her antics included torturing John Bell's children, and many believe that she gave him the vial of poison that caused his death.

Option 3 turns southwest on Hwy. 76 and crosses beautiful Sulphur Fork. Before this, you may want to stop for a short walk along an old road at mile 20.4, now a footpath, to an alluring truss bridge just downstream from the remains of a large mill.

This option soon arrives at Port Royal State Historic Area located at the confluence of the Red River and Sulphur Fork. An important early center for trade and commerce, Port Royal was settled as early as 1784 and incorporated in 1797. Farmers brought their goods to be shipped down to the Cumberland River and points beyond. Because this was the furthest access point for the steamboats, Port Royal flourished as a thriving port in the mid-1800s. Also, the Cherokees set up camp here during The Trail of Tears. This historic area features a well-made reconstruction of the 1903 covered bridge that spanned the Red River years earlier. Hiking and picnicking are popular, and you may see (as we did) Mennonites playing ball in one of the fields.

The next 18 miles of Option 3 are "cycling at its best" as the route travels into Kentucky. Our tour continues north over increasingly level terrain and reaches Guthrie, Kentucky, a somewhat forgotten town that was once a busy railroad center with a large freight yard. From Guthrie, the ride rolls along seemingly endless, flat stretches with rarely a car infringing upon the solitude of these plains. Elegant white farm houses and tall grain silos stand among the fields of wheat, corn, and other crops.

Options 2 and 3 join in Keysburg and proceed further northeast into the Bluegrass State, encountering the blue-green rolling pastures for which Kentucky is famous. (Note—From Keysburg you may continue straight on Hwy. 102 which becomes Hwy. 161, then pick up the tour in Barren Plains. This shortens your entire trip by 4.5 miles.)

Upon reaching a community named Dot, our tour turns south, crosses the Red River, and winds its way over somewhat hilly county roads back into Tennessee. The farm community of Barren Plains has an old market/cafe complete with a porch swing for the weary cyclist.

As you roll into Springfield on Main St., notice the well-preserved homes, some of which date back to the early 19th century. All options join at the town square in Springfield. This thriving town was founded in 1796, and the stately courthouse (constructed in 1881) is considered one of the finest in the state. Most of the food services have moved to the new Hwy. 431, so it requires a two-block detour to replenish your energy.

Main St. continues through the more modest part of town and joins Hwy. 431, a busy highway with a good shoulders. And that completes the loop.

#37 LOWER RED RIVER LOOP

HOW TO GET THERE: Take I-24 West and exit at Hwy. 431 (Exit 35). Turn right at the end of the exit ramp and go north toward Springfield for 8 miles. Park at the gas station/market at the corner of Old Hwy. 431 and Hwy. 431. This is the second left after crossing Sycamore Creek. Be sure to get permission to park before beginning your ride.

Mile

0.0 Begin by cycling away from Hwy. 431 on Old Hwy. 431.

0.7 **Right** on Coopertown Rd. (Coopertown-Chestnut Rd.)(second right).

4.8 Cross Hwy. 49 in Coopertown and continue on Burgess Gower Rd.

6.2 Continue straight through the next 4-way intersection.

9.8 **Left** on Maxie Rd. (T-intersection).

10.6 **Right** on Ed Ross Rd. at the "Y" (first right) after descending to Millers Creek.

12.3 **Right** on Glen Raven Rd./Hwy. 256 (stop sign at the 4-way intersection).
Go to Option 1, Option 2, or Option 3

OPTION 1
33 miles

15.6 **Right** on Kenney Rd. toward Cedar Hill (first right after crossing Sulphur Fork).

25.5 **Left** on Hwy. 49/5th Ave. (stop sign) in the town of Springfield. Market.

26.2 **Right** on Main St. at the Robertson County Courthouse.

26.5 Market/restaurants (.2 mi. off the route) to the left (east) on 10th Ave. East immediately before crossing the RR tracks.

26.8 Bear **right** at the "Y" past the town square.
Go to All Options

OPTION 2
48 miles

15.6 **Left** on Hwy. 256/Kenney Rd. (first left after the hill past Sulphur Fork).

18.2 **Right** on Hwy. 76 (stop sign at the 4-way intersection).

18.6 **Right** on Hwy. 41/Hwy. 11 in the town of Adams. Market.

18.8 **Left** on Keysburg/Adams Rd. (Mint Springs Rd.)

19.9 Cross the Red River.

20.7 Bear **right** onto Keysburg Rd.

25.2 Bear **left** on Keysburg Rd. as Hugh Gill Rd. enters from the right.

25.7 **Right** on Hwy. 102 in the town of Keysburg (stop sign at the T-intersection).

25.8 **Left** on Hwy. 96/Orndorff Mill Rd.
Go to Options 2 and 3

OPTION 3
65 miles

15.6 **Left** on Hwy. 256/Kenney Rd. (first left after the hill past Sulphur Fork).

18.2 Straight onto Hwy. 76. Market (.4 mi. off the route) to the right on Hwy. 76 in the town of Adams.

22.2 Cross over Sulphur Fork. Market.

23.6   **Right** on Port Royal Rd./Hwy. 238. This is the Port Royal Rd. *after* crossing Sulphur Fork.

24.9   Port Royal State Park. Water/restrooms.

25.3   Market.

29.8   **Right** on Guthrie Rd. (easy to miss). Guthrie Rd. becomes Russel St. as it enters the town of Guthrie, Kentucky.

32.0   **Right** on 2nd St. immediately after crossing the RR tracks.

32.2   **Right** on Hwy. 41/Ewing St. Market/restaurant.

32.7   **Left** on Fairgrounds Rd. immediately after crossing the Montgomery County line. Market, restaurant. You will soon cross several railroad tracks.

34.8   **Left** on Allison Rd. by a large two-story farmhouse.

36.2   **Right** on Hwy. 848./Darnell Rd. (stop sign at the T-intersection).

41.8   **Right** on Hwy. 102 (stop sign at the T-intersection).

42.8   **Left** on Hwy. 96/Orndorff Rd. in Keysburg.

Go to Options "2 and 3"

OPTIONS " 2 and 3"

29.5, 46.5   **Right** on Dot Rd. (KY 1309) in the town of Dot (4-way intersection). Market. (KY 1041 goes to the left.)

29.7, 46.7   Cross Red River.

31.7, 48.7   Bear **left** where Smith Rd. enters from the right.

32.5, 49.5   **Right** on Barren Plain-Dot Rd./KY 1307 (stop sign at the T-intersection).

36.9, 53.9   Angle **left** onto Hwy. 161 South in the town of Barren Plains. Don't take a sharp left onto Hwy. 25. Market.

42.2, 59.2   **Right** on Hwy. 431 South (stop sign). Market.

42.5, 59.5   **Left** on Hwy. 41 (Hwy. 431 South runs together with Hwy. 41).

42.8, 59.8   **Right** on N. Main St. (first right) in the town of Springfield.

44.0, 61.0   Markets/restaurants (.2 mi. off the route) to the left (east) on 10th Ave East. immediately before crossing the RR tracks.

44.3, 61.3   Bear **right** at the "Y" past the town square.

Go to All Options

ALL OPTIONS

26.9, 44.4, 61.4   Cross Central Ave. (traffic light). Restaurant to the left on Central Ave. At least 2 markets in the next 2 miles.

28.9, 46.4, 63.4   **Right** on Hwy. 431 (stop sign at the T-intersection).

32.7, 48.2, 65.2   End of ride!

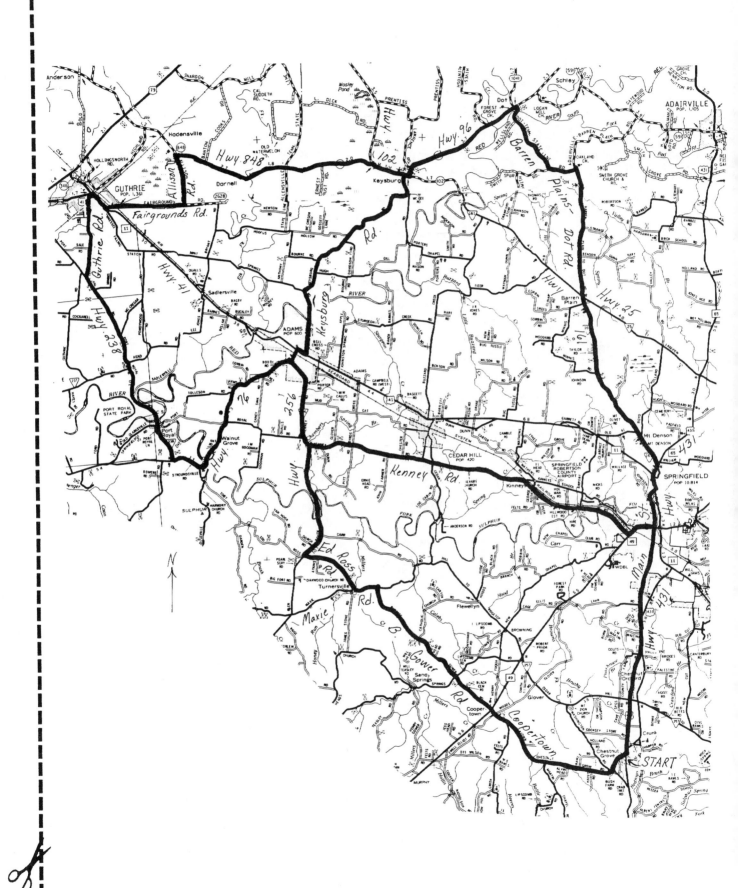

Ride # 38   CROSS PLAINS LOOP

Distance: 24 or 40 miles
Elevation Difference/Accumulated Climb: Option 1 - 265/1080 ft., Option 2 - 265/1580 ft.
Terrain: Mostly level with a few moderate hills.
Services: Option 1 has markets at miles 10.5, 13.6, and 18.3. Restaurant at mile 18.3. Option 2 has markets at miles 7.3, 13.9, 21.8, 26.1, 29.2, and 33.9. Restaurant at mile 33.9.
Traffic: Light to moderate on Hwy. 49. Light on all other roads.
Combining Rides: *# 37 Lower Red River Loop, # 39 Upper Red River Loop.*
Connector Routes: 1) 3.6 mi. to *# 32 North Sumner County Loop*--Bike east from the starting point toward White House on Hwy. 76. Caution: moderate to heavy traffic. **2)** 11.2 to *# 32 North Sumner County Loop*--Bike east on Hwy. 52 from Orlinda to Portland.
Alternate Parking Sites: Cross Plains.
Distance from Nashville: 25 miles

Have you ever had a craving for ice cream near the end of your bike ride? Well, this is the ride for you. Both options tour the flat-to-rolling farmlands of the Highland Rim and go right by Thomas Drugs, an old fashioned drugstore with black and white tile floors, decorative furnishings, and an incredible soda fountain boasting the best ice cream sodas and phosphates this side of 1955. This establishment (open until noon on Saturdays, closed Sundays) has faithfully served the residents of Cross Plains since 1930. Since there are only 6 miles to the end of the ride, a *small* banana split can't hurt anything...

This relatively easy tour starts at a market along Hwy. 76 where you need to ask permission before parking. A short distance to the south on Old Hwy. 31E there is a church where parking is possible. The ride begins by heading north, then west, along open fields. The wind can really blow up here on the exposed plains, especially in the winter, and we once renamed this the "crosswinds and headwinds ride." There is a wonderful feeling of expansiveness and solitude in this wide open area of distant horizons and large skies.

Option 1 splits from Option 2 and follows a particularly satisfying segment on Woodrow Wilson Rd. and Henry Rd., peaceful country lanes which wind their way through gently hilly land.

Option 2 continues west on Eden Corner Rd., drops into the lovely Beaver Dam Valley, climbs up to Hwy. 49, and then passes through a geological area of porous limestone where sink holes are common--creeks flow, only to disappear underground. The route also goes around a wooded wetland known as The Swamp. Hwy. 25 travels an enjoyable stretch over the gently rolling pastures dotted with barns, trailer homes, and white farm houses adorned with intricate wood trim. There is more of the same pleasant cycling on Hwy. 49 as you roll into the town of Milldale on the South Fork of the Red River where Option 1 has joined.

Both Options cross the river, tackle a steep 90-ft. climb, and proceed through the open plains to the town of Orlinda, "The sunniest spot in Tennessee" (as their sign reads). Our tour soon hooks up with East Robertson Rd., eventually dipping down and crossing the South Fork of the Red River. A moderate upgrade (140-ft.) is required to get to the ice cream stop in Cross Plains. (See *Ride # 39* for historical information.) From here, a fun descent and a few minor hills take you back to your starting point.

#38 CROSS PLAINS LOOP

HOW TO GET THERE: Take I-65 North and exit at Hwy. 76 (Exit 108). Turn left on Hwy. 76 going west toward Springfield and continue for 2 mi. Begin ride from the market (ask permission before parking) at 4-way intersection of Old Hwy. 31W/Cross Plains Rd. and Hwy. 76 in the community of Oakdale.

OPTION 1
24 miles

Mile

0.0	Begin ride by going right (north) on Old Hwy. 31W/Cross Plains Rd. from Hwy. 76.
2.8	**Left** on Eden Corner Rd. (easy to miss). Look for a sign to Owens Chapel United Methodist Church.
4.0	**Right** on Woodrow Wilson Rd. across from the fire tower.
7.1	Cross Hwy. 25 (stop sign) and continue on Henry Rd. (Robert Rd.)
10.5	**Right** on Hwy. 49 (stop sign at the T-intersection). Market in the town of Milldale.

Go to Both Options

OPTION 2
40 miles

0.0	Begin ride by going right (north) on Old Hwy. 31W/Cross Plains Rd. from Hwy. 76.
2.8	**Left** on Eden Corner Rd. (easy to miss). Look for a sign to Owens Chapel United Methodist Church.
7.3	Market.
10.2	**Right** on Hwy. 49 (stop sign at the T-intersection).
10.6	**Left** on William Woodard Rd. (first left).
13.8	**Left** on Hwy. 431 (stop sign at the T-intersection).
13.9	**Right** on Hwy. 161 (first right). Market.
14.8	**Right** on Boyd Holland Rd. (first right).
17.5	**Right** on Hwy. 25 West/Lakeview Rd. (stop sign).
18.9	Cross Hwy. 431 (stop sign).
21.8	**Left** on Hwy. 49 (still Hwy. 25) (stop sign at the T-intersection). Market.
22.4	Bear **left** on Hwy. 49 as Hwy. 25 goes straight.
26.1	Market in the town of Milldale.

Go to Both Options

BOTH OPTIONS

13.6, 29.2	**Right** on Hwy. 52 (4-way stop) in the town of Orlinda. Market.
13.8, 29.4	Go straight onto Elm Springs Rd. (E. Church St.) (first intersection) as Hwy. 52 bends to the left.
15.4, 31.0	**Right** on E. Robertson Rd. (stop sign at the T-intersection).
18.3, 33.9	**Right** on Hwy. 25/Main St. (stop sign at the T-intersection) in the town of Cross Plains. Markets/restaurant/drugstore with soda fountain (yum!) and lunch counter.
18.4, 34.0	**Left** on Cedar St. (Old Hwy. 31W/Cross Plains Rd.)(first left).
19.1, 34.7	**Left** on Kilgore Trace Rd. (Old Hwy. 31W/Cross Plains Rd.) (stop sign at the T-intersection).
24.2, 39.8	End of ride!

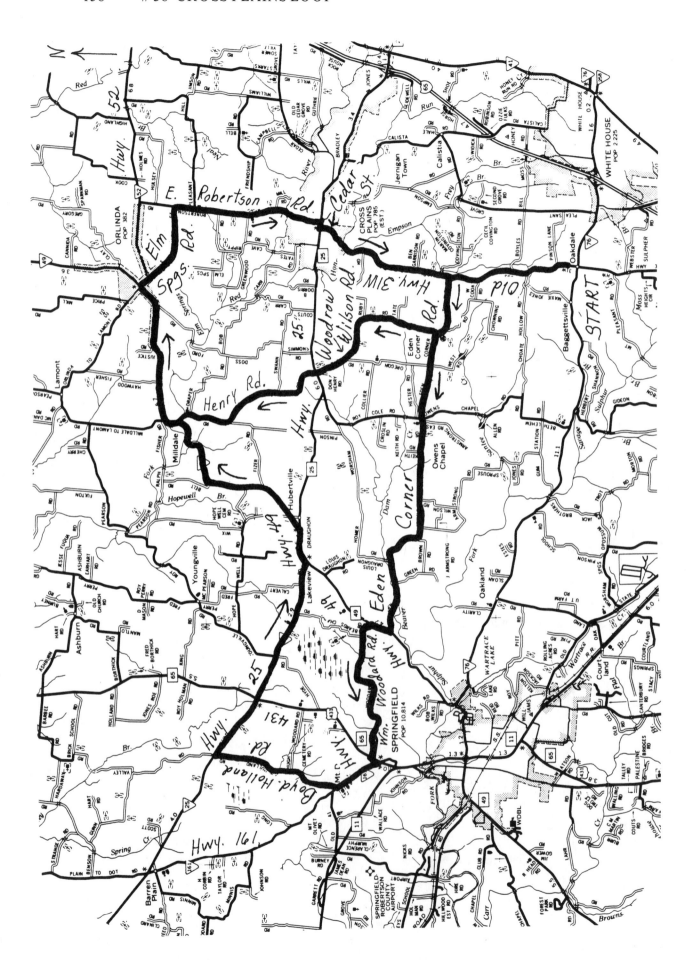

Ride # 39 UPPER RED RIVER LOOP

Distance: 39 or 44 miles
Elevation Difference/Accumulated Climb: Option 1 - 260/1360 ft., Option 2 - 260/1655 ft.
Terrain: Mix of rolling terrain and long flat stretches with only a few short climbs.
Services: Option 1 has markets at miles 6.4, 13.3, 22.5, and 33.8. Option 2 has markets at miles 6.4, 13.3, 22.5, and 38.7.
Traffic: Light to moderate on the first 6 mi. of Hwy. 25, and also on Hwy. 49. Light on all other roads.
Combining Rides: *# 37 Lower Red River Loop, # 38 Cross Plains Loop.*
Connector Routes: 11 mi. to *# 32 North Sumner County Loop*--From the town of Orlinda, bike east on Hwy. 52 to Portland.
Alternate Parking Sites: Springfield (7 mi. to loop)--Bike north on Hwy. 431 and go left on Hwy. 161 to Barren Plains. Boyd Holland Rd. also connects Hwy. 161 to the *Upper Red River Loop.*
Distance from Nashville: 31 miles

We enjoy going up to Cross Plains, not because it's just a pretty town with friendly people, but because we also love the chocolate ice cream sodas at Thomas Drugs (open until noon on Saturdays, closed Sundays). This traditional small town drugstore, in operation since 1930, makes an excellent stop just before the end of your ride. Down the street stands the Randolph Inn, originally built of logs in 1819 and expanded in 1833 to its present condition of white clapboard over the original logs.

The *Upper Red River Loop* traverses scenic northeastern Robertson County while traveling over wonderfully flat open stretches in southern Kentucky before returning through the town of Orlinda. Along this route, there are several lovely, well-kept old homes with intricate gingerbread trim and picket fences. Since our trip stays entirely on the Highland Rim, you will find it to be much flatter than many of the rides in the Central Basin.

The tour begins by heading west from Cross Plains and soon passing a historical sign marking the sight of Kilgore's Station. Thomas Kilgore, who arrived on foot from North Carolina in 1778, spent much of his first year in a nearby cave to hide from hostile Indians. The following year, he returned to the area with his wife and several other families and constructed a stockade. Despite the dangers and hardships of frontier life, Thomas Kilgore lived to the age of 108! It is hard to imagine that this region of expansive fields and pastures was once a thick virgin forest full of wild animals and unfriendly Indians.

Within the first 3 miles, animal lovers may opt to take a 1-mile side trip to the Wild Horse and Burro Adoption Center run by the Bureau of Land Management. Here you can see the cutest burros and beautiful horses of all sizes. The first 13 miles of the *Upper Red River Loop* follow Hwy. 25 from Cross Plains to Barren Plains. You may feel as if you are truly cycling across the plains, for the rolling pastures seem to go forever and, as on the plains, the wind often blows relentlessly hard here as we have discovered on winter bike rides.

Next, the tour heads north from Barren Plains, following the meandering Barren Plains-Dot Rd. over minor hills and across the unmarked Kentucky border. Kentucky Rd. 1307 drops into a small valley and crosses the South Fork of the Red River on an old metal truss bridge. This a peaceful spot to enjoy a snack (if you brought one) and be temporarily lazy.

You soon roll into Adairville, Kentucky, a small town with a pleasant little park located in the town square and a market across the street. As you leave town, 4-11 miles of cycling bliss await as you pedal flat and smooth Hwy. 591. The countryside is a patchwork of tobacco, corn, and soybean fields separated by strips of forests. Old barns, grain silos, and quaint farm houses dot the sparsely populated farmland.

Option 1 turns off of Hwy. 591 and travels south on remote backroads, passing by several antebellum homes. Option 2 continues east, crosses the North Fork of the Red River in the community of Prices Mill, and climbs back up to the rim (100 ft.).

Options 1 and 2 come together in Orlinda, a peaceful little town established in the latter part of the 19th century. In an elegant home approximately 3 miles east on Hwy. 52 is the lovely Aurora Inn, a bed and breakfast built in 1858 by William Stringer. The hosts are the nicest folks and love to have cyclists stay with them. (See *Appendix.*) From Orlinda, this trip cruises down to the South Fork of the Red River and conquers a moderate hill (140 ft.) before returning to Cross Plains.

Proper pedaling technique (often referred to as "ankling") is an important factor in efficiently utilizing your energy. Toe clips (straps) or cleats are needed to ankle, and stiff sole shoes are also helpful. Think of pedaling in small circles rather than mashing down on each downstroke. From the 12:00 position (pedal at the top), pedal by pushing *forward* to the 3:00 position, then press down to the 6:00 position. Next, point your toe slightly down and pull *back* to the 9:00 position, and then relax for the rest of the stroke.

39 UPPER RED RIVER LOOP

HOW TO GET THERE: Take I-65 North from Nashville and exit on Hwy. 25 (Exit 112). Go left (west) on Hwy. 25 toward Cross Plains. Continue 4 mi. into Cross Plains and park at the municipal building on the right or at the high school on the left.

Mile

0.0	Begin ride by biking west (away from I-65) on Hwy. 25/Main St.
5.7	Continue on Hwy. 25 at the stop sign where Hwy. 49 joins Hwy. 25.
6.4	**Right** on Hwy. 25/Lakeview Rd. after passing a market.
9.3	Cross Hwy. 431 (stop sign).
13.3	Sharp **right** on Barren Plains-Dot Rd. (stop sign) which becomes KY 1307. Do not continue on Hwy. 161. Market in the community of Barren Plains.
17.0	Continue straight on KY 1307 at the 3-way intersection.
19.6	Cross the South Fork of the Red River.
20.1	**Right** on Hwy. 591 (stop sign at the T-intersection).
22.5	Cross Hwy. 431 in the town of Adairville. Market. Benches/water in the town square.

Go to Option 1 or Option 2

OPTION 1
39 miles

26.8	**Right** (almost straight) on Lamont Rd./KY 765 (Pearson Rd.).
30.9	**Left** on Orlinda to Lamont Rd. (stop sign at the T-intersection).
33.8	Straight onto Hwy. 52 at the 4-way stop in the town of Orlinda. Market.

Go to Both Options

OPTION 2
44 miles

30.9	**Right** (staying on Hwy. 591) after crossing the Red River in the town of Prices Mill.
33.8	**Right** on Hwy. 383 (stop sign at the T-intersection) which becomes Hwy. 49 as you enter Tennessee.
34.3	Cross the Red River.
38.6	**Left** on Hwy. 52 (4-way stop). Market in the town of Orlinda.

Go to Both Options

BOTH OPTIONS

34.0, 38.9	Straight onto Elm Springs Rd. (E. Church St.)(first intersection) as Hwy. 52 bends to the left.
35.5, 40.4	**Right** on E. Robertson Rd. (stop sign at the T-intersection).
38.4, 43.3	**Right** on Hwy. 25 (stop sign at the T-intersection) in the town of Cross Plains. Drugstore with soda fountain/hot plates. Markets/restaurant (.2 mi. off the loop) to the left on Hwy. 25.
38.8, 43.7	End of ride!

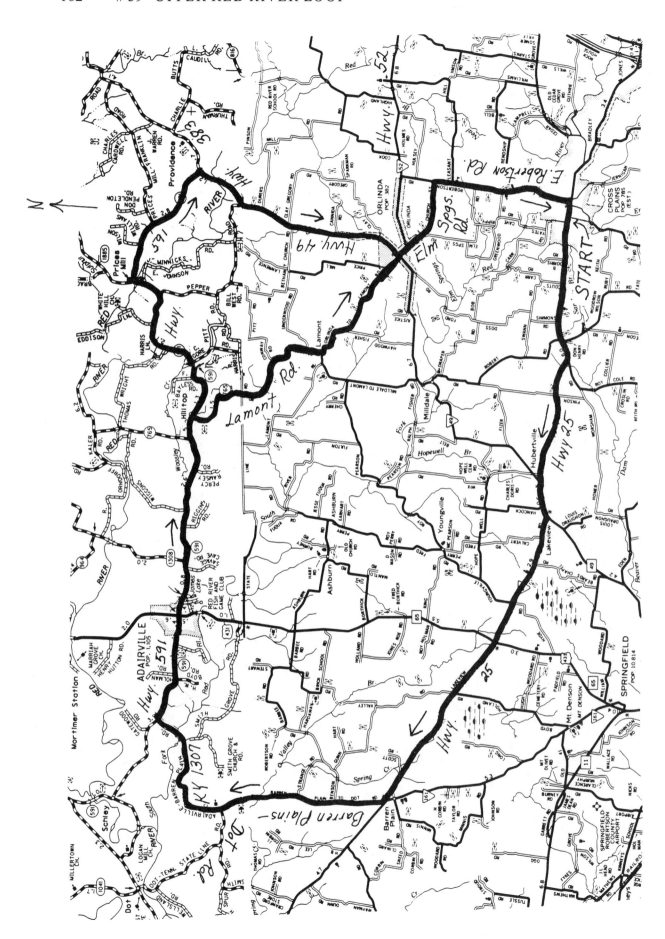

MOUNTAIN BIKING MIDDLE TENNESSEE

Mountain biking in Middle Tennessee is better than many folks would expect for a non-mountainous region. Although areas of the Cumberland Plateau, such as the Big South Fork National Recreation Area and Sewanee, have become the hot places for mountain biking in the southeast, Middle Tennessee has many fine possibilities for short excursions and all day trips.

We have explored the current *legal* places to ride on the public land in our seven county area and have discovered numerous narrow trails, steep hills, stream crossings, and occasional tough technical spots. Also, there are fine jeep roads for those who like to look around at the scenery more than down at the trail.

Keep in mind that with this growing sport, there are bound to be changes in the near future. There are current possibilities of building mountain bike trails at Montgomery Bell State Park, Cedars of Lebanon State Forest, and the Cheatham Wildlife Management Area, and in most cases, this will occur only if mountain bike enthusiasts plan, construct, and maintain the trails themselves. Check with a local bike shop or the Mountain Trails Bicycle Club to learn about the latest developments. We also encourage you to volunteer for trail construction and maintenance. (See *Appendix.*)

On the dark side, mountain biking may be banned from areas where it is currently permitted. This occurs not only because of the behavior of unsympathetic trail users and government officials, but also irresponsible and unmannerly mountain bikers. Please, for everyone's sake, be a courteous and responsible off-road cyclist and always share the trail.

International Mountain Biking Association Rules of the Trail:

1. RIDE ON OPEN TRAILS ONLY. Respect trail and road closures (ask if not sure), avoid possible trespassing on private land, obtain permits and authorization as may be required. Federal and state wilderness areas are closed to cycling. Additional trails may be closed because of sensitive environmental concerns or conflicts with other users. Your riding example will determine what is closed to all cyclists!

2. LEAVE NO TRACE. Be sensitive to the dirt beneath you. Even on open trails, you should not ride under conditions where you will leave evidence of your passing, such as on certain soils shortly after rain. Observe the different type of soils and trail construction and practice low impact cycling. This also means staying on the trail and not creating any new ones. Be sure to pack out at least as much as you pack in.

3. CONTROL YOUR BICYCLE. Inattention for even a second can cause disaster. Excessive speed maims and threatens people; there is no excuse for it!

4. ALWAYS YIELD TRAIL. Make known your approach well in advance. A friendly greeting (or bell) is considerate and works well; startling someone may cause loss of trail access. Show your respect when passing others--slow down to a walk or even stop. Anticipate that other trail users may be around corners or in blind spots.

5. NEVER SPOOK ANIMALS. All animals are startled by an unannounced approach, a sudden movement, or a loud noise. This can be dangerous for you, others, and the animals. Give animals extra room and time to adjust to you. In passing, use special care

and follow the directions of horseback riders. Running cattle and disturbing the wild animals are serious offenses. Leave gates as you found them, or as marked.

6. PLAN AHEAD. Know your equipment, your ability, and the area in which you are riding and prepare accordingly. Be self-sufficient at all times, keep your machine in good repair, and carry necessary supplies for changes in weather or other conditions. A well-executed trip is a satisfaction to you and not a burden or offense to others. Keep trails open by setting an example of responsible cycling for all other mountain bicyclists.

Rides # 40

Note: The three rides listed here as #40 are not located near each other, but are the result of incorporating these new mountain bike opportunities into the space alloted in this edition. Maps are usually available at the trailheads.

BOWIE NATURE PARK
(City of Fairview)

Distance: 1 to 4.5-mile loops
Elevation Difference: 140 ft.
Terrain: Small hills with a few steep climbs. Much of the trail is smooth dirt with only a few rocky spots. Slippery creek crossings. Extremely muddy after heavy rains.
Distance from Nashville: 25 miles

Bowie Nature Park in Fairview is an extremely popular spot for off-road cycling and has a variety of old dirt roads and single track trails within an 800-acre preserve. The terrain is suitable for most beginners, yet challenging enough to attract hard-core, off-road cyclists. The area was recovered from eroded and overly-cut farmland by the late Dr. Evangeline Bowie who worked for many years to restore the land before donating it to Fairview. With the help of local children, she packed the gullies with tree limbs and grass, and planted approximately 500,000 pine trees. Large areas of natural mixed hardwood forests are interspersed among the pine groves. Several attractive ponds created for erosion control and wildlife habitat are situated in the park.

This land, although abused, is recovering nicely, and the shady forests, hills, and streams make Fairview Nature Park a fun and scenic place to mountain bike. The park also has a nature center, picnic tables, grills, flush toilets, and a playground. Our son used to enjoy the elaborate playland before he learned to ride the trails with us.. Remember that hikers, joggers, and equestrians also use this park and that the privilege to ride these trails depends on responsible behavior. The City of Fairview hopes to make their park an example of how multi-use trails can work—please do your part to contribute to this goal. Be very careful when crossing the streams, because the flat rock stream bed can be very slick. (We found this out the hard way!)

A labyrinth of trails crisscross the park, allowing for a large variety of trips. Most cyclists follow the 4.5-mile perimeter trail, but don't miss our son's favorite "whoopty-doos" that come off the dome trail. The trail system is often revamped with certain areas being closed for reforestation and new trails opened. The park superintendent told us these trails will be better marked in the future. Don't rely completely on trail markers, because they may be turned around, vandalized, or removed. If you miss the loop markers, you may decide simply to head down an enticing trail until you get to the next junction, then go explore another trail. Should you become disoriented (a more comforting word than "lost"), head east, keeping the afternoon sun to your back, and you will find your way out.

The trails are closed to bikes on Wednesday and whenever the ground is saturated. You may call (615) 799-5544 ext. 1 for current trail conditions. Also, a $2 user fee is charged to bicyclists who do not live in Fairview.

HOW TO GET THERE: Take Hwy. 100 South from Nashville and continue through the city of Fairview. Go 1.6 mi. past Hwy. 96 West (not East) and turn right on Bowie Lake Rd. immediately past the France Factory. Follow the gravel road .5 mi. and park.

LONG HUNTER STATE PARK/BRYANT GROVE
(South of Mt. Juliet)

Distance: 2 to 6-mile loops
Elevation Difference: 140 ft.
Terrain: First loop is beginner terrain with a few gentle climbs. The second loop has a
    hill climb and slightly rougher terrain.
Distance from Nashville: 23 miles

Long Hunter State Park is the place to go for easy single track. Even advance riders will find the trails are fun as they twist in and out of the forests and cedar glades. The intermediate loop features a nice stretch on the side of a hill above Percy Priest Lake. Of course the long gradual climb will make you work for this segment. Best of all, if you want to relax after the ride, continue down the road to the picnic area and swim beach. If you are into attempting trail stunts (hopping and balancing on rocks with a bike), there is a rock garden a very short distance from the traihead. More trails are being planned.

HOW TO GET THERE: Take I-40 East and exit on Mt. Juliet Rd./Hwy. 171 (Exit 226A) going south. Turn left on South Mt. Juliet Rd. and left on Couchville Pk. Go right on Barnette Rd. which leads to Bryant Grove Picnic Area of Long Hunter State Park. The trailhead is on the right.

CHICKASAW TRACE
(North of Columbia)

Distance: Loops up to 7 miles
Elevation Difference: 200 ft.
Terrain: The inner loop is suitable for beginners and the outer loop is very challenging.
Distance from Nashville: 35 miles

This city park just outside Columbia attracts hard core racers and families alike. Views of the Duck River certainly add to the beauty of this place. We suggest you ride the trail clockwise from the mountain bike parking lot so the first 4 miles will be relatively flat and easy along the Duck River and Knob Creek. The next 4 miles are known as the "Trail of Tears" so the less enthusiastic riders might want to skip this part! This segment is considered very difficult and technical. Beginners may want to start on the River Trail by the boat launch rather than starting on the intermediate Creek Trail segment. There are shortcuts that bypass the more technical sections.

HOW TO GET THERE: Drive south on the Natchez Trace Parkway until the Hwy. 7 exit at milepost 416. Go left on Hwy. 7 toward Columbia. Chickasaw Trace Park will be on your right.

Ride #41   HAMILTON CREEK RECREATION AREA

Distance: East Loop - 2.5 miles (beginner/intermediate trail). West Loop - 5.8 miles (advance trail)
Elevation Difference: 150 ft.
Terrain: No big hills, but occasional short, steep grades. East Loop is mostly smooth, single track with a few minor hills and rocky spots. West Loop has very demanding technical spots, steep climbs, and rocky terrain.
Distance from Nashville: 11 miles

When mountain biking was officially banned from the Warner Parks, the Metro Parks Board recognized, amid all the controversy, that mountain biking was a growing sport and that we needed trails to ride. Although there was much grumbling amongst mountain bikers, we think that most off-road cyclists have come to realize Hamilton Creek is an excellent place to ride.

The *Mountain Trails Bicycle Club* has worked hard in designing and maintaining the trail system at Hamilton Creek, and we can't stress enough how important it is that all off-road cyclists volunteer to help maintain the trails in order to continue having trail access.

The Hamilton Creek trail system consists of an easy/intermediate East Loop (2.5 miles) and a very challenging advance West Loop (5.8 miles). A .2-mile connector which runs through a culvert under Bell Rd (please walk your bike) allows you to ride the entire system uninterrupted. Much of the area is covered with second growth forest occasionally interrupted with cedar thickets and bushy clearings. There is a particularly nice section of hardwood forests on the East Loop. Several interesting geological formations can be seen on the West Loop, but you may be too busy navigating over and through limestone rock outcrops to notice.

The MTBC was very ambitious while constructing the west trail, and they must have looked for the most difficult route they could find. They even put the trail through a sink hole! Not to worry, even mortal mountain bikers such as we can enjoy this loop if we don't mind occasionally walking our bikes. (Hike 'n bike!) In your efforts to participate with trail maintenance, please don't think that removing the tree trunks from across the path is being helpful—they were purposefully placed there so that experienced riders can practice the art of stump jumping.

FUTURE MOUNTAIN BIKING IN NASHVILLE

With a generous gift from the Beaman family, Metro Nashville is planning a 1,500 acre nature park in northwest Davidson County near the intersection of Old Hickory Blvd. and Eatons Creek Rd. Although the master plan had not been written at the time of this printing, it seems likely that mountain biking will be permitted in this rugged ridgetop forest. Call 862-8400 for current information on Beaman Park.

41 HAMILTON CREEK RECREATION AREA

HOW TO GET THERE: Take I-40 East to Stewarts Ferry Pk. (Exit 219) and go right. Continue straight (road will become Bell Rd.) 3.5 mi. to the sign for Hamilton Creek Marina and Recreation Area. For the East Trailhead, turn left into the Recreation Area and take the first right to the parking lot by the swim area. For the West Loop, turn right on Ned Shelton Rd. and take the first left to the parking area.

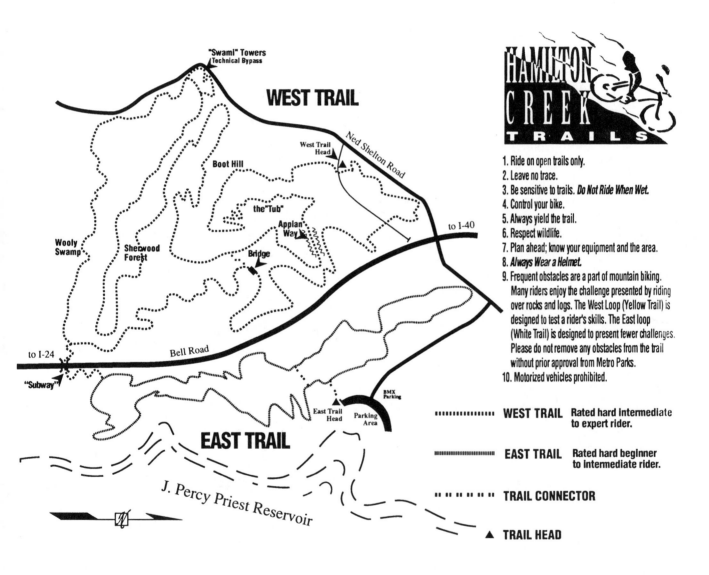

1. Ride on open trails only.
2. Leave no trace.
3. Be sensitive to trails. *Do Not Ride When Wet.*
4. Control your bike.
5. Always yield the trail.
6. Respect wildlife.
7. Plan ahead; know your equipment and the area.
8. *Always Wear a Helmet.*
9. Frequent obstacles are a part of mountain biking. Many riders enjoy the challenge presented by riding over rocks and logs. The West Loop (Yellow Trail) is designed to test a rider's skills. The East loop (White Trail) is designed to present fewer challenges. Please do not remove any obstacles from the trail without prior approval from Metro Parks.
10. Motorized vehicles prohibited.

•••••••••••••• **WEST TRAIL** Rated hard intermediate to expert rider.

||||||||||||||||||||| **EAST TRAIL** Rated hard beginner to intermediate rider.

■ ■ ■ ■ ■ ■ ■ **TRAIL CONNECTOR**

▲ **TRAIL HEAD**

Map provided by Paul Tosh
Mountain Trails Bicycle Club

Ride #42   CHEATHAM WILDLIFE MANAGEMENT AREA

The Cheatham Wildlife Management Area consists of 21,000 acres of dense forests, fields, cascading streams, and rugged hills along a steep ridge separating the Cumberland and Harpeth watersheds. This large area is administered by the Tennessee Wildlife Resource Agency and currently boasts a healthy deer population. This brings us to the most important advice we can give: DON'T EVEN THINK OF RIDING HERE DURING DEER OR TURKEY HUNTING SEASON!!! (It's not permitted during this time anyway.) Deer hunting season usually lasts from the end of September to January 1st, and turkey season occurs in the early spring, but call (615) 781-6622 for details. A few windows of opportunity for autumn mountain biking occur when the entire area is closed to hunting for as many as 5 days at a time. We suggest that you always wear bright colors (orange is best) when you mountain bike in any area which permits hunting, even during closed-season.

From Germantown on Hwy. 250, an improved gravel/dirt road follows the ridge southeast through the wildlife management area to Sams Creek Rd. Numerous jeep trails branch off the main road and follow the different fingers of the ridge. The majority of these trails dead-end in 1-3 miles, but they make nice excursions if you don't mind the large stone-size gravel on some of them. Adventurous cyclists can occasionally find and explore the overgrown single track trails which have numerous deadfalls. Due to the well-drained soil and gravel roads, this is an ideal place to mountain bike when Fairview and Hamilton Creek Park are too muddy. Currently mountain bikes are not restricted on any of the trails, and it is requested that we do not ride in the open fields where clover, corn, etc. is grown. Please take care to ride in a manner that does not disturb wildlife or vegetation.

After several exploratory expeditions, we have mapped out three enjoyable rides, but there are several other possibilities. Free maps are usually available at the market in Germantown or outside the game checking station on Headquarters Rd.

NARROWS OF THE HARPETH MOUNTAIN BIKE RIDE

Distance: 13 miles
Difficulty: Moderate to easy. Maintained gravel roads. Suitable for hybrid bikes when dry.
Elevation Difference: 250 ft. (350 ft. if you go all the way down to the river.)
Terrain: Moderately rolling along the ridge. Long steady grade with a few steep sections from the ridge to the Harpeth River.
Services: None.
Combining Rides: #42 Dry Creek Loop, #22 Narrows of the Harpeth Loop (road bike).
Distance from Nashville: 22 miles

The *Narrows of the Harpeth Mountain Bike Ride* is almost entirely on maintained dirt roads and suitable for hybrid bikes except when it is muddy. This ride is also a good choice in the summer when you want an off-road experience without ticks and poison ivy. The Narrows of the Harpeth State Park is an interesting geological and historical area as well as an ideal lunch stop. (See *#22* for more historical information.)

BRUSH CREEK LOOP

Distance: 9 miles
Difficulty: Moderate. Mostly non-technical jeep roads and maintained gravel roads. A
   difficult descent and climb are encountered in addition to creek crossings.
Elevation Difference: 330 ft.
Terrain: An extremely steep descent to Brush Creek is followed by a very tough climb
   back to the ridge. The rest of the trip is mostly rolling terrain..
Services: None.
Distance from Nashville: 26 miles

The *Brush Creek Loop* replaces a unique trail, decribed in our first edition, along Big Bluff Creek that was obliterated by downed trees from the 1994 ice storms. While much of this new trek is on jeep roads along the ridges, a portion of this ride is also in a remote hollow with a clear gurgling stream. If you want a secluded wilderness bike trip where you are exploring a large uninhabited area rather than weaving around in a small mountain bike park, this ride fits the bill.

After four easy miles of ridgetop riding, a hair raising descent leads into a beautiful valley where a sparkling creek flows through a large clearing reminiscent of an Appalachian cove. From here, a faint and often brushy trail heads up the hollow for .6 miles before a grueling climb crests another finger of the ridge. While the descent and ascent are challenging even to experienced cyclists, the more timid (or sane!) rider can easily walk these two short sections of jeep trail.

DRY CREEK LOOP

Distance: 12 miles
Difficulty: Moderate. Mostly non-technical jeep roads and maintained gravel roads.
   A difficult descent and semi-technical climb are encountered in addition to creek
   crossings.
Elevation Difference: 330 ft.
Terrain: Mostly rolling ridgetop except for 1.5 miles of extremely steep terrain near
   Dry Creek.
Services: None.
Distance from Nashville: 22 miles

This trek utilizes the first four miles of the *Narrows of the Harpeth Mountain Bike Ride* before turning north on Pipeline Rd. which transits a long finger of the Cumberland-Harpeth Ridge. The rolling and twisting road follows a narrow clearing surrounded by dense forests. A seemingly vertical descent (use extreme caution if you choose not to walk this one!) plunges down to a beautiful remote hollow 300 ft. below the ridge. After two back-to-back creek crossings, our route climbs Cedar Creek Rd., currently a seldom-used foot/horse trail. We found this old rutted road to be extremely challenging when covered with a light snow! Before climbing out of the hollow, you may opt to explore the jeep road that continues downstream along Dry Creek. After climbing back to the ridge, our route joins Headquarters Rd. which returns us to our starting point.

NARROWS OF THE HARPETH MOUNTAIN BIKE

HOW TO GET THERE: Take I-40 West to Bellevue/Hwy 70S (Exit 196) and turn right (west) on Hwy. 70S. Continue for 1.8 mi., turn left on Hwy. 70, go another 5.5 mi., and turn right on Sams Creek Rd./Hwy. 249. From here, watch your odometer carefully and continue 2.7 mi. On the left, look for a gated jeep road. This road lies shortly after the first TVA powerlines, but before the second TVA powerlines. There are a few places to park on either side of Sams Creek Rd.

Mile

0.0	Begin by biking west on the gated gravel road.
3.5	**Left** on Cedar Hill Rd. shortly past a pipeline route.
6.4	Stay **right** at the fork by a white house.
6.6	New Cedar Hill Rd. (paved) Narrows of the Harpeth State Park. Several roads crisscross the small state park. Return the way you came.
13.2	End of ride!

BRUSH CREEK LOOP

HOW TO GET THERE: Take I-40 West to Charlotte Pk./Hwy. 70 (Exit 209), go right (west) on Charlotte Pk. for .4 mi., and turn right on River Rd. Go 1.5 mi., turn right at the stop sign, and continue on what is still River Rd. Continue for another 12 mi. and turn left on Willie Pardue Rd. which goes behind the Lakeview Market across the road from the Brush Creek Recreation Area. Take Willie Pardue Rd. (which becomes gravel) to the market on Hwy. 250. Park at the market (with permission) or at the State Forest Fire Tower.

Mile

0.0	Begin by biking back toward River Rd. on Willie Pardue Rd.
0.1	**Right** on Griffintown Rd. (maintained gravel).
1.5	**Left** on Headquarters Rd. (maintained gravel).
2.1	**Left** on Brush Creek Rd. (easy to miss).
4.6	Bear **left** and descend to Brush Creek.
4.9	Cross the creek and continue upstream.
5.6	Bear **right** and begin climbing out of the valley.
6.7	**Left** on Willie Pardue Rd. (maintained gravel)
8.6	End of ride!

DRY CREEK LOOP

HOW TO GET THERE: Same as *Narrows of the Harpeth Mountain Bike*.

Mile

0.0	Begin by biking west on the gated gravel road.
3.5	**Right** on Pipeline Rd. past the cable fence. There are also gas line markers.
5.9	Bear **left** into a lesser used jeep road as Pipeline Rd. nears the crest of a short climb (easy to miss). You will soon go through an area which has been partially logged.
6.7	Cross Dry Creek and immediately turn **left**, cross another creek and continue uphill on Cedar Hill Rd. (currently a foot/horse trail).
8.0	**Left** on Headquarters Rd. at the T-intersection.
12.2	End of ride!

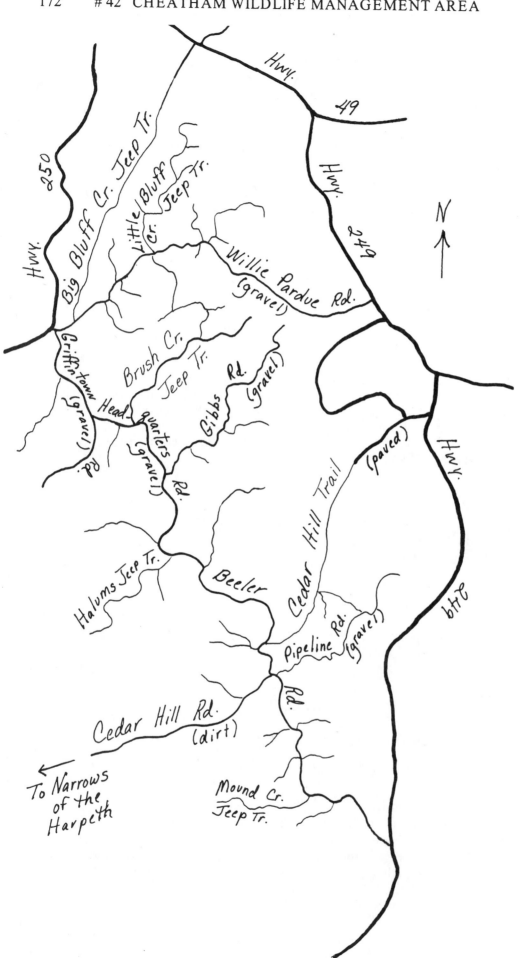

Ride # 43   CEDARS OF LEBANON STATE FOREST

Distance: East Loop--13 miles. West Loop--11 or 15 miles
Elevation Difference: East Loop--170 ft.; West Loop--130 ft.
Terrain: Varies from flat cedar glades to steep knobs. Very rocky in spots. After rains, possible gooey mud which can cake on tires to the point that they will no longer spin. Mud holes are common on the jeep roads, even several days after a rain. Suitable, although challenging, for hybrid bikes when trails are dry.
Services: Market in Norene on the East Loop.
Distance from Nashville: 36 miles

Cedars of Lebanon State Park and Forest consist of an unique geological and botanical landscape which is very different from what one normally sees in Tennessee. The thick cedar forest growing on the dry rocky soil is vaguely reminiscent of the Southwest high desert areas. The rocky limestone is seen in numerous sink holes and rock outcroppings, and because of its porous nature, almost no streams flow through this area. The cedars grow well in the poor, rocky soil where many hardwoods cannot survive. The open cedar glades are host to approximately 29 rare and endemic plants and flowers which grow nowhere else in the world. In the late spring and early summer, the grassy glades are a beautiful sight with multitudes of wild flowers in bloom.

Off-road cycling is currently prohibited in the state park, but is not restricted on the jeep roads in the state forest. The one exception is the motorcross trail in the southeastern part of the state forest (off-limits to bicycling). Several miles of jeep trails cross the forest reserve and provide fun and sometimes very challenging mountain biking. These jeep trails are used by equestrians, hikers, and 4-wheel drives, but we have rarely encountered anyone in the area. The gravel roads are fine for hybrid bikes and so would most of the jeep trails when they are dry. Some "hike and bike" for hybrids may be required on muddy or rocky sections, so be prepared to encounter mud holes which rarely dry out.

Although there are lovely areas of dense forests and open glades, beer cans and fast food packaging are frequent eyesores, and a few illegal dumps are even more infuriating. In some areas, 4-wheel drives have torn up fragile cedar glades. In spite of such negligence, it is well-worth your effort to spend time in this unique natural area.

The portion of the state forest north of Cedar Forest Rd. and west of Hwy. 231 is always closed to hunting. In other areas, hunting is allowed during hunting season, so we recommend strongly that you also avoid cycling these areas from late fall to early winter. Stop by the park office (.3 mile from the state park entrance) for more information, current mountain bike regulations, and an essential, free topographical map of the park and forest. Many of the jeep trails and roads are not marked, so you will need to pay close attention to the map and to our directions. Even so, you may get off track anyway, but that's often the nature of the sport! Again, for environmental reasons, please do not ride out on the open glades unless you are on a designated trail.

The East Loop is a mix of gravel roads, jeep trails, and paved roads. This trip begins in the predominately cedar forest, then follows Burnt House Jeep Trail up a rocky hillside through lush hardwood forests. Near the state park border, Burnt House Trail passes an interesting rock crevice where a wet weather spring rises and flows into a sink hole. On the left immediately past the Knight Trail, notice the huge old oak which, for some unknown reason, escaped the ax when this area was logged early in this century. Shortly after leaving the state forest, Burnt House Trail becomes gravel and then pavement before reaching Hwy. 266. Two and a half miles of paved road take you to the quaint community of Norene, with an old country store complete with inviting benches out front. With the rocks and mud behind you, the remainder of the trip is a pleasing spin on quiet paved roads.

The West Loop is predominately a collection of jeep trails which run along the periphery of the state forest. Several rock-strewn sections of jeep road along with occasional mud holes that never dry out are guaranteed to provide a challenge. Thick cedar forests, open glades, wild flowers, and rock formations all make this an enjoyable ride.

HOW TO GET THERE: Take I-40 East from Nashville and go south on Hwy. 231 (Exit 238). Continue 6.5 mi. to Cedars of Lebanon State Park Forest. For the West Loop, park near the Tennessee Forest Service building across the highway from the state park. For the East Loop, turn left into the state park, bear left at the "Y", and park by the swimming pool or the picnic area along the road to the horse stables.

CEDARS OF LEBANON FOREST WEST LOOP

0.0   Begin by biking west on Cedar Forest Rd.
1.3   **Right** on Thompson Jeep Trail near the bottom of a small hill.
2.6   **Right** on Richmond Shop Rd. (Moccasin Rd.) (T-intersection, paved road).
3.8   Murphy Jeep Trail goes to left (easy to miss) shortly after the road you are on bends to the left. If not overgrown (it was in 1998), this trail can be used to connect to Proctor Trail.
4.3   **Left** on Moccasin Rd. (stop sign at the T-intersection).
Go to Option 1 or Option 2

OPTION 1
11 Miles

4.8   Bear **left** on Proctor Jeep Trail where the county-maintained road ends.
5.4   Cross Cedar Forest Rd. (gravel).
6.4   **Left** on James Jordon Jeep Trail which goes into the woods near the top of a hill.
Go to Both Options

OPTION 2
15 Miles

4.8   Bear **right** on E. McPeak Jeep Trail where the county-maintained road ends.. Generally stay to the right where a few unmarked trails go to the left.
6.1   Bear **right** at the "Y" after going down the second big hill as an unnamed jeep trail goes left. The trail you are on will start going uphill again.
7.2   **Right** on Cedar Forest Rd. (T-intersection, gravel road).
7.7   **Left** on Sanders Jeep Trail (before arriving at paved Gladeville Rd.). Sanders Trail is currently dirt barricaded to motor traffic.
9.1   **Left** on Foutch Trail(Moccasin Rd.) (T-intersection, gravel road).
9.8   Bear **left** on Proctor Jeep Trail (dirt, easy to miss) after the road finishes a "S" curve. A private road continues straight.
10.0   **Right** on James Jordon Jeep Trail after going over a small hill.
Go to Both Options

BOTH OPTIONS

7.1, 10.7   Stay **right** on James Jordon Jeep Trail where Harris Jeep Trail goes straight.
7.7, 11.3   Continue straight on Spencer Jordon Jeep Trail as James Jordon Trail goes left.
9.0, 12.6   **Right** on Richmond Rd. (T-intersection, gravel road).
9.4, 13.0   **Left** on Robinson Jeep Trail.
10.2, 13.8   **Right** on Cedar Forest Rd. (T-intersection, gravel road).
11.3, 14.9   End of ride!

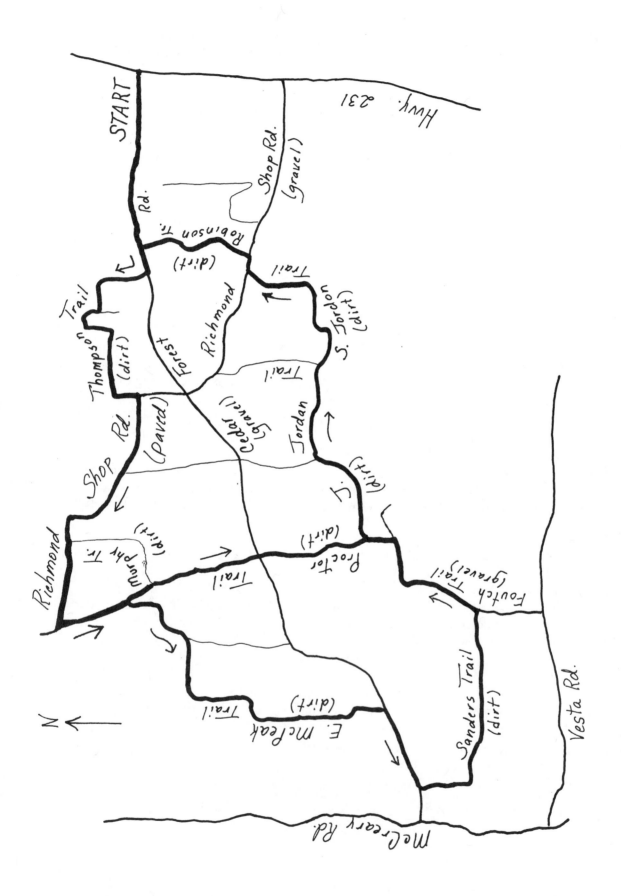

CEDARS OF LEBANON FOREST EAST LOOP
13 Miles

0.0   Begin ride by biking east on Cedars Forest Rd. from the picnic area.

0.8   **Left** on S. Warren Jeep Trail (gated) at the state park/state forest boundary. If you cross the metal bridge, you have gone too far.

1.2   **Right** on a mud hole bypass immediately past where the hiking trail crosses the S. Warren Trail. Stay to the left after making this turn.

1.4   **Right** on what is still the Warren Trail in a small clearing.

1.6   **Right** on Burnt House Jeep Trail.

1.9   Bear **right** on Burnt House Trail where the Tom Bond Jeep Trail goes left.

2.2   Bear **left** (going uphill) where the horse trail goes straight.

2.6   Stay **left** where the Knight Jeep Trail goes right.

3.2   Road becomes gravel.

4.5   Road becomes paved.

5.8   **Right** on Hwy. 266/Cainsville Rd. (stop sign at the T-intersection).

8.4   **Right** on Norene Rd. immediately past the market.

10.7   Bear **right** on Cedars Forest Rd. (T-intersection).

13.4   End of ride!

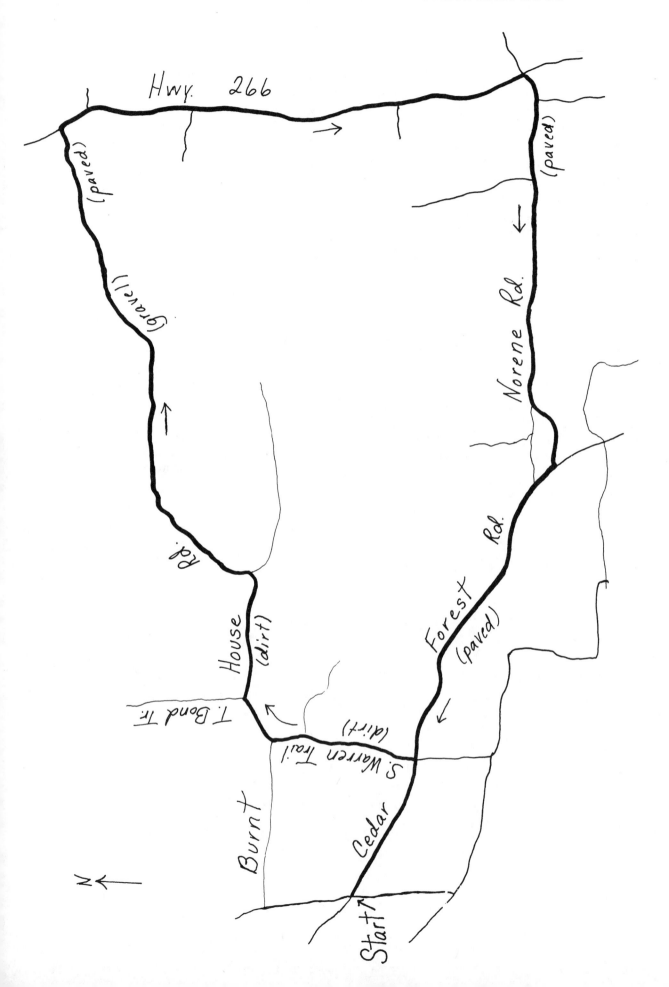

Ride # 44   LOCK FOUR PARK

Distance: Up to 8 miles of trails.
Elevation Difference: 60 ft.
Terrain: Mostly smooth intermediate single track with a few technical sections which have optional by-passes. No big hills, but several short steep climbs.
Distance from Nashville: 35 miles

Both beginners and die-hard mountain bikers can enjoy the trails created in this undeveloped city park by the Lock 4 Trailblazers under the direction of Sam Poyner and David Hardin, owner of Biker's Choice. Most of the trail is smooth single track (muddy after rain, of course) with a few rocky sections added for entertainment. The trails meander up and down the hills forested with hardwood groves and cedar thickets. A couple of very challenging sections (both with by-passes) drop down the rocky ledges to the edge of Old Hickory Lake and then tackle seemingly vertical ascents back up. This network of trails basically forms a variety of loops giving cyclist several route possibilities. The loops are color coded and the technical bypasses are also marked. As always, do not ride when the trails are wet.

HOW TO GET THERE: Take I-65 North to Vietnam Veteran Blvd./Hwy. 386 (Exit 95) toward Gallatin. Stay on Vietnam Veteran Blvd. until it terminates on Hwy. 31E north going toward Gallatin. Continue on Hwy. 31E and turn right on Lock 4 Rd. immediately before Hwy. 109. Follow this road to its end and park in the lot by the old concrete silo at the entrance of Lock Four Park. The trailhead is at the far end of the lot.

Ride # 45   MONTGOMERY BELL STATE PARK

Distance: 6-12 miles
Terrain: Single track over hilly terrain
Distance from Nashville: 32 miles

Montgomery Bell State Park offers what some claim to be the finest mountain biking in Middle Tennessee. These trails were built by volunteers who gave literally thousands of hours of sweaty-dirty labor to create this challenging trail system in a very pristine setting. The mountain biking area, situated north of Hwy. 70, basically consists of two loops totalling 12 miles. The left loop is better suited for intermediate riders. The single track trails wind among mature hardwood forests, rocky bluffs, and clear creeks. The mountain bike trails will accommodate intermediate-to-advanced riders. The soil here drains better than other mountain biking locations, so it is often permissable to ride 24 hours after a rain unless it is unusually heavy. For further information, call (931) 797-3101.

HOW TO GET THERE: Take I-40 West from Nashville to Bellevue/Hwy 70 (Exit 196) and turn right (west) toward Dickson. Continue approximately 19 mi. through the town of White Bluff. Turn right on Jones Creek Rd. which is shortly past the grocery store in White Bluff. The parking area is just beyond the boat factory. If a parking permit is required, you may need to take Hwy 70 to the main entrance of the state park.

GREENWAYS AND SHORT RIDES

Paved multi-use paths known as greenways are being constructed all over the region, allowing folks to bike, walk, run, or skate in an auto-free setting. Most are relatively short in length, but provide an ideal place for kids to discover cycling as well as for the kids-at-heart who desire peaceful excursions. Nashville has nearly 30 miles of greenways and plans to double that in the near future. Greenways can be found in all the surrounding counties as well. Check out these websites to discover where these gems can be found:

www.nashville.gov   www.brentwood-tn.org   www.murfreesborotn.gov
www.cityofwhitehouse.com   www.townofsmyrna.org
(click on City Departments and then Parks)

Greenways in this book: *Ride #1 Shelby Bottoms Greenway* (4 mi. one-way), *Ride #14B Brentwood Greenway* (5-6 mi. one-way), *Ride #15B Mill Creek Greenway* (two 1-mi. segments), *Ride #20B Stones River Greenway* (5 mi. one-way), *Ride #33B Cumberland River Bicentennial Trail* (7-8 mi. one-way). Check out the ride descriptions to learn about the premier greenways in the area.

Other Greenways:

Stones River Greenway—Nashville's Stones River Greenway runs 10 miles from Percy Priest Dam to Two Rivers Park near Opryland. This greenway provides a peaceful escape from the bustling suburbs of Donelson and Hermitage. The stretches along the river are very tranquil, but a few steep hills will certainly get your heart rate up. In the Fall of 2007, a pedestrian bridge will span the Cumberland River connecting the Stones River Greenway with the Shelby Bottoms Greenways. The 14 miles of non-stop trail will comprise the majority of the *Music City Bikeway* (See Ride #1).

Richland Creek Greenway—This 2-mile greenway is only a stone's throw from the Harding Rd. gridlock and allows cyclists to freely pedal from trailheads on White Bridge and Cherokee Rd. plus other access points at the Target on White Bridge Rd., Hill Shopping Center, and 54th Ave.

Smyrna and La Vergne Greenway System—Smyrna already has 7 miles of greenways available and neighboring La Vergne is also planning greenways. These greenways connect the city center to various parks and Percy Priest Lake. Plans are underway to connect these greenways with the system in Nashville and Murfreesboro so cyclists can pedal from downtown Nashville to Murfreesboro almost entirely on greenways.

White House Greenway—Beginning at White House Municipal Park on Hwy. 76 just east of I-65, a 3.5-mile greenway heads south from Hwy. 76. When complete, this 7-mile greenway will provide a nice way to start and end *Ride #32 North Sumner County Loop.*

Ride #2 Radnor Lake Excursion—While not an official greenway, this 1.2-mile section of road between the East and West Trailheads at Radnor Lake is ideal for cycling. This narrow road running along the beautiful lake is flat and and is closed to general auto traffic. Plus, there are many opportunities to stop and watch the waterfowl and resident turtles.

Other Short Rides: For short road rides, try biking the Natchez Trace from the parking area 2 miles past the northern terminus to milepost 432 which is 8 miles away. Expect rolling hills. Closer to town is Old Natchez Trace and Del Rio (Ride #7). If you park 3 miles into the ride near Temple Rd., you will avoid the hills. The first 6 miles of Ride #10 to Fernvale is absolutely delightful. Also try Big East Fork Rd. until the big uphill. In Hendersonville, try Station Camp Rd. (Ride #30) for the first 3 miles or continue on the rolling hills to the north.

FRANKLIN/NATCHEZ TRACE CENTURY

This challenging 100-mile tour encompasses sections of the *# 7 Old Natchez Trace/Del Rio Ride, # 8 Harpeth Loop, # 10 Fernvale Loop, # 12 Snow Creek Loop, # 13 Burwood Loop, and # 17 Williamson County Loop*. (See these rides for maps.) It also features 21 miles of the Natchez Trace Parkway. Although this century is 2 miles under the magic number, the hills will more than make up for this shortcoming.

HOW TO GET THERE: Begin at the town square in Franklin. Hillsboro Pk., Franklin Pk., and I-65 all lead south to Franklin from Nashville. Parking is available on residential streets near the square.

Mile

0.0	Begin ride by biking west on Main St./Hwy. 31 South.
0.2	Continue straight (don't veer to the left) onto W. Main St. at the busy intersection at 5th St. As you leave town, W. Main St. becomes Carters Creek Pk./Hwy. 246.
4.0	Market in the town of Southall.
7.8	**Left** on West Harpeth Rd. (easy to miss).
11.5	**Right** on Sedberry Rd. (first right).
14.7	**Right** on Thompson Station-Burwood Rd. (stop sign at the T- intersection).
14.5	**Left** on Evergreen Rd. (Martin Rd)(first left).
17.1	Bear **right** (staying on Evergreen Rd.) as Lavender Rd. goes straight ahead.
18.1	**Right** on Pope's Chapel Rd. (stop sign at the T- intersection).
19.3	**Left** on Carters Creek Pk./Hwy. 246 in the town of Burwood (stop sign at the T-intersection). Market.
22.6	**Right** on Hwy. 247.
24.9	Market in the town of Theta.
31.4	Cross Hwy. 7 at Santa Fe. Market/restaurant.
37.7	**Right** on Hwy. 50 (stop sign at the T-intersection).
40.7	**Right** onto the Natchez Trace Parkway on-ramp. Take the Parkway north toward Nashville. Colbert Ferry historic site and picnic area (water/restrooms) are .4 mi. to the south on the Parkway.
60.2	Garrison Creek Picnic Area (water/restrooms).
61.8	Exit onto Hwy. 46/Pinewood Rd.
62.1	**Left** on Pinewood Rd. at the bottom of the ramp.
69.4	Market.
71.8	**Right** on Deer Ridge Rd. (easy to miss) in a small residential area of brick homes.
73.3	**Right** on Caney Fork Rd. (second right). There are two confusing intersections on this road so be sure to follow the creek down to the South Harpeth River.
78.8	**Right** on Old Hwy. 96 and immediately cross the bridge over the South Harpeth River at Fernvale.
78.9	**Left** on Old Harding Rd. (3-way stop).
83.8	**Right** on Hwy. 96 (stop sign at the T-intersection).
89.9	**Left** on Hwy. 46/Old Hillsboro Rd. (flashing light).
92.0	**Right** on Del Rio Pk. (easy to miss).
93.9	**Right** (staying on Del Rio Pk.) at the 3-way stop.

95.5	**Left** (staying on Del Rio Pk.) at the next 3-way stop.
97.1	**Right** on Magnolia Ln. at the cemetery. Market/fast food restauants.
97.4	**Left** on Hope St. (first left).
97.8	**Right** on Fifth Ave. North (Hillsboro Pk.).
98.1	End of Ride!

RED RIVER CENTURY

This century is not as hilly as the *Franklin/Natchez Trace Century*, but it still has enough climbing to keep you entertained for 100 miles. There are plenty of long, open flat stretches so you can easily get into a good cycling rhythm. This century combines portions of the *# 37 Lower Red River Loop, # 38 Cross Plains Loop,* and *# 39 Upper Red River Loop.*

HOW TO GET THERE: Take I-65 North and exit at Hwy. 76 (Exit 108). Turn left on Hwy. 76 going west toward Springfield and continue 2 mi. The ride begins at the 4-way intersection of Old Hwy. 31W/Cross Plains Rd. in the community of Oakdale. We have been able to park at the market at this intersection in the past. Always ask permission before parking on private property.

Mile
0.0	Begin ride by going right (north) on Old Hwy. 31W/Cross Plains Rd. from Hwy. 76.
2.8	**Left** on Eden Corner Rd. (easy to miss). Look for a sign to Owens Chapel United Methodist Church.
7.3	Market.
10.2	**Right** on Hwy. 49 (stop sign at the T-intersection).
10.6	**Left** on William Woodard Rd. (first left).
13.8	**Left** on Hwy. 431 (stop sign at the T-intersection).
13.9	Market.
14.2	**Left** on Hwy. 41 (Hwy. 431 South runs together with Hwy. 41)
14.5	**Right** on N. Main St. (first right) in the town of Springfield.
15.7	Market/restaurant (.2 mi. off the route) to the left (east) on 10th Ave East. immediately before crossing the RR tracks.
16.0	Bear **right** at the "Y" past the town square.
16.1	Cross Central Ave. (traffic light). There are at least 2 markets in the next 2 mi.
18.1	**Right** on Hwy. 431 (stop sign at the T-intersection).
19.9	**Right** on Old Hwy. 431 just before Chevron Station (easy to miss). Market.
20.6	**Right** on Coopertown Rd. (Coopertown-Chestnut Rd.)(second right).
24.7	Cross Hwy. 49 in Coopertown and continue on Burgess Gower Rd.
26.1	Continue straight at the next 4-way intersection.
29.7	**Left** on Maxie Rd. at the T-intersection.
30.5	**Right** on Ed Ross Rd. (first right) at the "Y" after descending and crossing a creek.
32.2	**Right** on Glen Raven Rd./Hwy. 256 (stop sign at the 4-way intersection).
34.8	**Left** on Hwy. 256/Kenney Rd. (first left after the hill past Sulphur Fork).
36.8	Straight onto Hwy. 76. There is a market (.4 mi. off the route) to the right on Hwy. 76 in the town of Adams.
40.6	Cross Sulphur Fork.
42.0	**Right** on Port Royal Rd./Hwy. 238. This is the Port Royal Rd. *after* crossing Sulphur Fork.
43.3	Port Royal State Park (water/restrooms).
43.7	Market.
48.2	**Right** on Guthrie Rd. Guthrie Rd. becomes Russel St. as you enter the town of Guthrie, Kentucky.
50.4	**Right** on 2nd St. immediately after crossing the RR tracks.

50.6	**Left** on Ewing St. Market/restaurant.
50.7	**Right** on Park St. (first right where Hwy. 79 and Hwy. 41 go to the left.) Park St. becomes Highland Rd.
53.1	**Right** on Hwy. 848/Darnell Rd. (stop sign at the T-intersection).
60.2	**Right** on Hwy. 102 (stop sign at the T-intersection).
61.2	**Left** on Hwy. 96/Orndorff Rd. in the town of Keysburg.
64.9	**Right** on Dot Rd. (County Rd. 1309) in the town of Dot (4-way intersection). Market.
65.1	Cross the South Fork of the Red River.
67.1	Bear **left** where Smith Rd. enters from the right.
67.9	**Left** on Barren Plain-Dot Rd./KY 1307 (stop sign at the T-intersection).
70.5	Cross the South Fork of the Red River.
71.0	**Right** on Hwy. 591 (stop sign at the T-intersection).
73.4	Cross Hwy. 431 in the town of Adairville. Market/park with drinking fountains at the town square.
81.8	**Right** (staying on Hwy. 591) after crossing the Red River in the town of Prices Mill.
84.7	**Right** on Hwy. 383 (stop sign at the T-intersection) which becomes Hwy. 49 as you enter Tennessee.
85.2	Cross the Red River.
89.5	**Left** on Hwy. 52 at the 4-way stop. Market in the town of Orlinda.
89.8	Straight onto Elm Springs Rd. (E. Church St.)(first intersection) as Hwy. 52 bends to the left.
91.3	**Right** on E. Robertson Rd. (stop sign at the T-intersection).
94.2	**Right** on Hwy. 25 in the town of Cross Plains (stop sign at the T-intersection). Drugstore with soda fountain/hot plates. Markets/restaurants to the left on Hwy. 25 (.2 mi. off the loop).
94.3	**Left** on Cedar St. (Old Hwy. 31W/Cross Plains Rd.) (first left, flashing red light).
95.0	**Left** on Kilgore Trace Rd. (Old Hwy. 31W/Cross Plains Rd.) (stop sign at the T-intersection).
100.1	End of ride!

OVERNIGHT TOURING

Bicycling takes on a whole different aspect when you tour for two or more days. No longer is the outing merely a pleasant ride where you simply return to your starting point that same day—it is now an adventure with an actual destination. Touring by bicycle is also a challenge, because everything you need (food, clothing, camping gear, tools, etc.) is carried on your bicycle. Visit a bike shop for advice or buy a book on bike touring if you have never before pedaled a loaded bicycle. (We find it very satisfying being totally self-contained on two wheels.)

The Tennessee Bicycle Routes and the Natchez Trace Parkway make excellent one-way (or out and back) bicycle tours. Many of our rides have camping and/or lodging along the route, providing for overnight loop tours of one or more days. (See *Appendix* for information on routes, campgrounds, bed & breakfasts.)

The following tours are only a sample of the excellent possibilities for bike touring and weekend getaways:

Port Royal/Cumberland River Camping Tour
120 miles/2-3 days

This camping tour combines highlights of *#34 Union Hill/Paradise Ridge Loop, #35 Lower Sycamore Creek Loop, #36 Upper Sycamore Creek Loop, #37 Lower Red River Loop, #38 Cross Plains Loop,* and *#39 Upper Red River Loop.* (See these rides for maps and food locations.) Day 2 of this tour can be combined with Day 1 or Day 3 for those desiring a one night excursion. Most of this tour travels through scenic rural areas on lightly traveled roads. In order to create a simple tour that heads directly to each day's destination, a few sections of highway which may be busy are encountered near the towns of White House, Cross Plains, and Ashland City. At Ashland City, you may opt to follow the *Lower Sycamore Creek Loop* directions for Option 3 to Joelton rather than bicycle on busy Hwy. 49 and Hwy. 249. This is longer and hillier, but a more pleasant route.

HOW TO GET THERE: Take I-65 North and exit at Hwy. 76 (Exit 108). Turn right on Hwy. 76 going toward White House. Turn left on Hwy. 31W (traffic light) and immediately right on Hwy. 258/College St. Park at the Municipal Center (ask permission).

Day 1
35 miles

0.0	Bike north on Hwy. 31W.
0.1	**Right** on Hwy. 76.
4.0	**Left** on Hwy. 25 (4-way stop).
20.3	**Right** on Hwy. 161 in Barren Plains. (This becomes Hwy. 102 in Kentucky.)
26.8	Continue straight as Hwy. 96/Orndorff Mill Rd. goes right in Keysburg, KY.
26.9	**Left** on Keysburg/Adams Rd. (first left after Hwy. 96).
27.4	Bear **right** on Keysburg/Adams Rd. as Hugh Gill Rd. goes straight.
32.7	Cross the Red River.

33.8	**Right** on Hwy. 41 in the town of Adams.
35.0	Red River Canoe & Campground

Day 2
34 miles

0.0	Continue north on Hwy. 41.
2.3	**Left** on Jones Rd. (Sadlersville Rd.) just before the farm co-op.
6.5	**Left** on Hwy. 238 (stop sign at the T-intersection).
7.6	Port Royal State Historic Area (water, restrooms).
8.7	**Left** on Hwy. 76 (stop sign at the T-intersection).
9.4	**Straight** (or bear **right**) onto Harmony Church Rd. (easy to miss).
14.0	**Right** on Stroudsville Rd. at the Stroudsville Church of Christ.
16.5	Cross Hwy. 41A and continue on Thomasville Rd.
19.5	**Left** on Old Clarksville Pk. (stop sign).
19.6	**Right** on Thomasville Rd. (first right).
25.9	**Right** on Sweet Home Rd. (4-way stop).
28.8	Cross Hwy. 12 and continue on Cheatham Dam Rd.
33.8	Cheatham Dam Recreation Area.

Day 3
51 miles

0.0	**Bike** back to Hwy. 12.
5.0	**Right** on Hwy. 12.
5.7	**Right** on Chapmansboro Rd. (first right).
11.4	**Right** on Hwy. 12.
12.5	**Left** on Hwy. 49 in Ashland City.
14.7	**Right** on Hwy. 249.
22.7	Straight (going east) on Old Clarksville Pk. as Hwy. 249 goes to the left.
24.8	**Right** on Clarksville Pk./Hwy 41A.
25.8	**Left** on Old Clarksville Pk. (easy to miss).
27.4	**Left** on Whites Creek Pk./Hwy. 431 in Joelton.
27.5	**Right** on Union Hill Rd. (first right).
27.8	Bear **left** staying on Union Hill Rd.
33.5	**Left** on Greer Rd. (stop sign).
38.9	Straight onto Hwy. 257 going east.
39.4	Cross Hwy. 41 in Ridgetop. Follow all signs for Hwy. 257 to Hwy. 31W.
45.8	**Left** on Hwy. 31W.
50.7	End of tour!

Natchez Trace/Tennessee Backroads Bed and Breadfast Tour
76-136 miles/2-4 days

Bicyclists often deserve to be pampered after a day of riding, and Tennessee's Bed and Breakfasts will do just that. The *Natchez Trace/Tennessee Backroads B & B Tour* combines one of the best cycling roads in the country, the Natchez Trace Parkway, with wonderful Tennessee backroads which travel through quaint communities. (See *Rides #7, #12,* and *#17* for maps and information.) Cyclists desiring a shorter 35-mile trip on Day 2 and 21 miles on Day 3 can stay at the Oak Springs Inn on Hwy. 50 near the Trace. This tour can also be reduced to two days by starting in Franklin and biking Day 2 and Day 3 plus an additional 10 miles from Leipers Fork to Franklin on Day 3. Camping is available at Leipers Fork and at Meriwether Lewis Campground for rough-and-tough cyclists. We start this tour at the Model Airplane Field of Edwin Warner Park, but check with the ranger before parking overnight here. (Break-ins are sometimes a problem; we recommend cycling here from your own parking location or arrange a shuttle.)

Day 1
13+ miles

Follow #7 *Old Natchez Trace/Del Rio Ride* to Franklin.

Day 2
52 miles

0.0	From downtown Franklin, bike west on W. Main St. which becomes Carters Creek Pk./Hwy. 246.
14.0	**Right** on Hwy. 247.
29.1	**Right** on Hwy. 50 (stop sign at the T-intersection).
32.1	Go south on the Natchez Trace Pkwy.
48.1	Take Hwy. 412 East (mile post 392).
52.1	Ridgetop B & B in Hampshire.

Day 3
50 miles

0.0	Return to the Natchez Trace Pkwy.
4.0	Go north toward Nashville.
48.0	**Exit** at Hwy. 46 (mile post 436) in Leipers Fork. Ask for directions when making reservations for either B & B near Leipers Fork. (Both are approximately 2.5 miles from Natchez Trace Pkwy.)

Day 4
21 miles

0.0	Return to Natchez Trace Pkwy.
2.0	**Enter** Natchez Trace Pkwy. going north toward Nashville.
10.7	**Exit** onto Hwy. 96 going east.
14.2	**Left** on Old Hillsboro Rd./Hwy. 46.
16.3	**Left** on Old Natchez Trace.
18.4	**Right** on Sneed Rd.
18.9	**Left** on Vaughn Rd.
21.0	Edwin Warner Park/Old Hickory Blvd. End of tour!

APPENDICES

PUBLICATIONS

Tennessee Atlas and Gazetteer. Delorme Mapping, P.O. Box 298, Freeport, ME 04032, (800) 227-1656; 1990; $16.95 plus $5.00 shipping. Color topographic maps of the entire state. Gives elevation contour. Shows which areas are forested, cleared, or urban. Recreational information. Shows all back roads but does not specify road surface. Available in some bookstores and bike shops.

County Maps. Tennessee Dept. of Transportation, Map Sales, Suite 1000, James K. Polk Bldg. (located above the Tennessee Performing Arts Center), 505 Deaderick St., Nashville, TN 37219, (615) 741-2195; $ .50 each. Detailed road maps which indicate road surfaces—paved, gravel, dirt, etc.

County Maps. Puetz Pl., Lyndon Station, WI 53944, $11.90 postpaid. Book of Tennessee county maps similar to the D.O.T maps. Brief historical and natural narratives on each county.

Cycling Tennessee's Highways. TN Dept. of Transportation, Suite 700, James K. Polk Bldg. Nashville, TN 37243-0349, Attn. Bicycle Coord. Free maps of 5 overnight touring routes that are also marked by road signs on state and county roads. The routes are "Cycling to Reelfoot," "Cycling the Tennessee River," "Cycling the Heartland," "Cycling the Highland Rim," and "Cycling the Mountains."

Bicycling the Natchez Trace by Glen Wanner, Pennywell Press, P.O. Box 50624, Nashville, TN 37205. A guide to the 450-miles Natchez Trace Parkway. Includes camping, lodging, and food locations as well as info on terrain and history. Also includes day rides and overnight loop tours. $15.95 plus $2 postage.

Touring the Middle Tennessee Backroads by Robert Brandt. John F. Blair, Publisher, 1406 Plaza Dr. Winston-Salem, NC 27103. $16.95. Auto tours featuring scenic, historic, and cultural attractions. Not all roads featured are well-suited for cycling.

LOCAL BICYCLING ORGANIZATIONS

Columbia Bicycle Club
1116 W 7th St., Suite 214
Columbia TN 38401
columbiacyclingclub.com

Greenways for Nashville
Centennial Park Office
Nashville, TN 37201
nashville.org/greenways

Harpeth Bicycle Club
P.O. Box 680802
Franklin, TN 37068-0802
harpethbikeclub.com

Murfreesboro Bicycle Club
P.O. 766
Murfreesboro, TN 37133
mborobike.com

Team Allanti
144 Franklin Rd.
Brentwood, TN 37027
(615) 373-4700

TN Parks and Greenways
1205A Linden Ave.
Nashville, TN 37212
(615) 386-3171
tenngreen.org

Veloteers (East Nashville and Wilson County)
5514 Old Hickory Blvd.
Hermitage, TN 37076

Walk/Bike Nashville
PO Box 50624
Nashville, TN 37205
walkbikenashville.org

NATIONAL BICYCLE ORGANIZATIONS

National Center for Bicycling
and Walking
1506 21st St. NW Ste. 200
Washington, DC 20036
(202) 463-6622
bikewalk.org

International Mountain Bicyling
Organization
P.O. Box 7578
Boulder, CO 80306
(888) 442-4622
imba.com

National Off-Road Bicycle Assoc.
1750 E. Boulder St.
Colorado Springs, CO 80909
(719) 578-4581
usacycling.org

Adventure Cycling Association
P.O. Box 8308
Missoula, MT 59807-9988
(800) 755-2453
adventurecycling.org

League of American Bicyclists
1612 K St. NW Ste. 800
Washington, DC 20006
(202) 822-1333
bikeleague.org

United States Cycling Federation
1750 E. Boulder St.
Colorado Springs, CO 80909
(719) 578-4581
usacycling.org

BICYCLE SHOPS

Bicycle Center of Clarksville
1450 Madison St.
Clarksville, TN 37040
(931) 647-2453

Bike Pedlar (formerly Allanti
Cycling Co.)
144 Franklin Rd.
Brentwood, TN 37027
(615) 373-4700

Bike Pedlar
2910 West End Ave.
Nashville, TN 37203
(615) 329-2453

Bike Pedlar (formerly The
Jolly Cyclist)
5514 Old Hickory Blvd.
Hermitage, TN 37076
(615) 885-0881

Biker's Choice
240C E. Main St.
Hendersonville, TN 37075
(615) 822-2512

Cumberland Transit
2807 West End Ave.
Nashville, TN 37203
(615) 321-4069

Eastside Cycles
1012 Woodland St.
Nashville, TN, 37206
(615) 469-1079

Franklin Bicycle Company
124 Watson Glen
Franklin, TN 37064
(615) 790-2702

Gran Fondo Cycles
5205 Harding Rd.
Nashville, TN 37205
(615) 354-1090

Harpeth Bicycles
1110 Hillsboro Rd.
Franklin, TN 37064
(615) 791-7959

Murfreesboro Outdoor and
Bicycle (MOAB)
310 N. Maple St.
Murfreesboro, TN 37130
(615) 893-7725

Nashville Bicycle Co.
2817 West End Ave. #36
Nashville, TN 37203
(615) 321-5510

REI
261 Franklin Rd.
Brentwood, TN 37027
(615) 376-4248

Sun & Ski Sports
501 Opry Mills
Nashville, TN 37214
(615) 514-3300

Trace Bikes
8400 Hwy 100
Nashville, TN 37221
(615) 646-2485

BED & BREAKFASTS
The following B & B's are located on or near the indicated rides:

Apple Brook B & B
(615) 646-5082
Rides 7, 8, & 10

Blue Moon Farm B&B
(800) 493-4518
Rides 17, 18, & 19

Chigger Ridge B & B
(615) 952-4354
Rides 21, 22, & 42

Clardy's Guest House
(615) 893-6030
Rides 19 & 20

English Manor B&B
(615) 373-4627
Rides 9 & 14

Hachland Hills Inn
(usually for groups of
10 or more)
(615) 876-1500
Rides 34 & 35

Homeplace B & B
(615) 776-5181
Rides 14, 15, 16, & 19

Magnolia House B & B
(615) 794-8178
Rides 7, 16, & 17
Natchez Trace B & B Tour

Namaste Acres B & B
(615) 791-0333
Rides 8, 10, 11, 12, & 13
Natchez Trace B & B Tour

Natchez Trace B & B Reservation Service
(931) 285-2777 (800) 377-2770
Ride 12
Natchez Trace B & B Tour

Old Marshall House B & B
(615) 591-4121
Rides 16 & 17

Peacock Hill Country Inn
(615) 368-7727
Rides 17 & 18

Rebel's Roost B & B
(615) 790-8140
Rides 7, 16, & 17
Natchez Trace B & B Tour

Ridgetop B & B
(931) 285-2777
Ride 12
Natchez Trace B & B Tour

Sumner's View B&B
(615) 395-4334 (888)326-4334
Rides 16, 17, 18, & 19

Sweeney Hollow B&B
(615) 591-0498
Rides 10, 11, 12, & 13
Natchez Trace B&B Tour

Watertown B & B
(615) 237-9999
Ride 27

Water Valley B&B
(931) 682-2266
Rides 11 & 12
Natchez Trace B&B Tour

Xanadu Farms
(615) 395-7327
Ride 19

CAMPING FACILITIES
The following campgrounds are on or near the indicated rides:
Several are closed in winter.

Bledsoe Creek State Park
(615) 532-0001
Ride 31

Cages Bend Recreation Area
(615) 824-4989
Rides 29 & 30

Cedars of Lebanon State Park
Cabins also available
(615) 443-2769
Rides 24, 26, & 27

Cheatham Dam Lock A
(615) 792-5697
Rides 33B & 35, Port Royal/Cumberland River Camping Tour

Cook Recreation Area
(615) 889-1096
Rides 24 & 25

Montgomery Bell State Park
Cabins/inn also available
(615) 741-1537
Rides 23 & 45

Red River Canoe & Campground
(private)
(615) 696-2768
(800) 762-8408
Ride 37, Port Royal/Cumberland River Camping Tour

Seven Points Recreation Area
(615) 889-5198
Rides 24 & 25

CHAMBERS OF COMMERCE

Ashland City, P.O. Box 354, Ashland City, TN 37015, (615) 792-6722
Bellevue, 156 Belle Forest Cir., Suite 156A, Bellevue, TN 37221, (615) 662-2737
Brentwood, 5211 Maryland Way, Suite 180, Nashville TN 37027, (615) 373-1595
Clarksville/Montgomery County, 180 Holiday Rd., Clarksville, TN 37040, (931) 647-2331
Dickson, P.O. Box 339, Dickson, TN 37056, (615) 446-2349
Donelson/Hermitage, 3051 Lebanon Rd., Nashville, TN 37214, (615) 883-7896
Fairview, 321 Fairview Blvd., Fairview, TN 37062, (615) 799-9290
Gallatin, 118 W Main St., P.O. Box 26, Gallatin, TN 37066, (615) 452-4000
Franklin/Williamson County, P.O. Box 156, Franklin, TN, 37065-0156, (615) 794-1225 or (800) 356-3445
Goodlettsville Area, 100 S. Main St., Suite D, Goodlettsville, TN 37072, (615) 859-7979
Hendersonville, P.O. Box 377, Hendersonville, TN 37077, (615) 824-2818
Lebanon/Wilson County, 149 Public Square, Lebanon, TN 37087, (615) 444-5503
Madison, 856 Madison Sq., Madison, TN 37116, (615) 865-5400
Mt. Juliet, 404 Mt. Juliet Rd., Mt. Juliet, TN 37122, (615) 758-3478
Murfreesboro/Rutherford, P.O. Box 864, Murfreesboro, TN 37133-0864, (615) 893-6565
Nashville, 161 4th Ave North, Nashville, TN 37219, (615) 259-4755
Portland, 111 S. Broadway, Portland, TN 37148-0387, (615) 325-9032
Springfield, 100 5th Ave W., Springfield, TN 37172, (615) 384-3800
White House, P.O. Box 521, White House, TN 37188, (615) 672-3937

AIRPORT/BUS INFORMATION

Getting To and From The Airport
You need to obtain a good city map (available at the airport) if you plan on cycling to and/or from the airport. Hwy. 255 (which is Donelson Pk. going north, or Harding Place going west) is the only surface road that goes by the terminal. It is usually busy and often shoulderless, yet tolerable to ride. Try to avoid peak traffic hours. Donelson Pk., Elm Hill Pk. and LaFayette St. connect the airport to downtown and points north. Harding Place and Franklin Pk. lead to points south. Harding Place and Hwy. 70S leads to points west. Bell Rd. leads to points east. Expect moderate to heavy traffic and little or no shoulder on all these routes. Station wagon and van taxis are usually available at the airport.

Getting To And From Nashville By Bus
The downtown bus station is located on 8th Ave S. at Demonbreun St. They do not have bike boxes, but local bike stores usually have free boxes. Greyhound also serves Murfreesboro, Lebanon, Columbia, Dickson, and Clarksville.

Additional copies of this book may be obtained by sending check
or money order for $16.95 to:

Pennywell Press
P.O. Box 50624
Nashville, TN 37205

Also by Pennywell Press: *Bicycling the Natchez Trace* $15.95